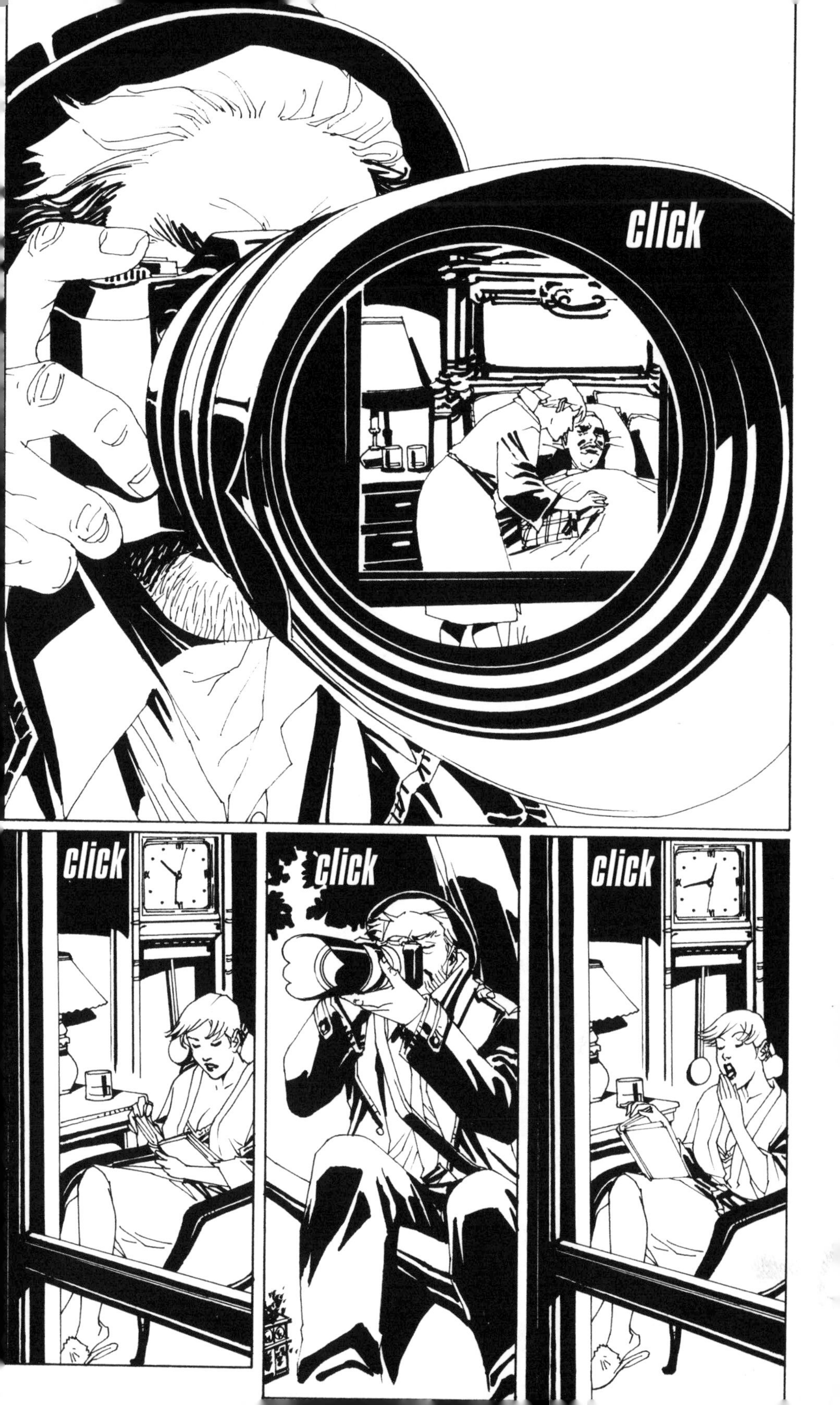
click
click
click
click

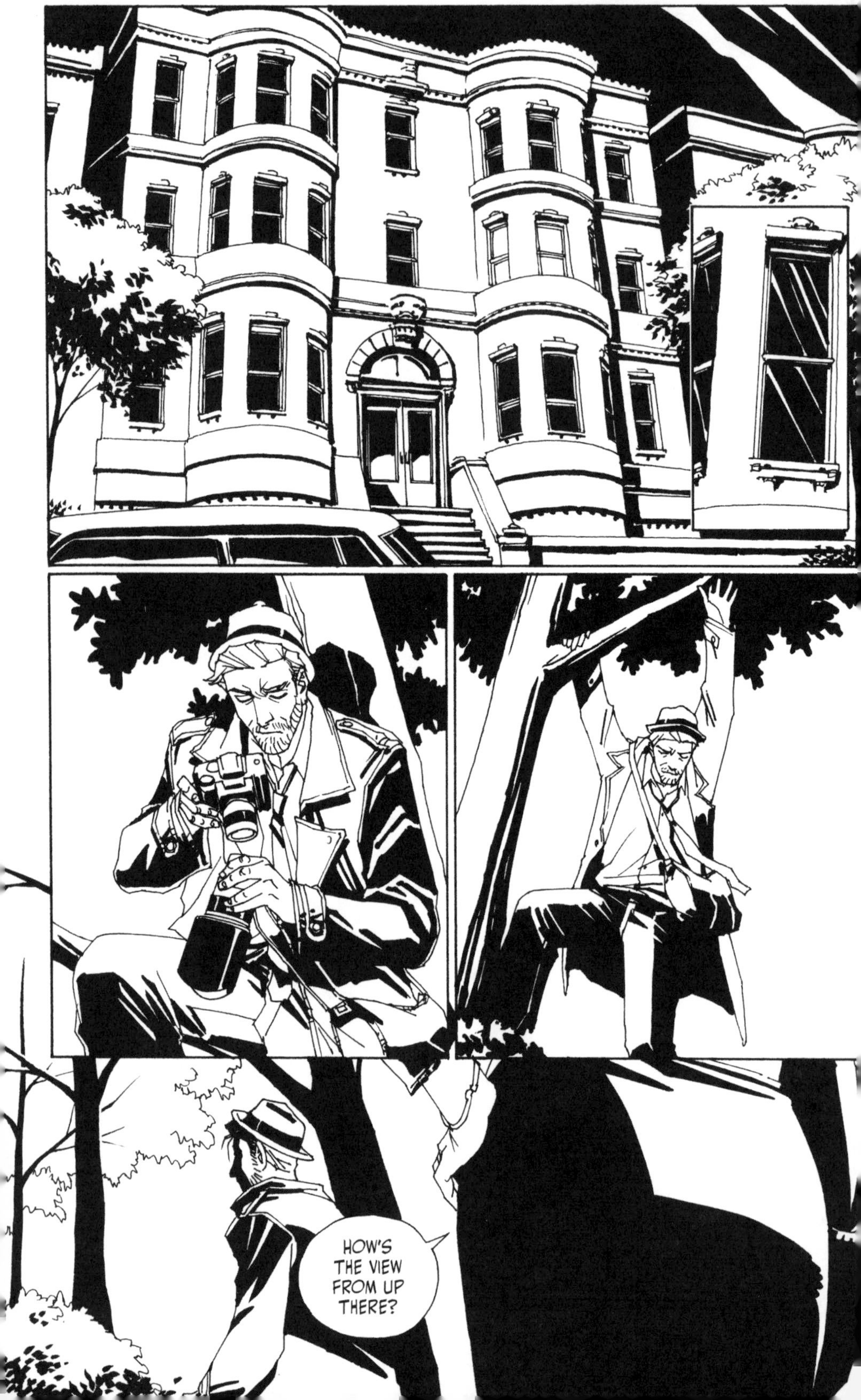
HOW'S THE VIEW FROM UP THERE?

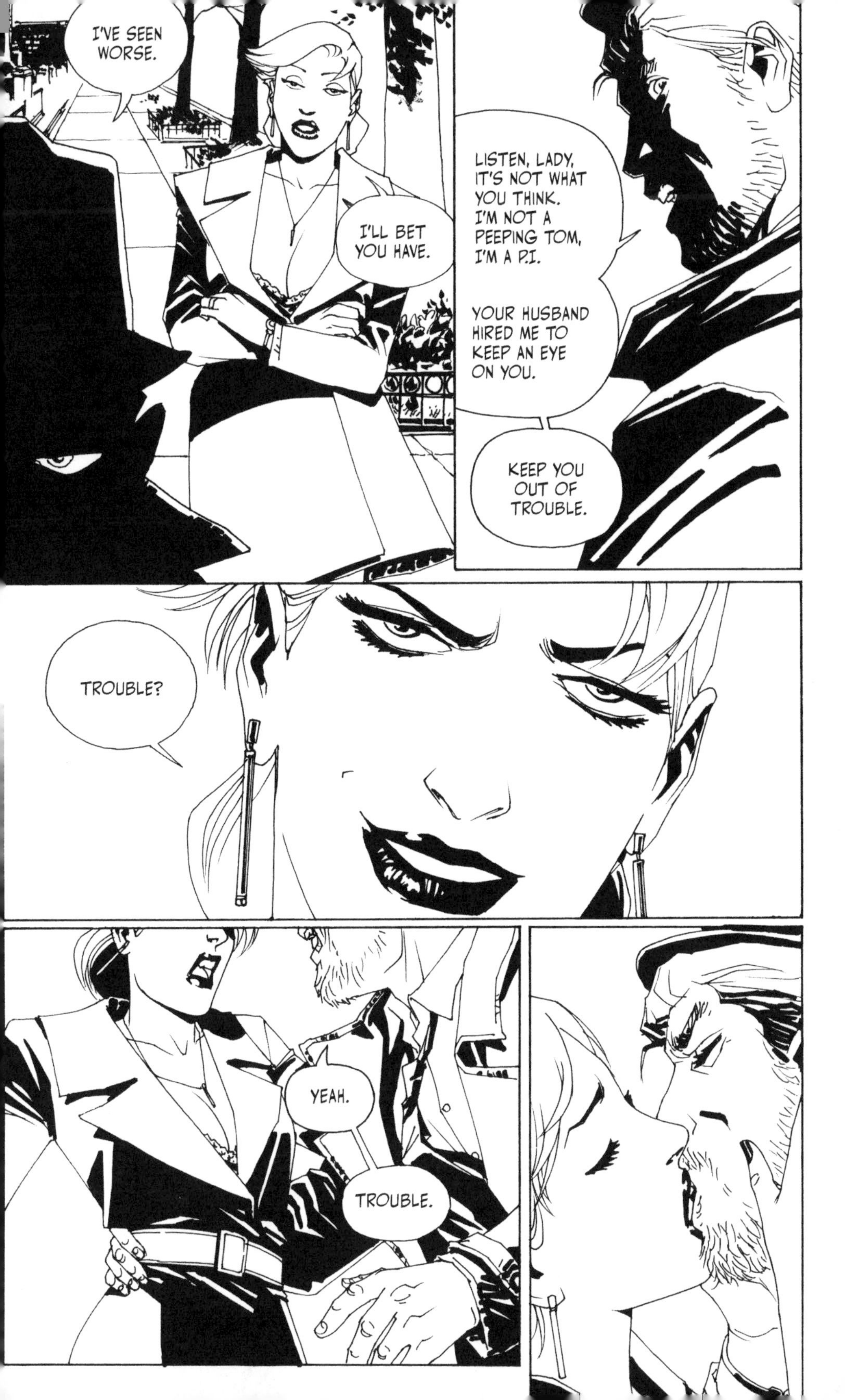
I'VE SEEN WORSE.
I'LL BET YOU HAVE.
LISTEN, LADY, IT'S NOT WHAT YOU THINK. I'M NOT A PEEPING TOM, I'M A P.I.
YOUR HUSBAND HIRED ME TO KEEP AN EYE ON YOU.
KEEP YOU OUT OF TROUBLE.
TROUBLE?
YEAH.
TROUBLE.

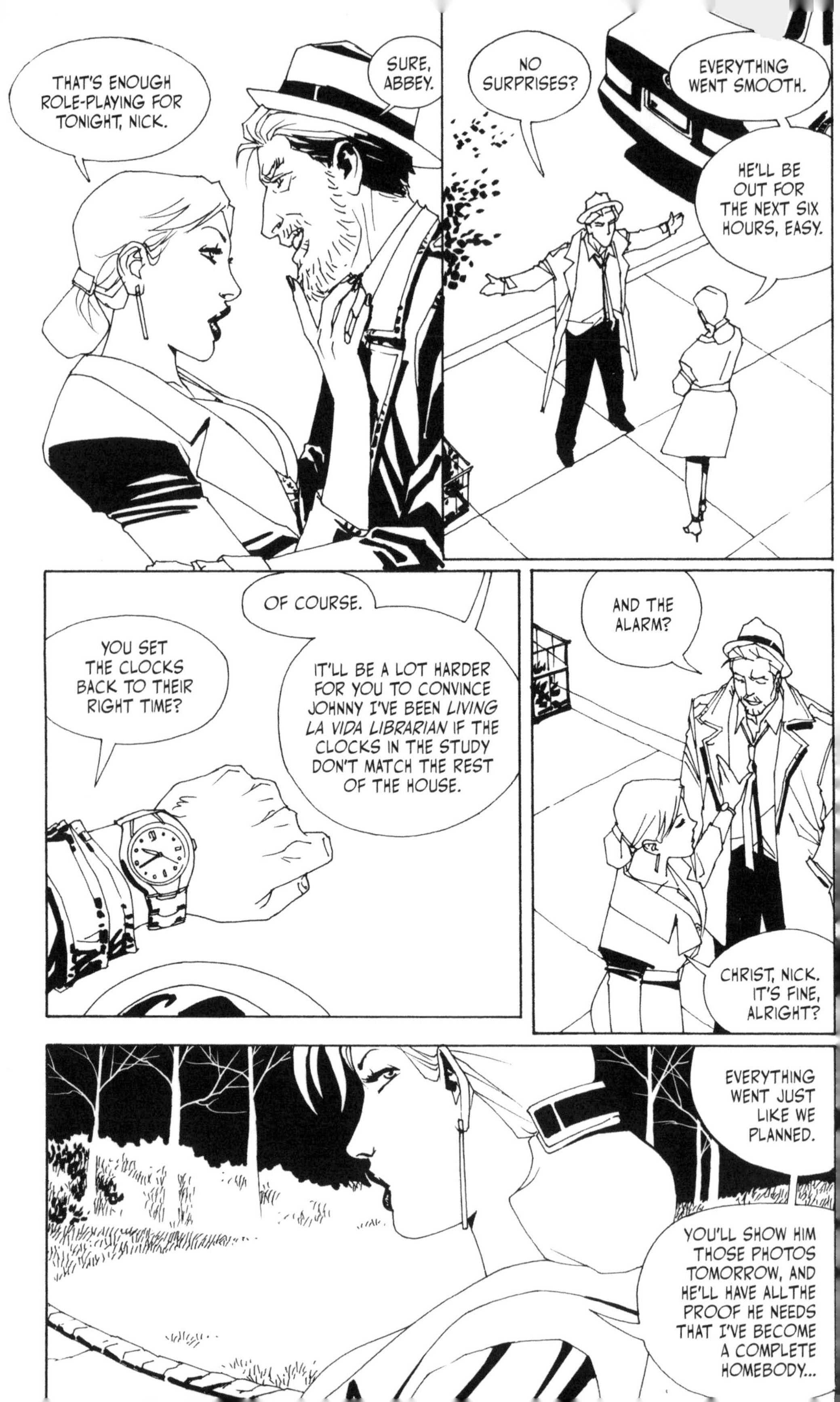
THAT'S ENOUGH ROLE-PLAYING FOR TONIGHT, NICK.
SURE, ABBEY.
NO SURPRISES?
EVERYTHING WENT SMOOTH.
HE'LL BE OUT FOR THE NEXT SIX HOURS, EASY.
YOU SET THE CLOCKS BACK TO THEIR RIGHT TIME?
OF COURSE.
IT'LL BE A LOT HARDER FOR YOU TO CONVINCE JOHNNY I'VE BEEN *LIVING LA VIDA LIBRARIAN* IF THE CLOCKS IN THE STUDY DON'T MATCH THE REST OF THE HOUSE.
AND THE ALARM?
CHRIST, NICK. IT'S FINE, ALRIGHT?
EVERYTHING WENT JUST LIKE WE PLANNED.
YOU'LL SHOW HIM THOSE PHOTOS TOMORROW, AND HE'LL HAVE ALLTHE PROOF HE NEEDS THAT I'VE BECOME A COMPLETE HOMEBODY...

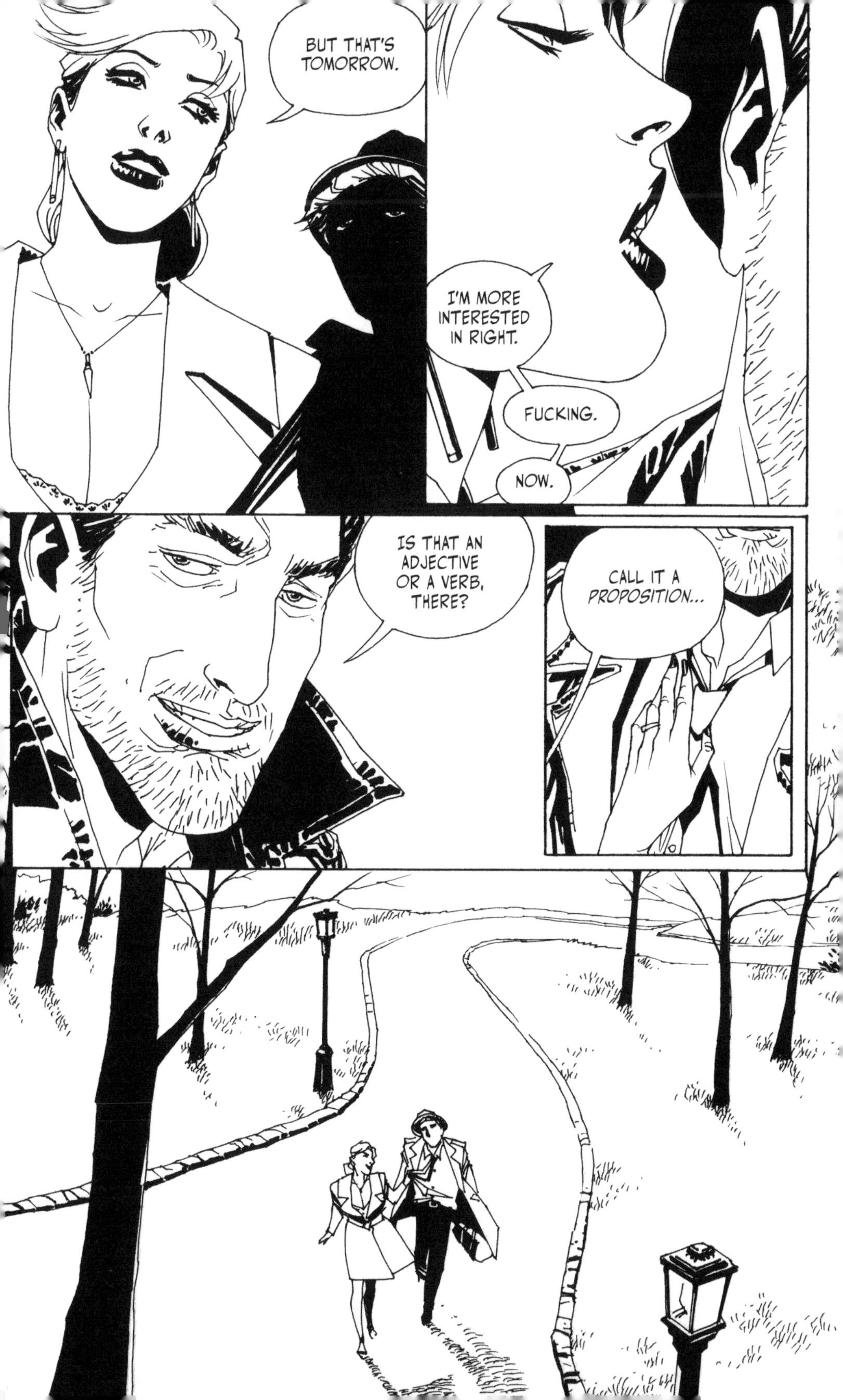
BUT THAT'S TOMORROW.
I'M MORE INTERESTED IN RIGHT.
FUCKING.
NOW.
IS THAT AN ADJECTIVE OR A VERB, THERE?
CALL IT A *PROPOSITION*...

TOP SHELF PRODUCTIONS **PRESENTS**

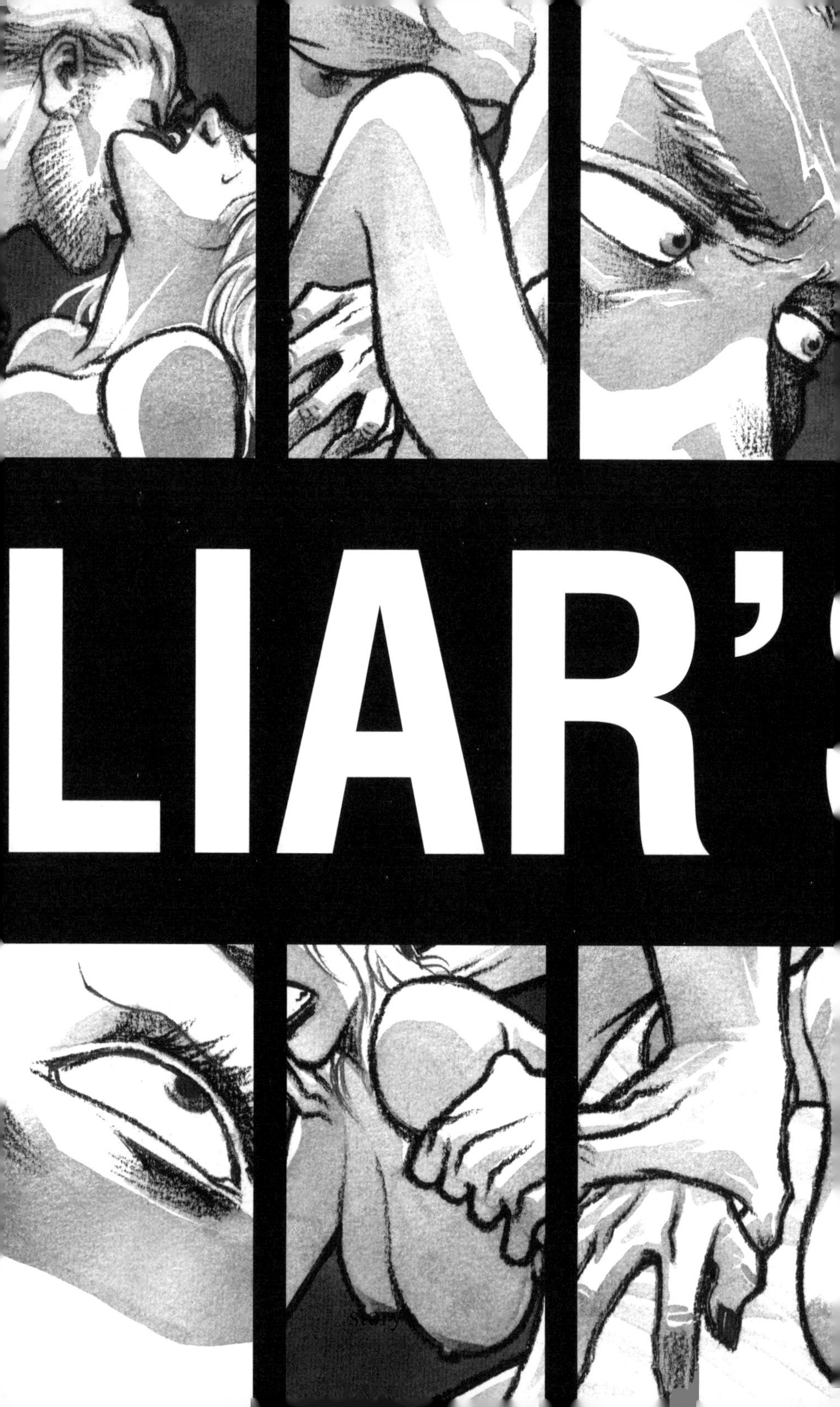
LIAR’

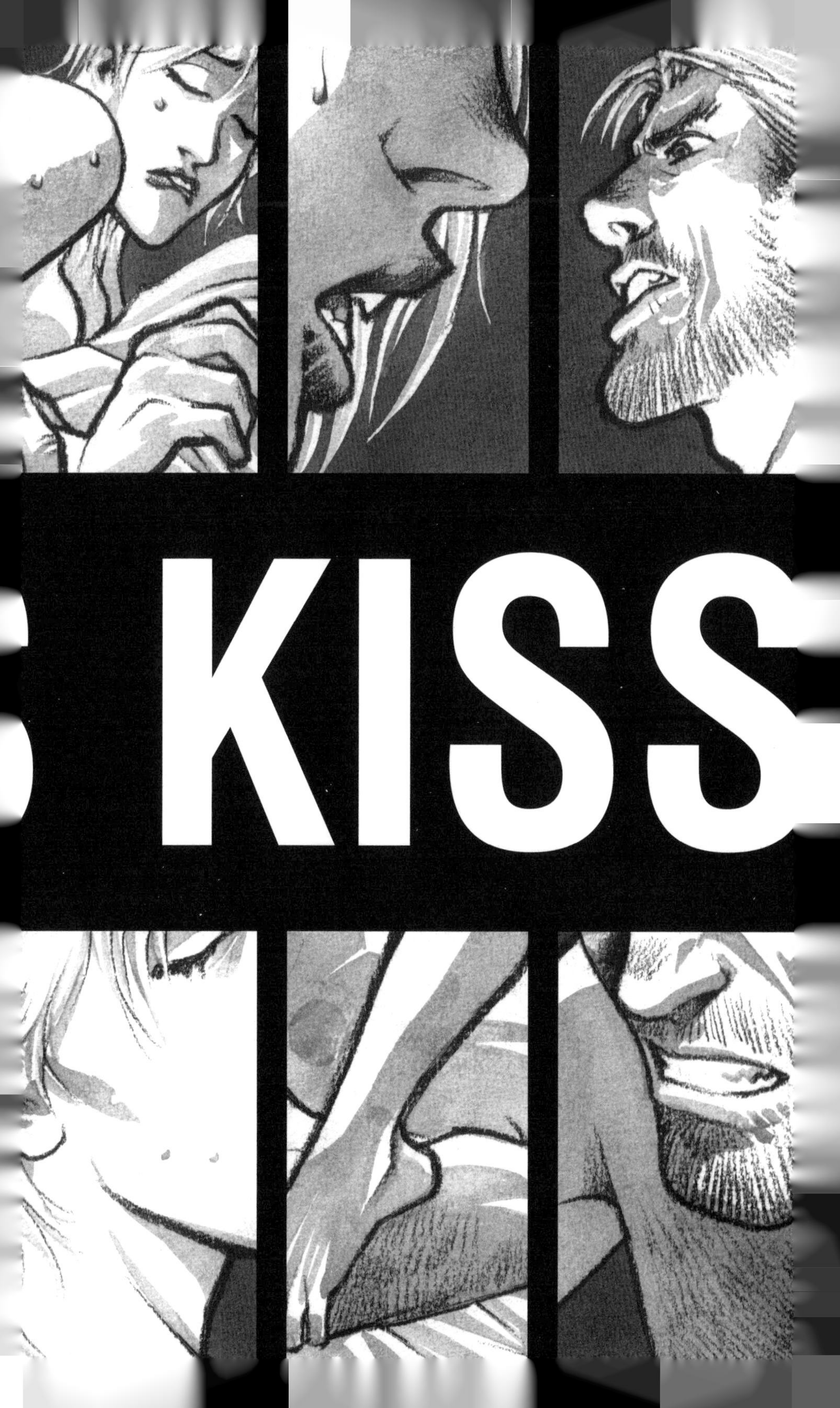
KISS

BY ERIC

& JHOMAR

SKILLMAN

SORIANO

ONE

**"DOESN'T EVERY WOMAN
CRAVE A LITTLE DANGER?"**

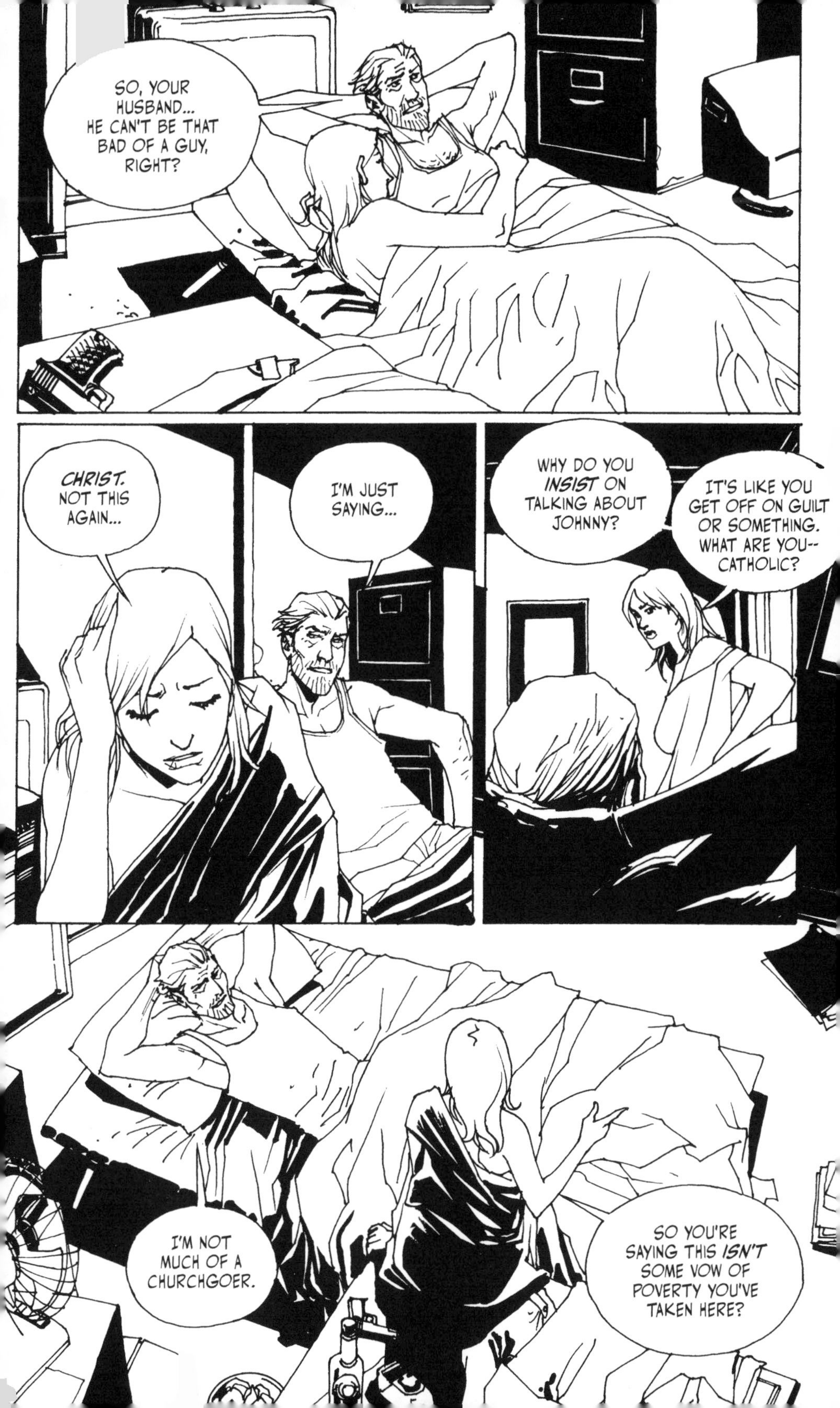
SO, YOUR HUSBAND... HE CAN'T BE THAT BAD OF A GUY, RIGHT?
CHRIST. NOT THIS AGAIN...
I'M JUST SAYING...
WHY DO YOU INSIST ON TALKING ABOUT JOHNNY?
IT'S LIKE YOU GET OFF ON GUILT OR SOMETHING. WHAT ARE YOU-- CATHOLIC?
I'M NOT MUCH OF A CHURCHGOER.
SO YOU'RE SAYING THIS ISN'T SOME VOW OF POVERTY YOU'VE TAKEN HERE?

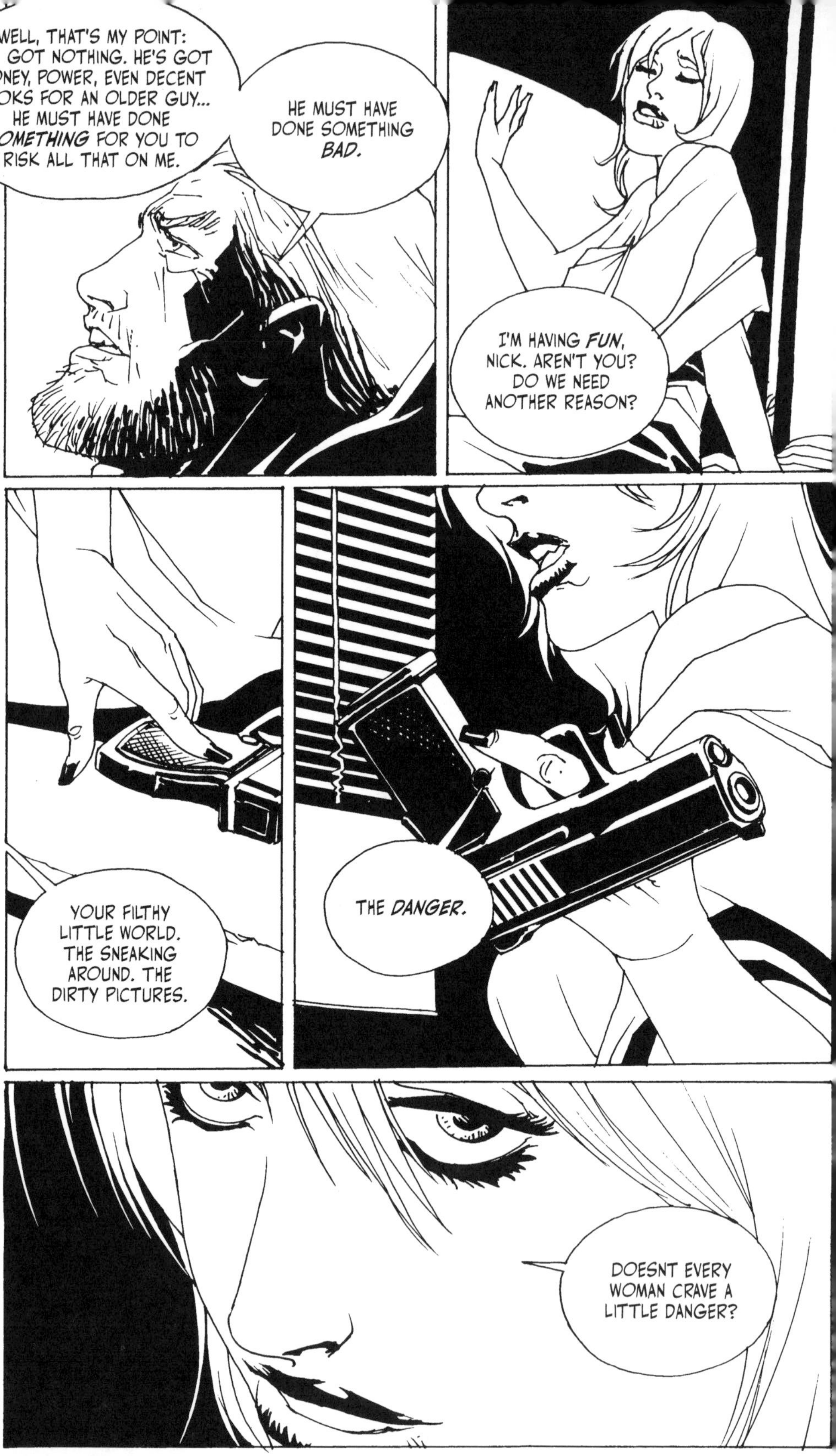
WELL, THAT'S MY POINT: I'VE GOT NOTHING. HE'S GOT MONEY, POWER, EVEN DECENT LOOKS FOR AN OLDER GUY... HE MUST HAVE DONE *SOMETHING* FOR YOU TO RISK ALL THAT ON ME.
HE MUST HAVE DONE SOMETHING *BAD.*
I'M HAVING *FUN*, NICK. AREN'T YOU? DO WE NEED ANOTHER REASON?
YOUR FILTHY LITTLE WORLD. THE SNEAKING AROUND. THE DIRTY PICTURES.
THE *DANGER.*
DOESNT EVERY WOMAN CRAVE A LITTLE DANGER?

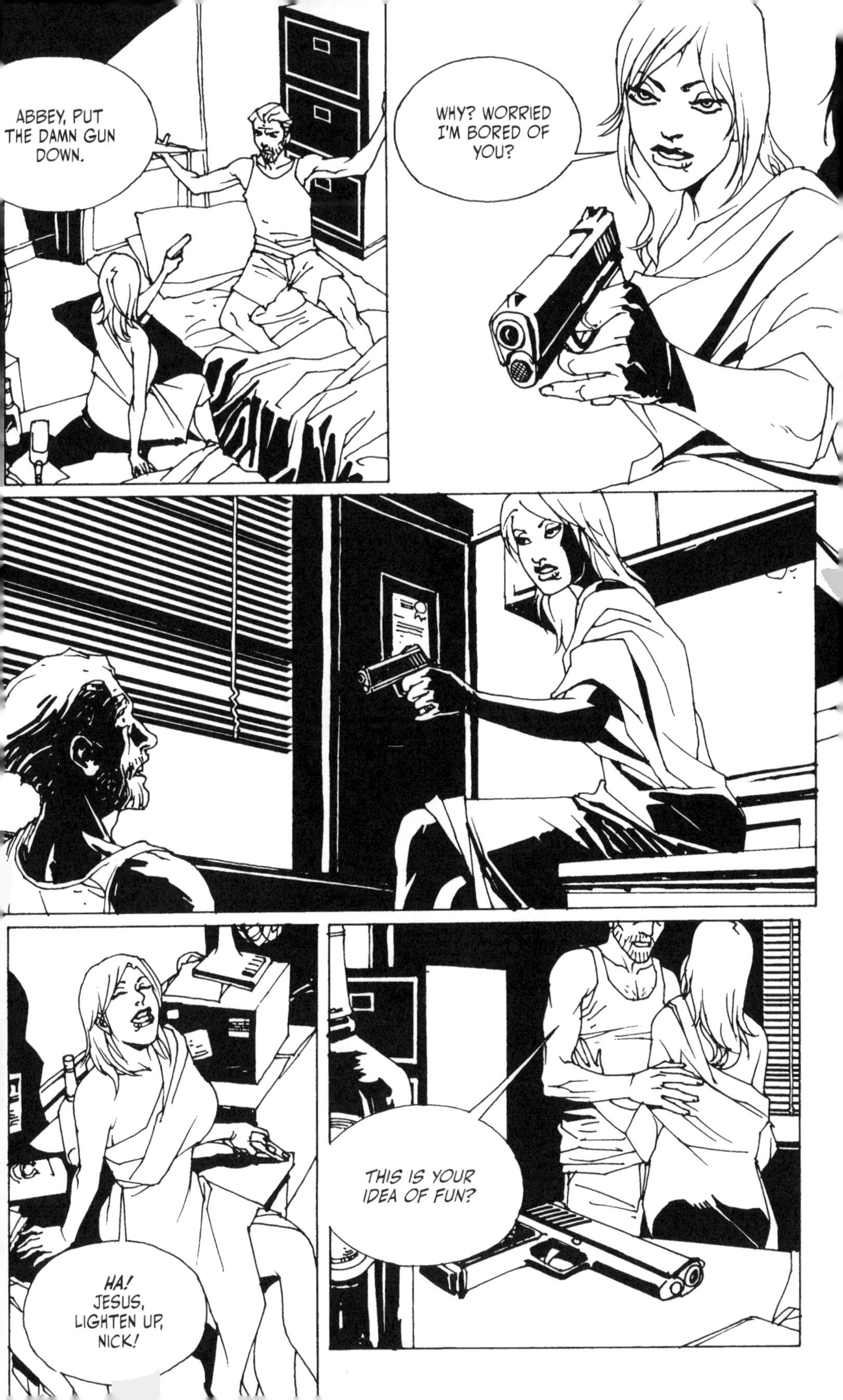
ABBEY, PUT THE DAMN GUN DOWN.
WHY? WORRIED I'M BORED OF YOU?
HA! JESUS, LIGHTEN UP, NICK!
THIS IS YOUR IDEA OF FUN?

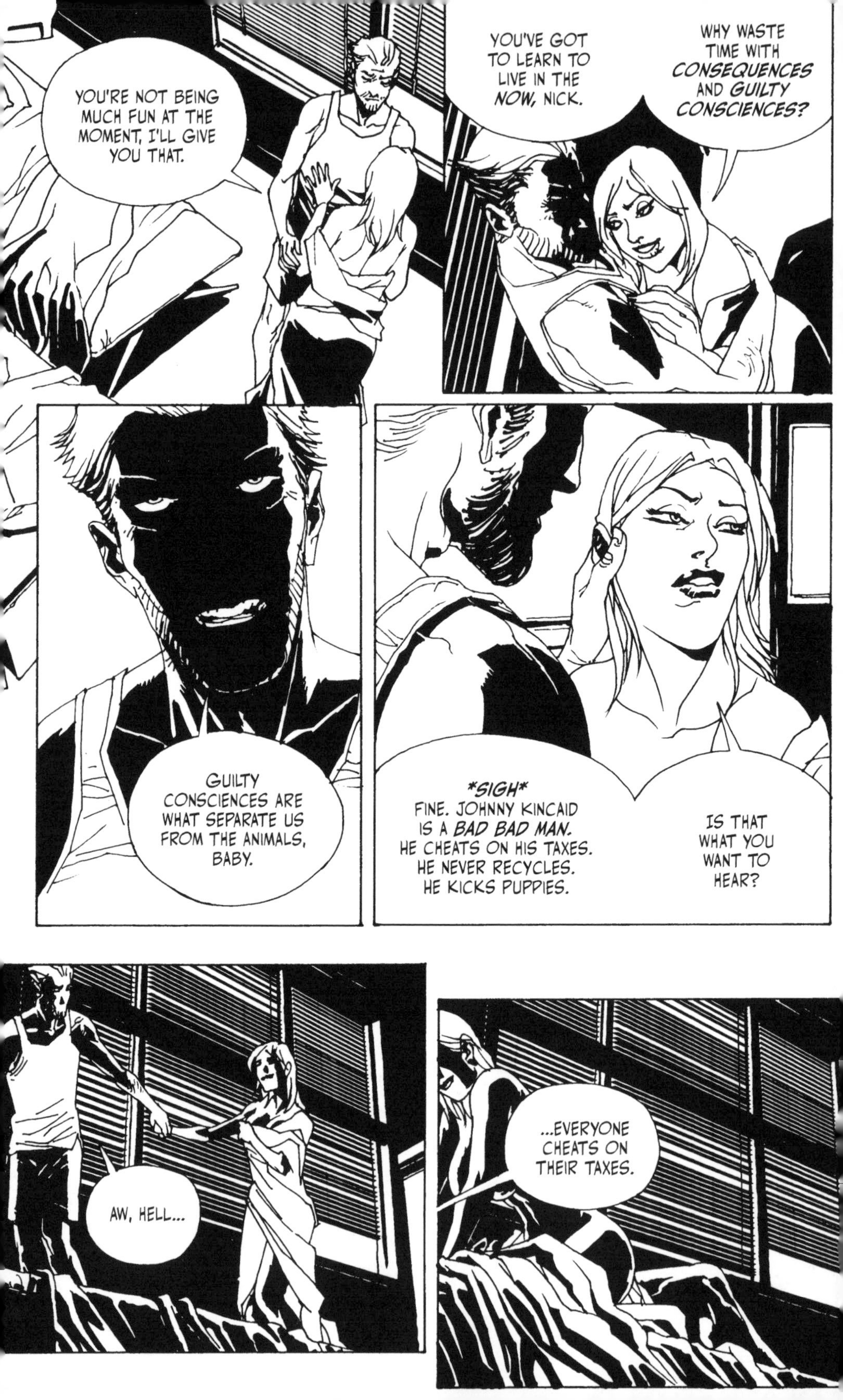
YOU'RE NOT BEING MUCH FUN AT THE MOMENT, I'LL GIVE YOU THAT.
YOU'VE GOT TO LEARN TO LIVE IN THE NOW, NICK.
WHY WASTE TIME WITH CONSEQUENCES AND GUILTY CONSCIENCES?
GUILTY CONSCIENCES ARE WHAT SEPARATE US FROM THE ANIMALS, BABY.
SIGH FINE. JOHNNY KINCAID IS A BAD BAD MAN. HE CHEATS ON HIS TAXES. HE NEVER RECYCLES. HE KICKS PUPPIES.
IS THAT WHAT YOU WANT TO HEAR?
AW, HELL...
...EVERYONE CHEATS ON THEIR TAXES.

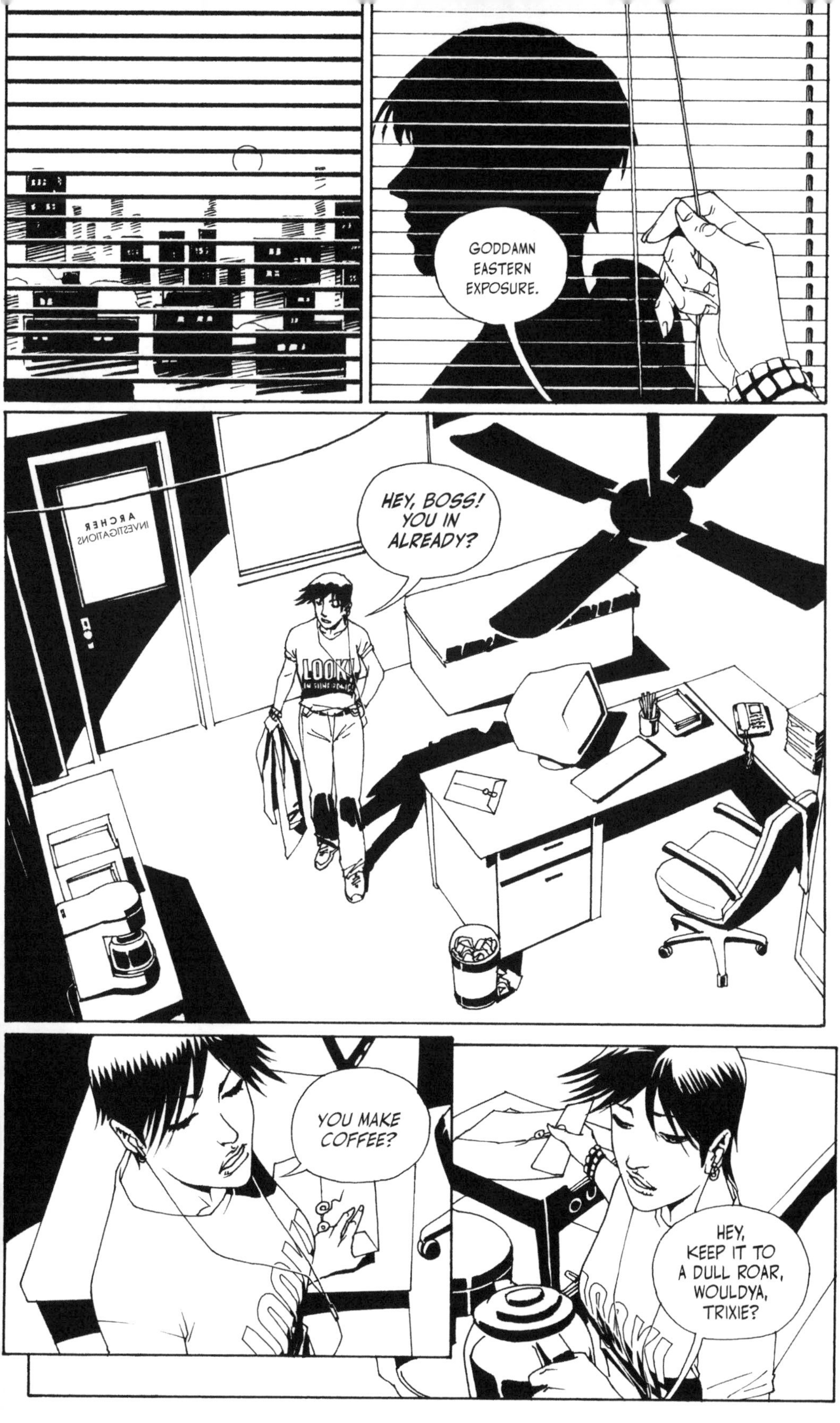
GODDAMN EASTERN EXPOSURE.
ARCHER INVESTIGATIONS
HEY, BOSS! YOU IN ALREADY?
YOU MAKE COFFEE?
HEY, KEEP IT TO A DULL ROAR, WOULDYA, TRIXIE?

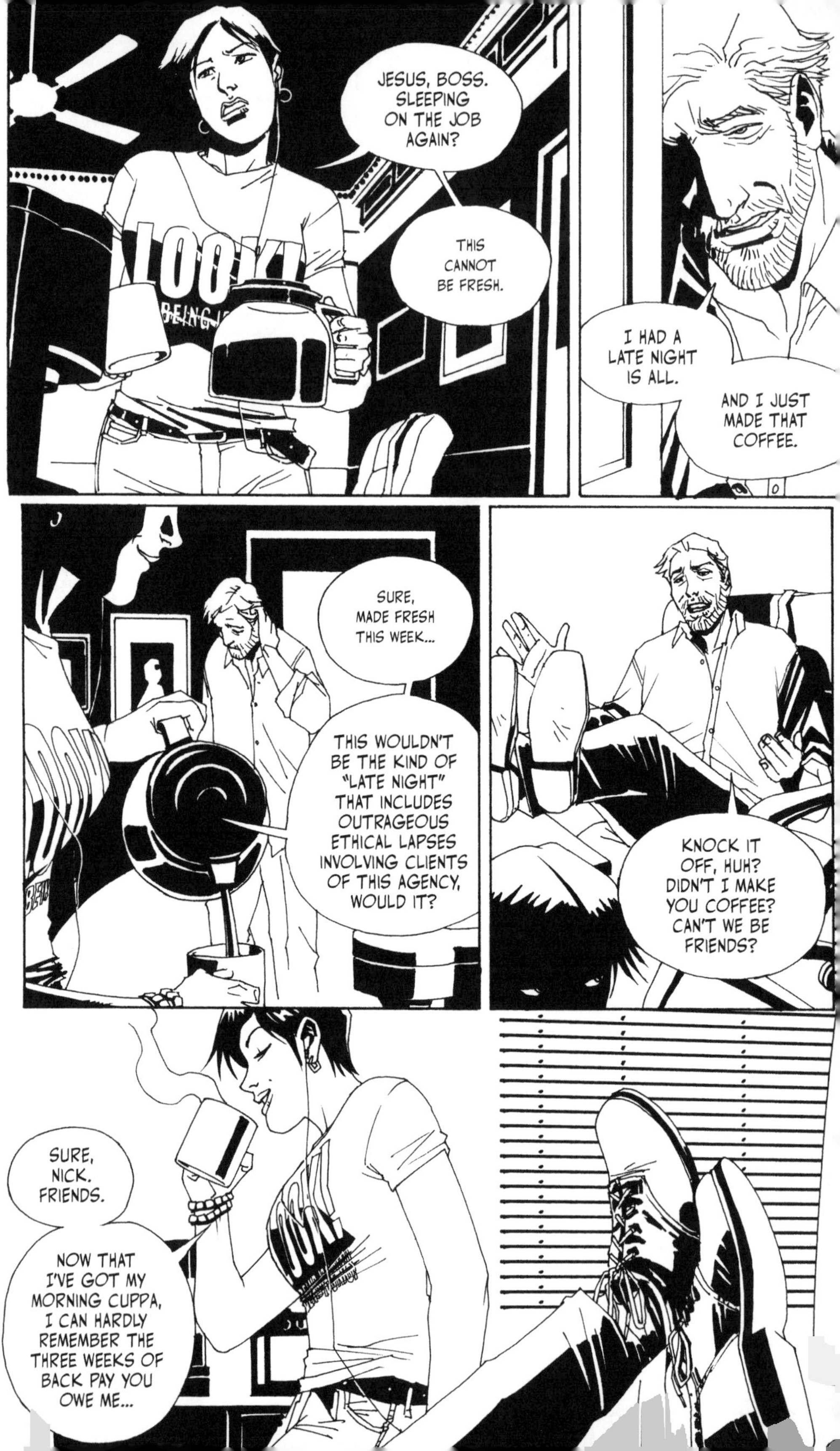
JESUS, BOSS. SLEEPING ON THE JOB AGAIN?
THIS CANNOT BE FRESH.
I HAD A LATE NIGHT IS ALL.
AND I JUST MADE THAT COFFEE.
SURE, MADE FRESH THIS WEEK...
THIS WOULDN'T BE THE KIND OF "LATE NIGHT" THAT INCLUDES OUTRAGEOUS ETHICAL LAPSES INVOLVING CLIENTS OF THIS AGENCY, WOULD IT?
KNOCK IT OFF, HUH? DIDN'T I MAKE YOU COFFEE? CAN'T WE BE FRIENDS?
SURE, NICK. FRIENDS.
NOW THAT I'VE GOT MY MORNING CUPPA, I CAN HARDLY REMEMBER THE THREE WEEKS OF BACK PAY YOU OWE ME...

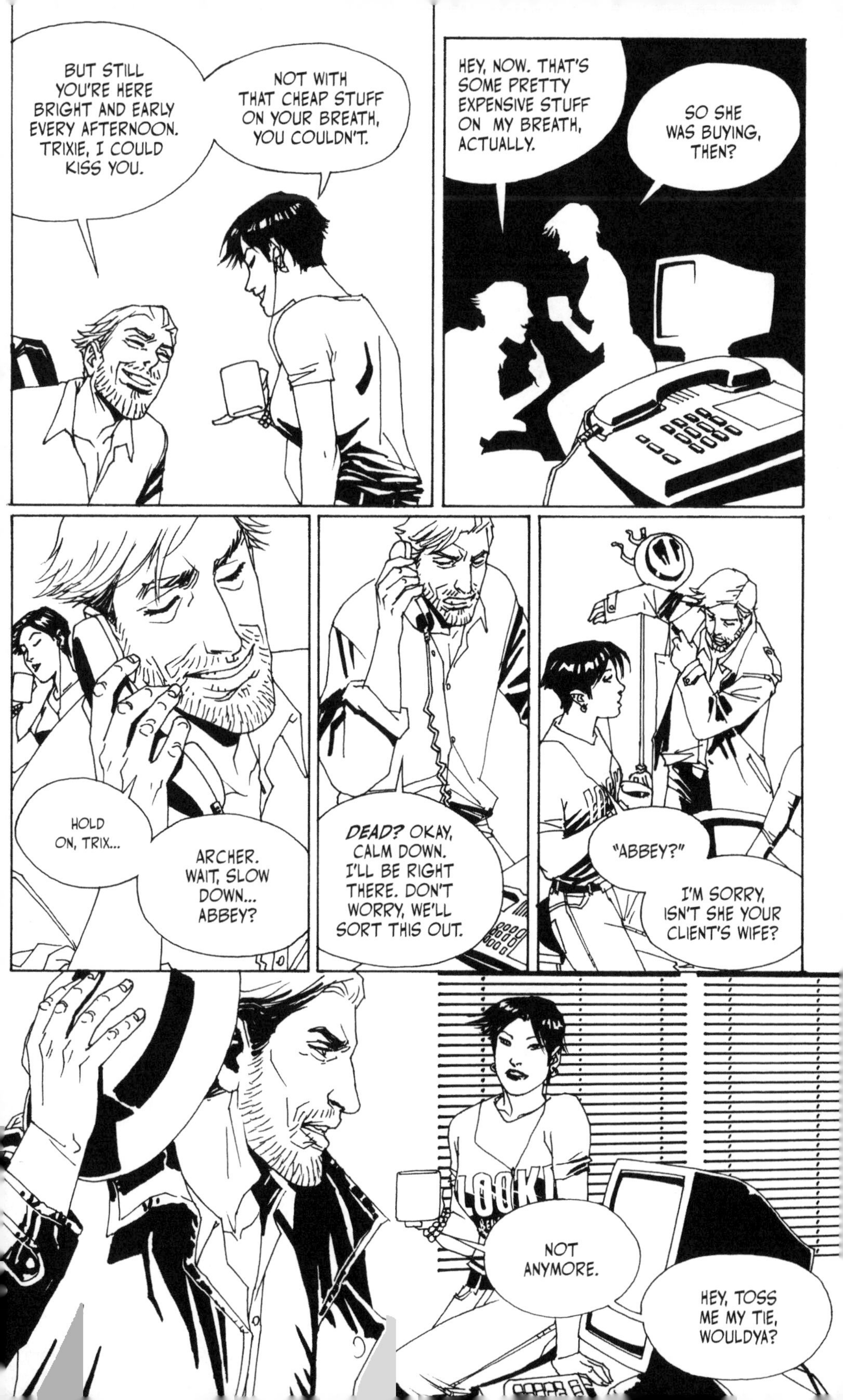
BUT STILL YOU'RE HERE BRIGHT AND EARLY EVERY AFTERNOON. TRIXIE, I COULD KISS YOU.
NOT WITH THAT CHEAP STUFF ON YOUR BREATH, YOU COULDN'T.
HEY, NOW. THAT'S SOME PRETTY EXPENSIVE STUFF ON MY BREATH, ACTUALLY.
SO SHE WAS BUYING, THEN?
HOLD ON, TRIX...
ARCHER. WAIT, SLOW DOWN... ABBEY?
DEAD? OKAY, CALM DOWN. I'LL BE RIGHT THERE. DON'T WORRY, WE'LL SORT THIS OUT.
"ABBEY?"
I'M SORRY, ISN'T SHE YOUR CLIENT'S WIFE?
NOT ANYMORE.
HEY, TOSS ME MY TIE, WOULDYA?

TWO "SLOW DOWN, BABY. START FROM THE BEGINNING."

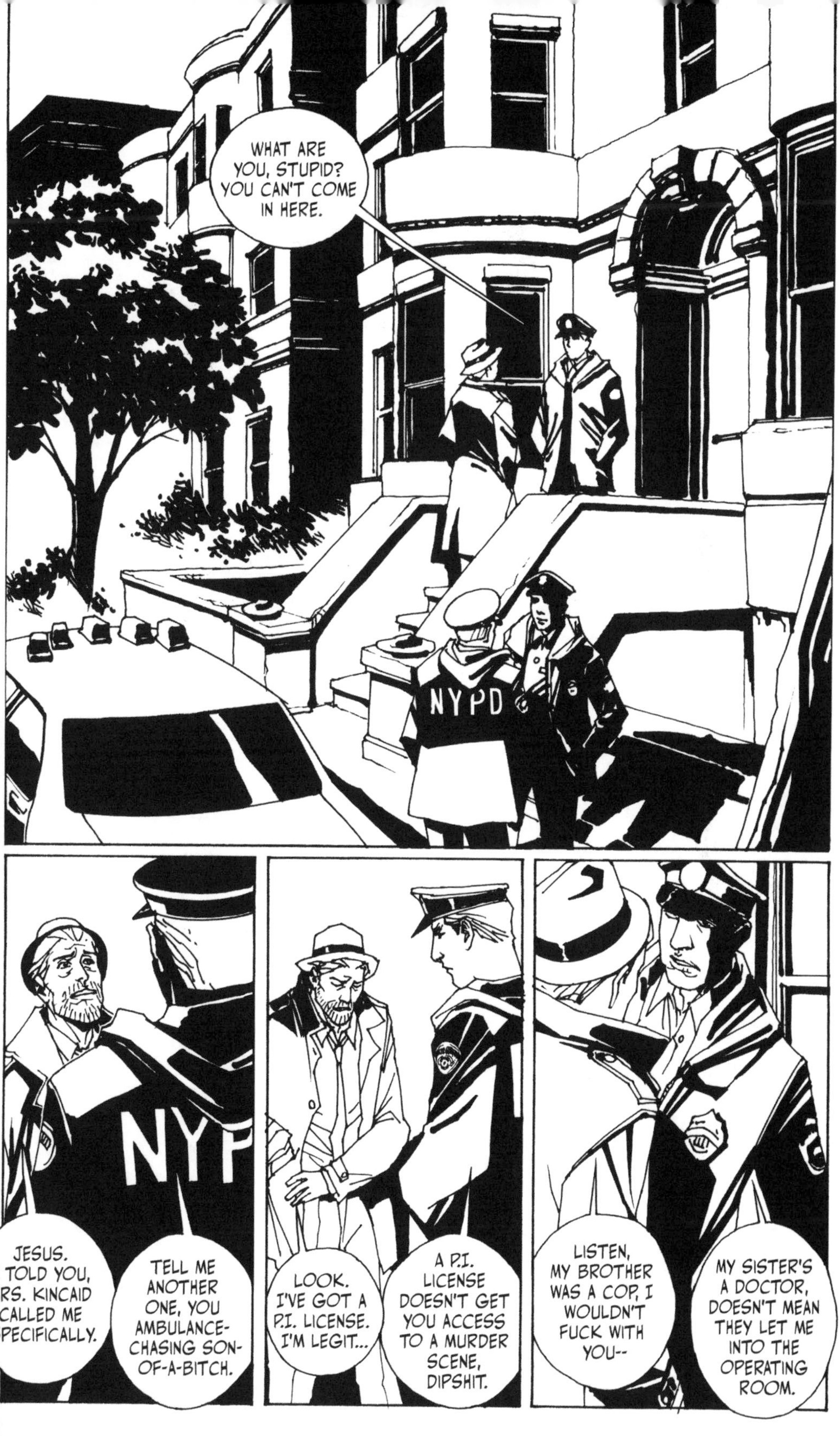

WHAT ARE YOU, STUPID? YOU CAN'T COME IN HERE.
JESUS. TOLD YOU, RS. KINCAID CALLED ME PECIFICALLY.
TELL ME ANOTHER ONE, YOU AMBULANCE-CHASING SON-OF-A-BITCH.
NYPD
LOOK. I'VE GOT A P.I. LICENSE. I'M LEGIT...
A P.I. LICENSE DOESN'T GET YOU ACCESS TO A MURDER SCENE, DIPSHIT.
LISTEN, MY BROTHER WAS A COP, I WOULDN'T FUCK WITH YOU--
MY SISTER'S A DOCTOR, DOESN'T MEAN THEY LET ME INTO THE OPERATING ROOM.

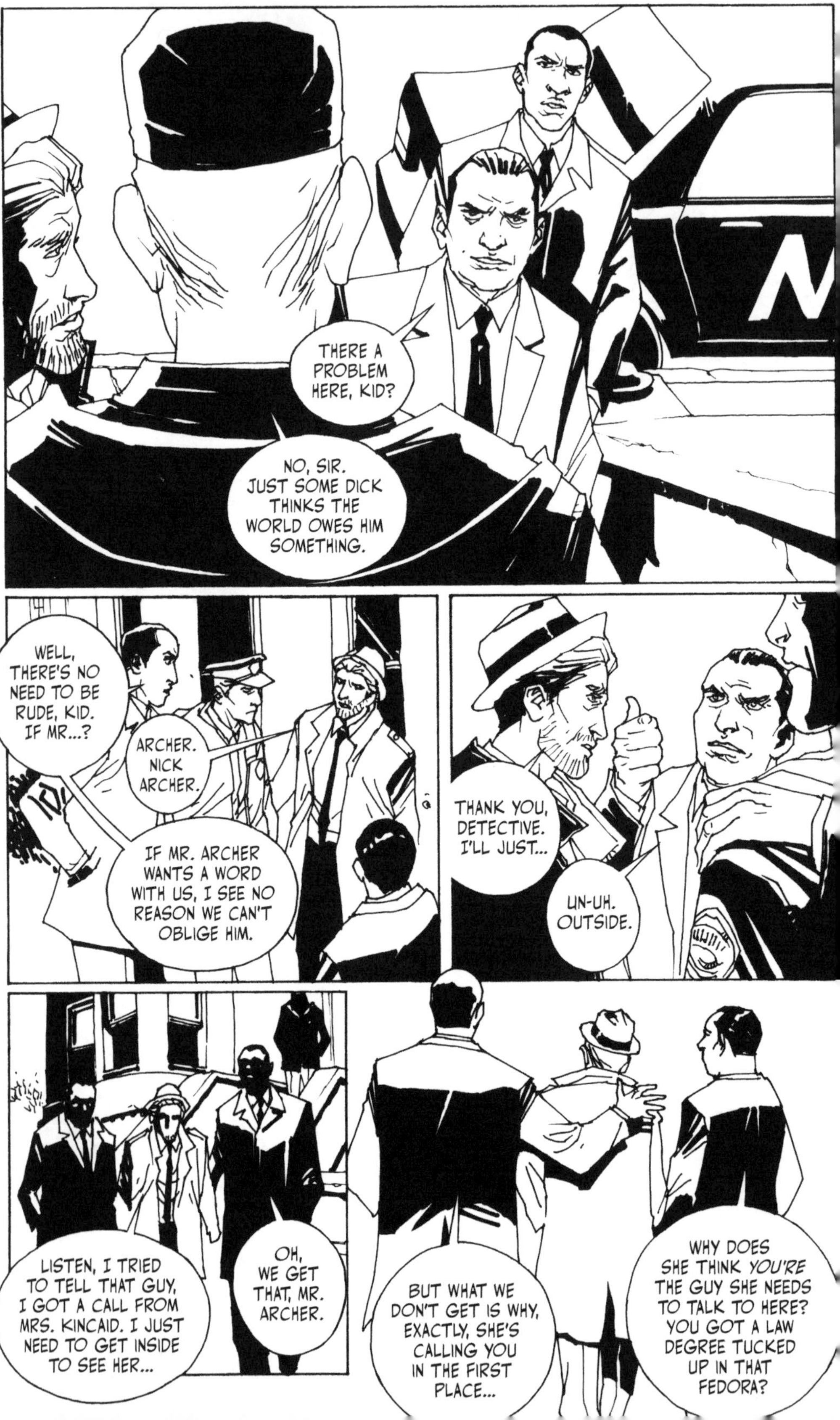
THERE A PROBLEM HERE, KID?
NO, SIR. JUST SOME DICK THINKS THE WORLD OWES HIM SOMETHING.
WELL, THERE'S NO NEED TO BE RUDE, KID. IF MR...?
ARCHER. NICK ARCHER.
IF MR. ARCHER WANTS A WORD WITH US, I SEE NO REASON WE CAN'T OBLIGE HIM.
THANK YOU, DETECTIVE. I'LL JUST...
UN-UH. OUTSIDE.
LISTEN, I TRIED TO TELL THAT GUY, I GOT A CALL FROM MRS. KINCAID. I JUST NEED TO GET INSIDE TO SEE HER...
OH, WE GET THAT, MR. ARCHER.
BUT WHAT WE DON'T GET IS WHY, EXACTLY, SHE'S CALLING YOU IN THE FIRST PLACE...
WHY DOES SHE THINK *YOU'RE* THE GUY SHE NEEDS TO TALK TO HERE? YOU GOT A LAW DEGREE TUCKED UP IN THAT FEDORA?

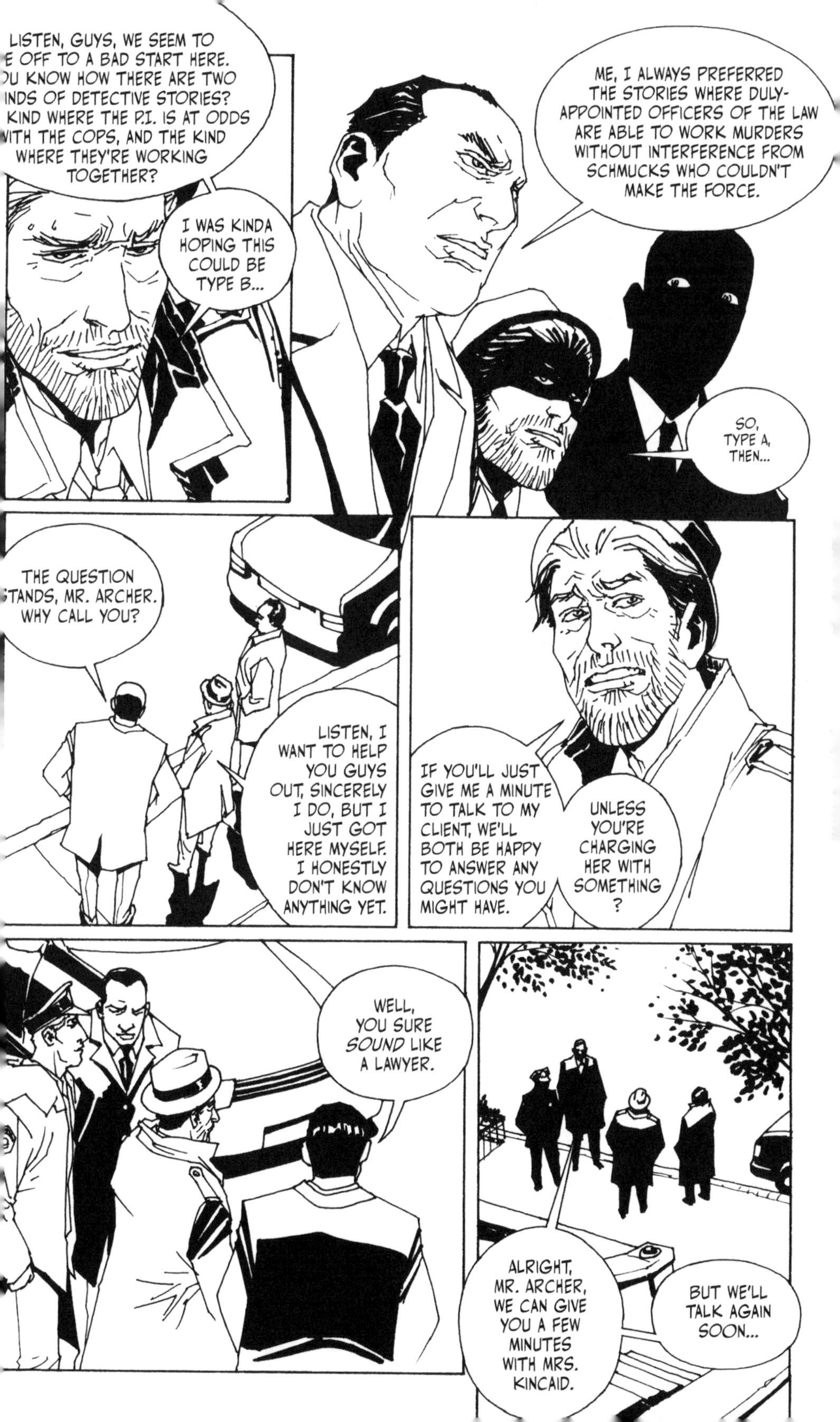
LISTEN, GUYS, WE SEEM TO
E OFF TO A BAD START HERE.
OU KNOW HOW THERE ARE TWO
INDS OF DETECTIVE STORIES?
KIND WHERE THE P.I. IS AT ODDS
WITH THE COPS, AND THE KIND
WHERE THEY'RE WORKING
TOGETHER?
I WAS KINDA HOPING THIS COULD BE TYPE B...
ME, I ALWAYS PREFERRED THE STORIES WHERE DULY-APPOINTED OFFICERS OF THE LAW ARE ABLE TO WORK MURDERS WITHOUT INTERFERENCE FROM SCHMUCKS WHO COULDN'T MAKE THE FORCE.
SO, TYPE A, THEN...
THE QUESTION
TANDS, MR. ARCHER.
WHY CALL YOU?
LISTEN, I WANT TO HELP YOU GUYS OUT, SINCERELY I DO, BUT I JUST GOT HERE MYSELF. I HONESTLY DON'T KNOW ANYTHING YET.
IF YOU'LL JUST GIVE ME A MINUTE TO TALK TO MY CLIENT, WE'LL BOTH BE HAPPY TO ANSWER ANY QUESTIONS YOU MIGHT HAVE.
UNLESS YOU'RE CHARGING HER WITH SOMETHING ?
WELL, YOU SURE *SOUND* LIKE A LAWYER.
ALRIGHT, MR. ARCHER, WE CAN GIVE YOU A FEW MINUTES WITH MRS. KINCAID.
BUT WE'LL TALK AGAIN SOON...

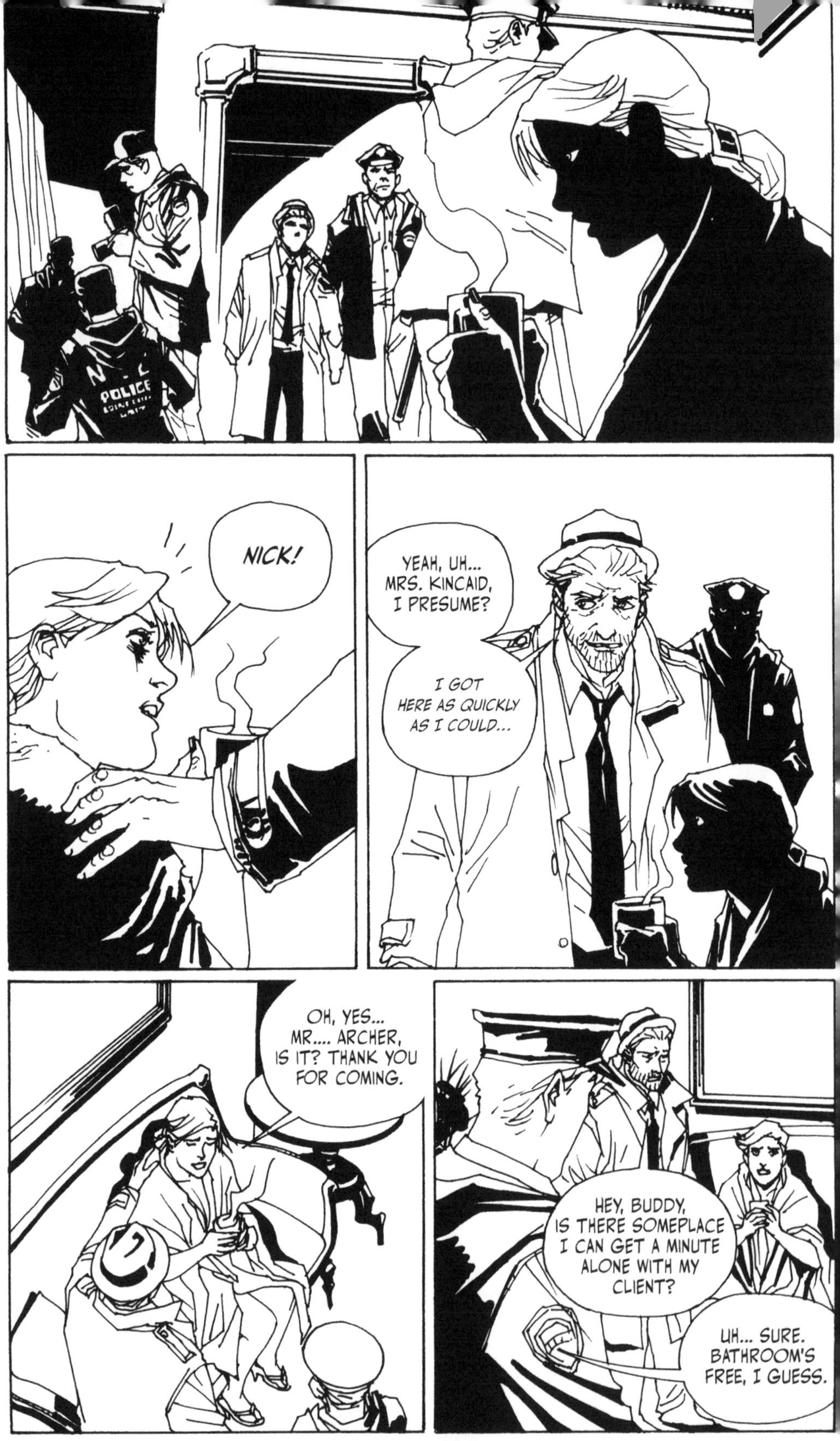
POLICE
NICK!
YEAH, UH... MRS. KINCAID, I PRESUME?
I GOT HERE AS QUICKLY AS I COULD...
OH, YES... MR.... ARCHER, IS IT? THANK YOU FOR COMING.
HEY, BUDDY, IS THERE SOMEPLACE I CAN GET A MINUTE ALONE WITH MY CLIENT?
UH... SURE. BATHROOM'S FREE, I GUESS.

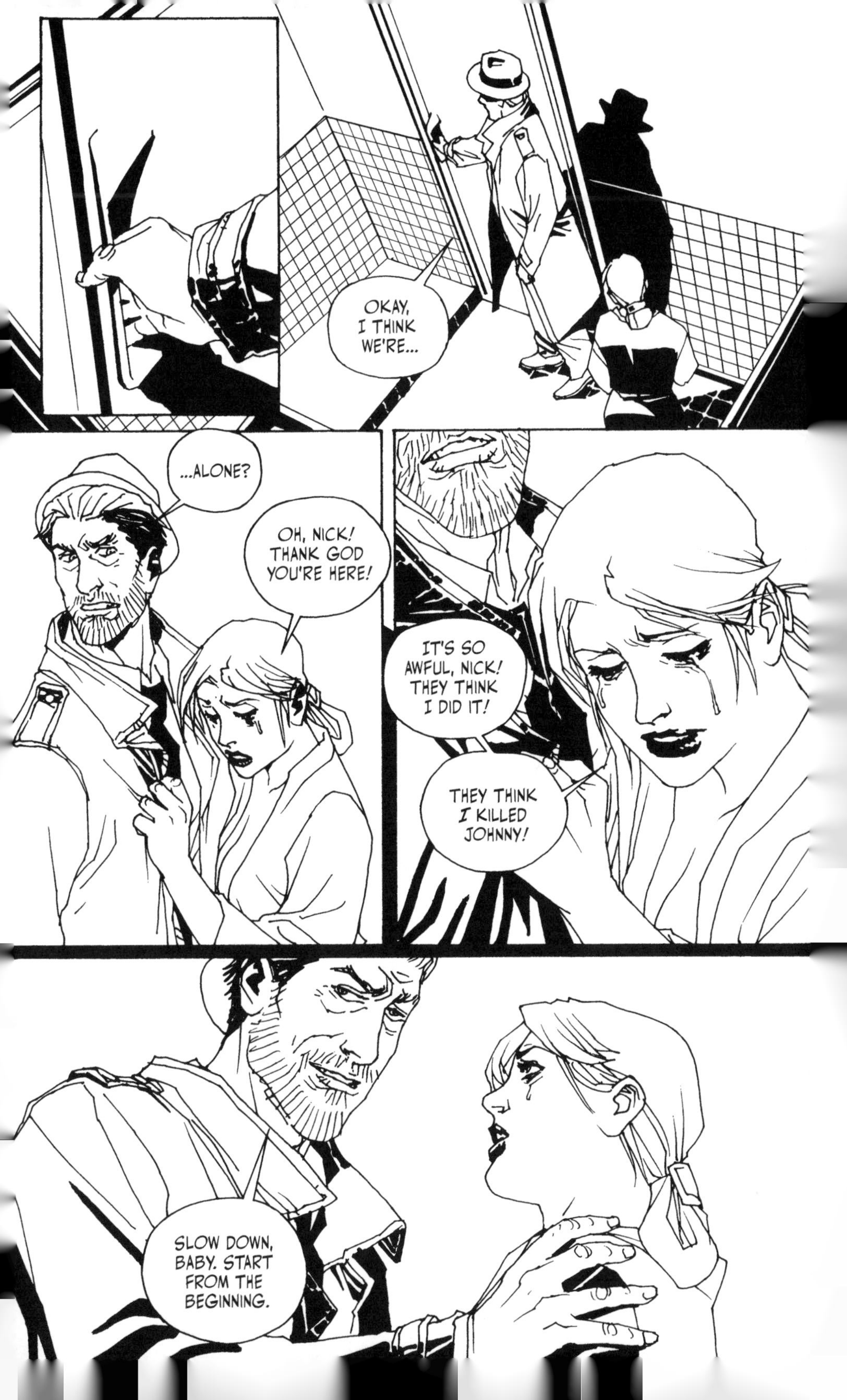

OKAY, I THINK WE'RE...
...ALONE?
OH, NICK! THANK GOD YOU'RE HERE!
IT'S SO AWFUL, NICK! THEY THINK I DID IT!
THEY THINK *I* KILLED JOHNNY!
SLOW DOWN, BABY. START FROM THE BEGINNING.

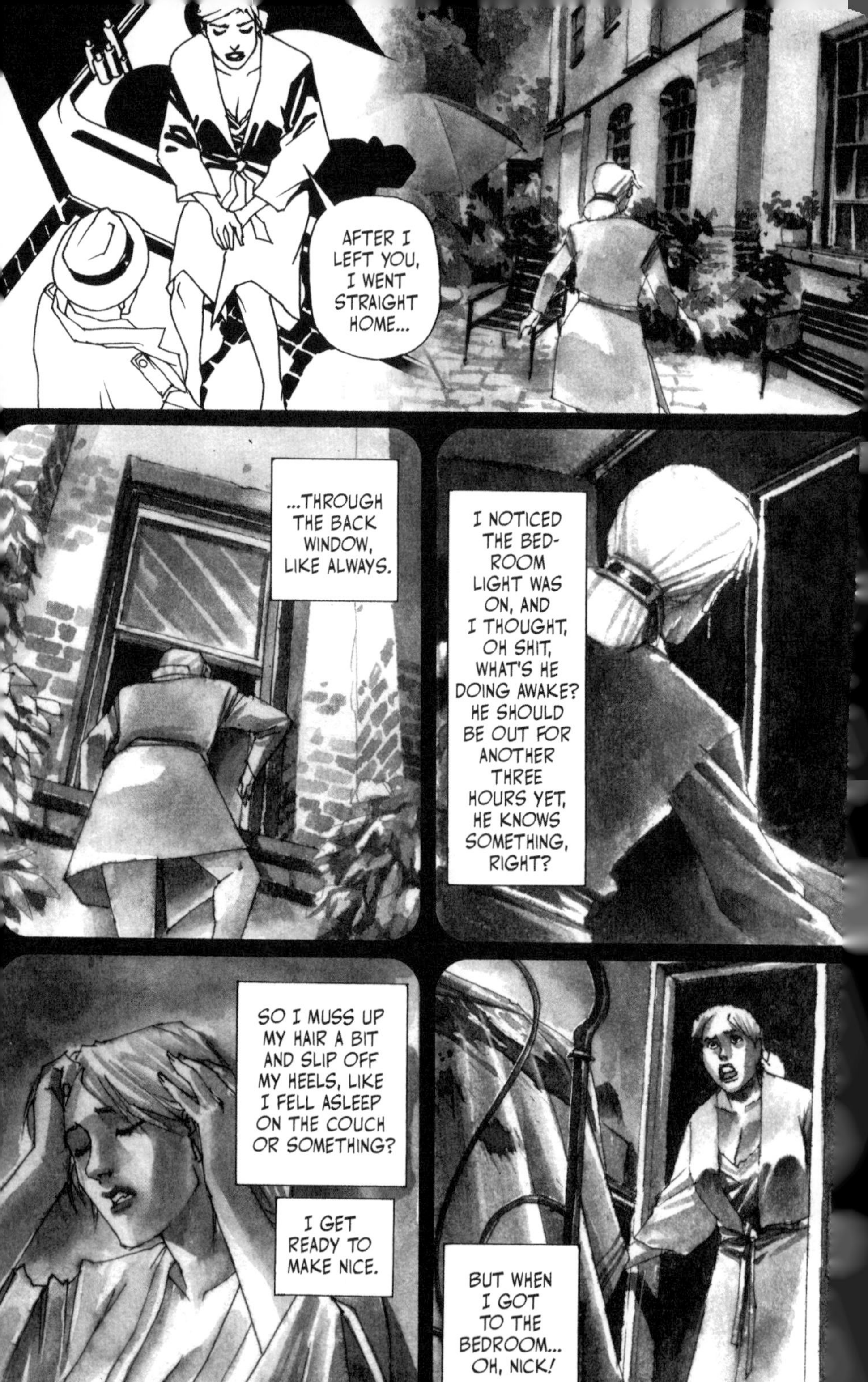
AFTER I LEFT YOU, I WENT STRAIGHT HOME...
...THROUGH THE BACK WINDOW, LIKE ALWAYS.
I NOTICED THE BED-ROOM LIGHT WAS ON, AND I THOUGHT, OH SHIT, WHAT'S HE DOING AWAKE? HE SHOULD BE OUT FOR ANOTHER THREE HOURS YET, HE KNOWS SOMETHING, RIGHT?
SO I MUSS UP MY HAIR A BIT AND SLIP OFF MY HEELS, LIKE I FELL ASLEEP ON THE COUCH OR SOMETHING?
I GET READY TO MAKE NICE.
BUT WHEN I GOT TO THE BEDROOM... OH, NICK!

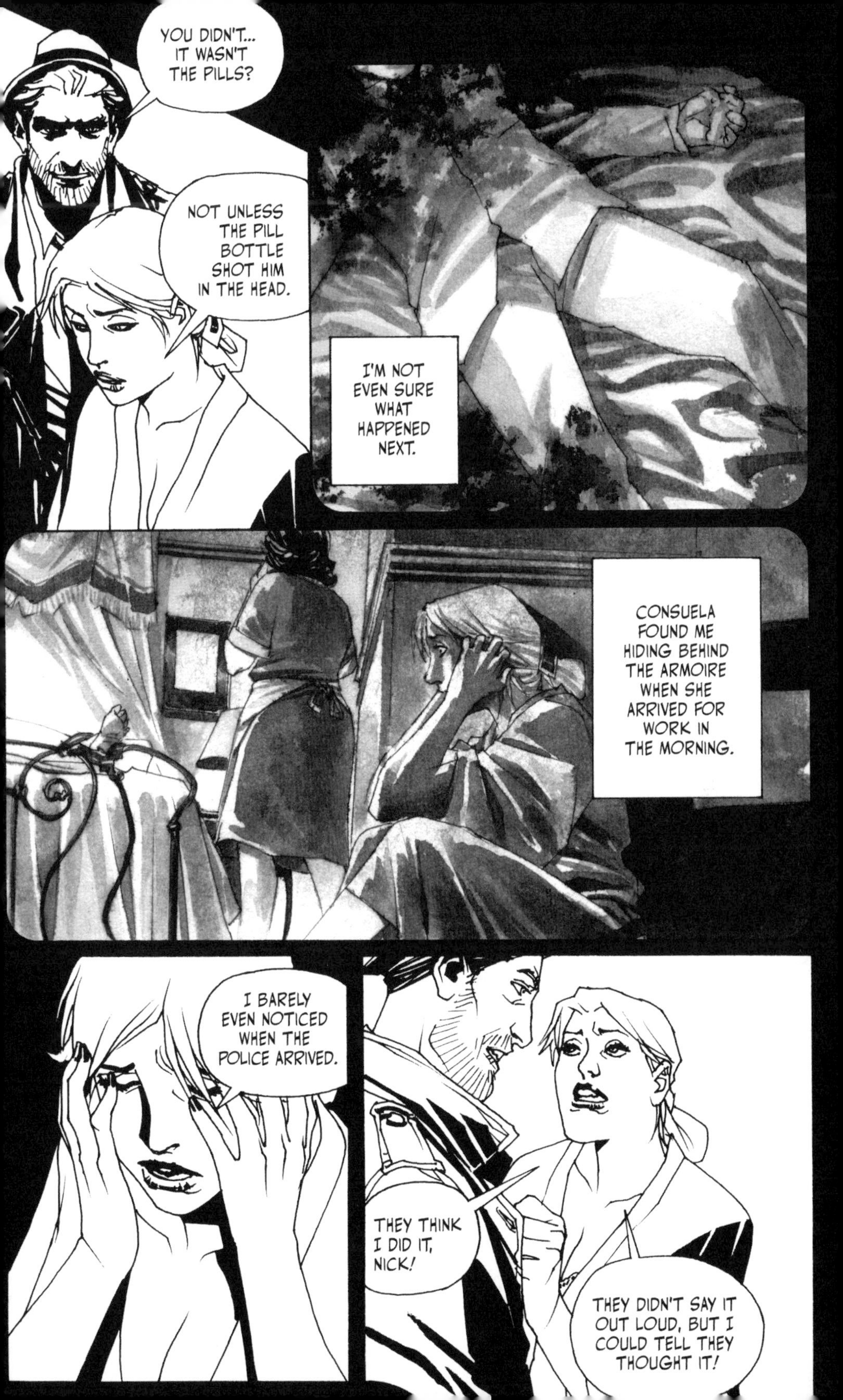

YOU DIDN'T... IT WASN'T THE PILLS?
NOT UNLESS THE PILL BOTTLE SHOT HIM IN THE HEAD.
I'M NOT EVEN SURE WHAT HAPPENED NEXT.
CONSUELA FOUND ME HIDING BEHIND THE ARMOIRE WHEN SHE ARRIVED FOR WORK IN THE MORNING.
I BARELY EVEN NOTICED WHEN THE POLICE ARRIVED.
THEY THINK I DID IT, NICK!
THEY DIDN'T SAY IT OUT LOUD, BUT I COULD TELL THEY THOUGHT IT!

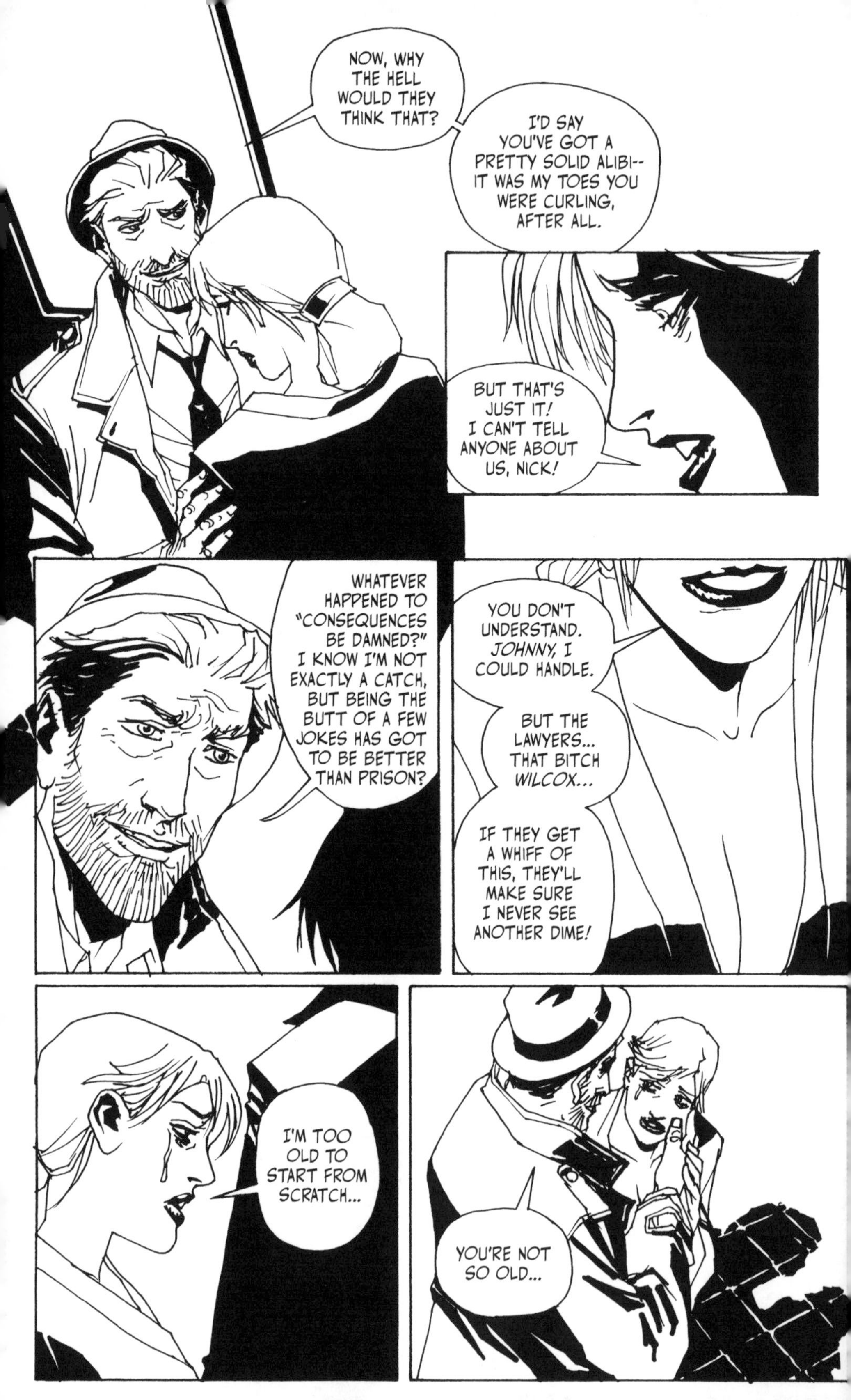
NOW, WHY THE HELL WOULD THEY THINK THAT?
I'D SAY YOU'VE GOT A PRETTY SOLID ALIBI-- IT WAS MY TOES YOU WERE CURLING, AFTER ALL.
BUT THAT'S JUST IT! I CAN'T TELL ANYONE ABOUT US, NICK!
WHATEVER HAPPENED TO "CONSEQUENCES BE DAMNED?" I KNOW I'M NOT EXACTLY A CATCH, BUT BEING THE BUTT OF A FEW JOKES HAS GOT TO BE BETTER THAN PRISON?
YOU DON'T UNDERSTAND. *JOHNNY*, I COULD HANDLE.
BUT THE LAWYERS... THAT BITCH *WILCOX*...
IF THEY GET A WHIFF OF THIS, THEY'LL MAKE SURE I NEVER SEE ANOTHER DIME!
I'M TOO OLD TO START FROM SCRATCH...
YOU'RE NOT SO OLD...

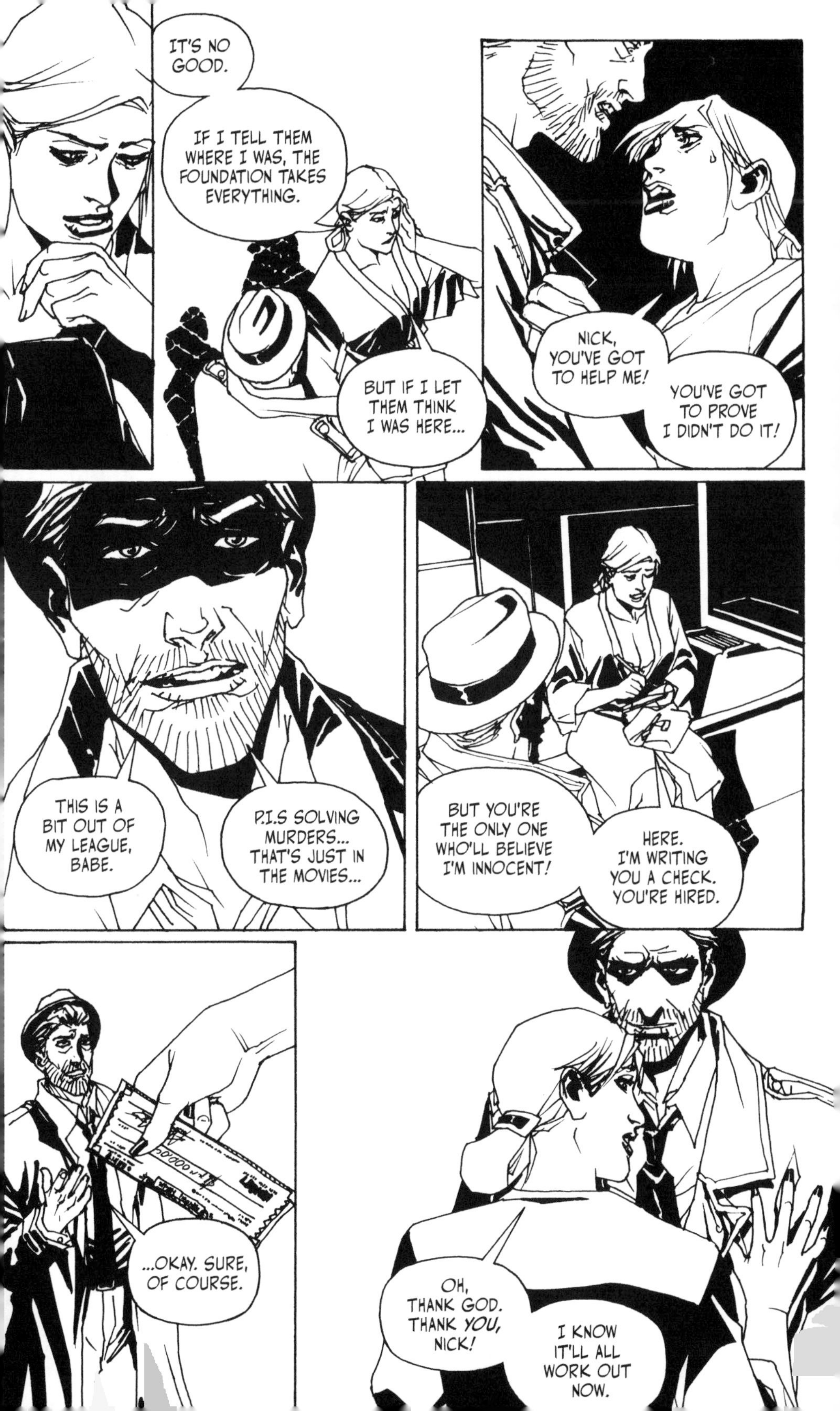
IT'S NO GOOD.
IF I TELL THEM WHERE I WAS, THE FOUNDATION TAKES EVERYTHING.
BUT IF I LET THEM THINK I WAS HERE...
NICK, YOU'VE GOT TO HELP ME!
YOU'VE GOT TO PROVE I DIDN'T DO IT!
THIS IS A BIT OUT OF MY LEAGUE, BABE.
P.I.S SOLVING MURDERS... THAT'S JUST IN THE MOVIES...
BUT YOU'RE THE ONLY ONE WHO'LL BELIEVE I'M INNOCENT!
HERE. I'M WRITING YOU A CHECK. YOU'RE HIRED.
...OKAY. SURE, OF COURSE.
OH, THANK GOD. THANK *YOU*, NICK!
I KNOW IT'LL ALL WORK OUT NOW.

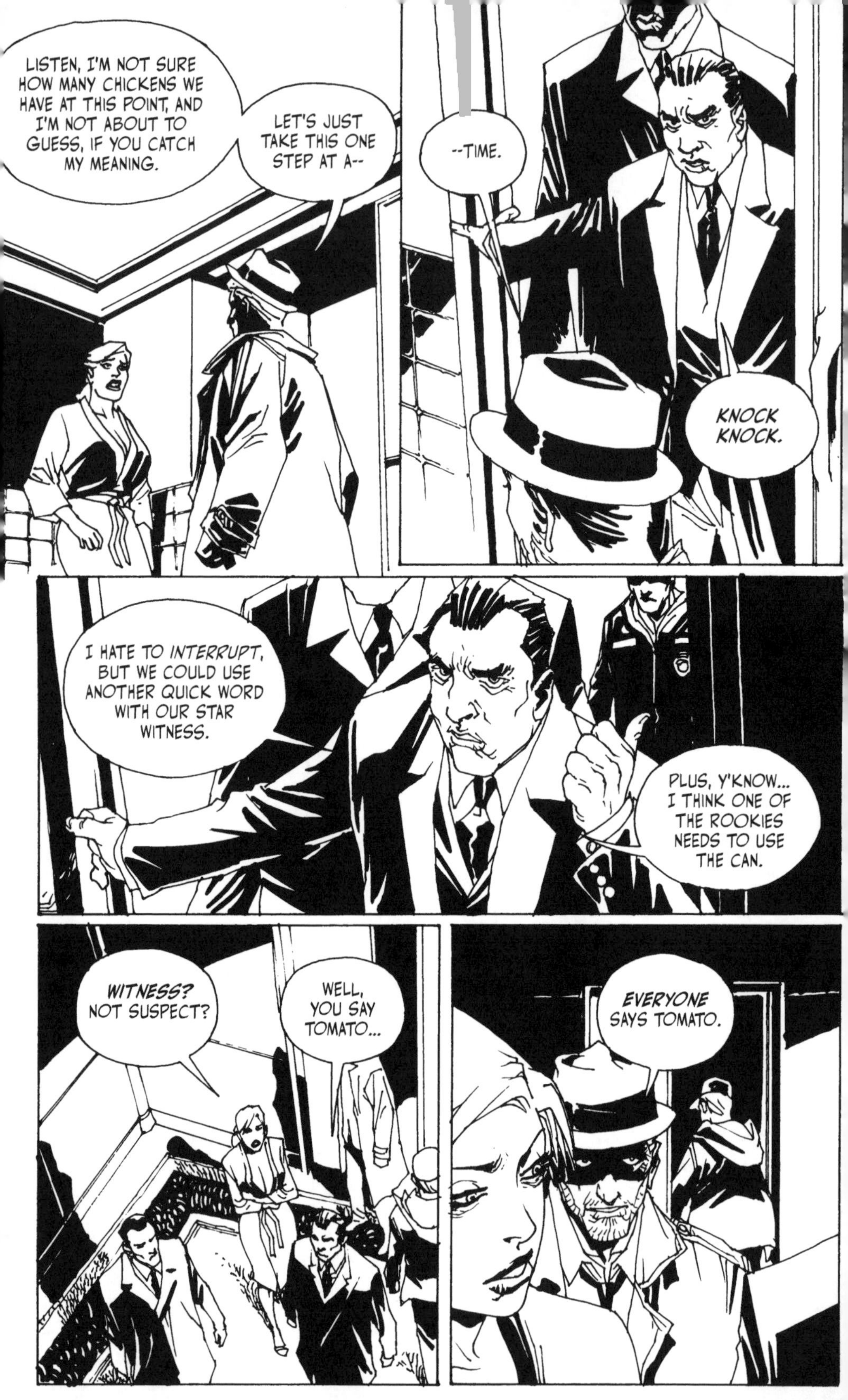
LISTEN, I'M NOT SURE HOW MANY CHICKENS WE HAVE AT THIS POINT, AND I'M NOT ABOUT TO GUESS, IF YOU CATCH MY MEANING.
LET'S JUST TAKE THIS ONE STEP AT A--
--TIME.
KNOCK KNOCK.
I HATE TO *INTERRUPT*, BUT WE COULD USE ANOTHER QUICK WORD WITH OUR STAR WITNESS.
PLUS, Y'KNOW... I THINK ONE OF THE ROOKIES NEEDS TO USE THE CAN.
WITNESS? NOT SUSPECT?
WELL, YOU SAY TOMATO...
EVERYONE SAYS TOMATO.

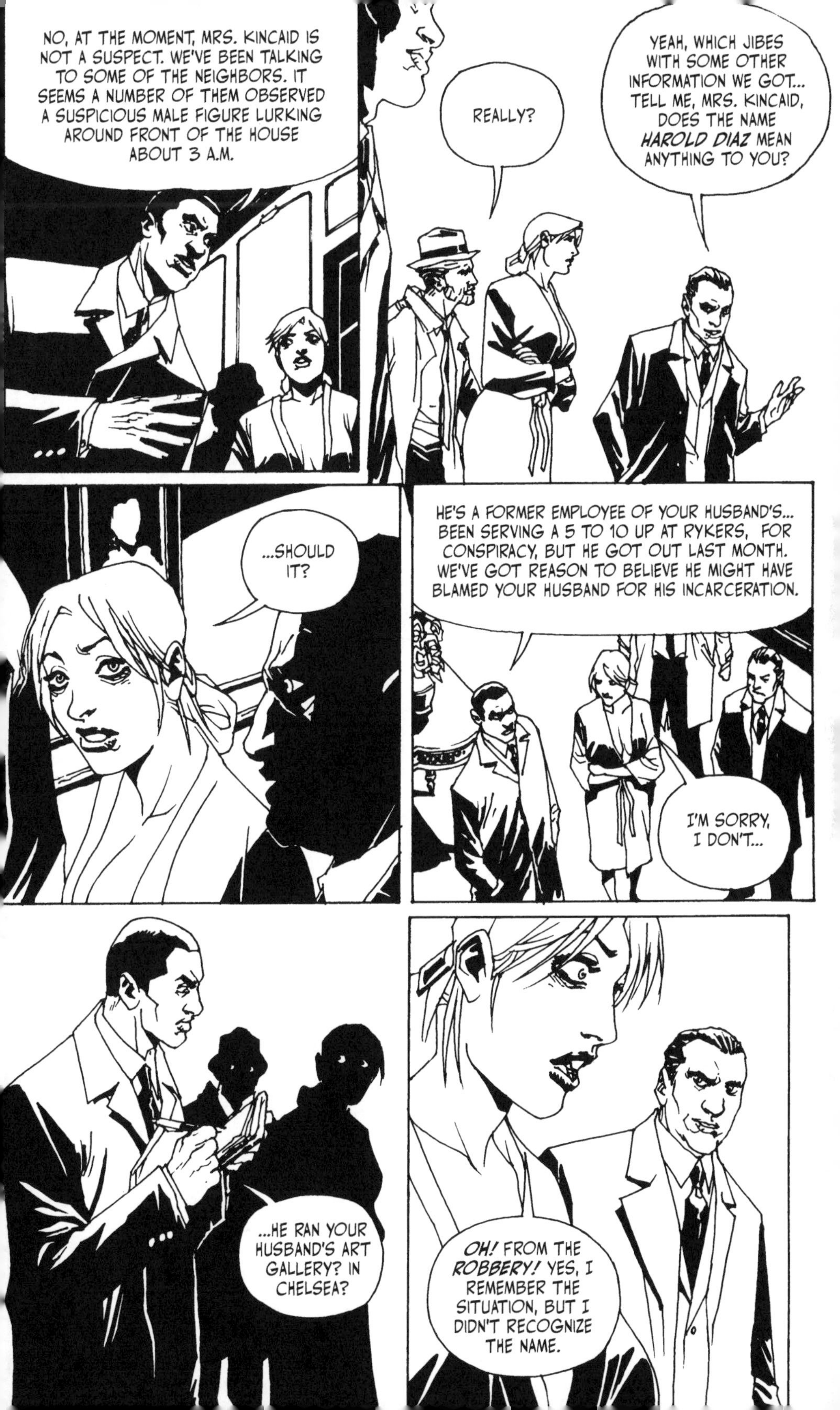
NO, AT THE MOMENT, MRS. KINCAID IS NOT A SUSPECT. WE'VE BEEN TALKING TO SOME OF THE NEIGHBORS. IT SEEMS A NUMBER OF THEM OBSERVED A SUSPICIOUS MALE FIGURE LURKING AROUND FRONT OF THE HOUSE ABOUT 3 A.M.
...
REALLY?
YEAH, WHICH JIBES WITH SOME OTHER INFORMATION WE GOT... TELL ME, MRS. KINCAID, DOES THE NAME HAROLD DIAZ MEAN ANYTHING TO YOU?
...SHOULD IT?
HE'S A FORMER EMPLOYEE OF YOUR HUSBAND'S... BEEN SERVING A 5 TO 10 UP AT RYKERS, FOR CONSPIRACY, BUT HE GOT OUT LAST MONTH. WE'VE GOT REASON TO BELIEVE HE MIGHT HAVE BLAMED YOUR HUSBAND FOR HIS INCARCERATION.
I'M SORRY, I DON'T...
...HE RAN YOUR HUSBAND'S ART GALLERY? IN CHELSEA?
OH! FROM THE ROBBERY! YES, I REMEMBER THE SITUATION, BUT I DIDN'T RECOGNIZE THE NAME.

OKAY, THEN WHY DON'T YOU TELL US WHAT YOU REMEMBER ABOUT THE ROBBERY AT YOUR HUSBAND'S GALLERY?

WELL, FIRST OFF, IT WASN'T REALLY *JOHNNY'S* GALLERY. IT WAS A PET PROJECT OF HIS FIRST WIFE.

EVELYN.

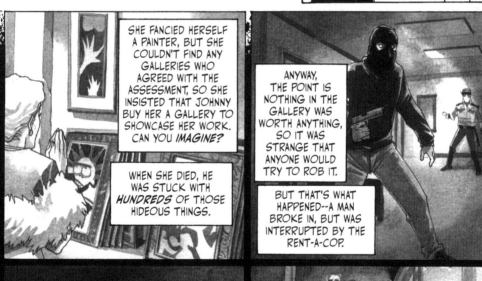

SHE FANCIED HERSELF A PAINTER, BUT SHE COULDN'T FIND ANY GALLERIES WHO AGREED WITH THE ASSESSMENT, SO SHE INSISTED THAT JOHNNY BUY HER A GALLERY TO SHOWCASE HER WORK. CAN YOU *IMAGINE?*

WHEN SHE DIED, HE WAS STUCK WITH *HUNDREDS* OF THOSE HIDEOUS THINGS.

ANYWAY, THE POINT IS NOTHING IN THE GALLERY WAS WORTH ANYTHING, SO IT WAS STRANGE THAT ANYONE WOULD TRY TO ROB IT.

BUT THAT'S WHAT HAPPENED--A MAN BROKE IN, BUT WAS INTERRUPTED BY THE RENT-A-COP.

THE GUARD GOT HIMSELF SHOT, AND SO DID THE BURGLAR, SO THE WHOLE THING BECAME A TABLOID STORY FOR A LITTLE WHILE.

BURGLARY

KATE CARTER TO BEGIN PROSECUTION TOMORROW

THEY TRIED TO PIN IT ON JOHNNY, SAID HE SET THE WHOLE THING UP FOR THE INSURANCE, BUT THEY COULDN'T MAKE IT STICK.

I GUESS THIS "HAROLD" IS THE ONE THEY FINALLY PUT AWAY FOR IT?

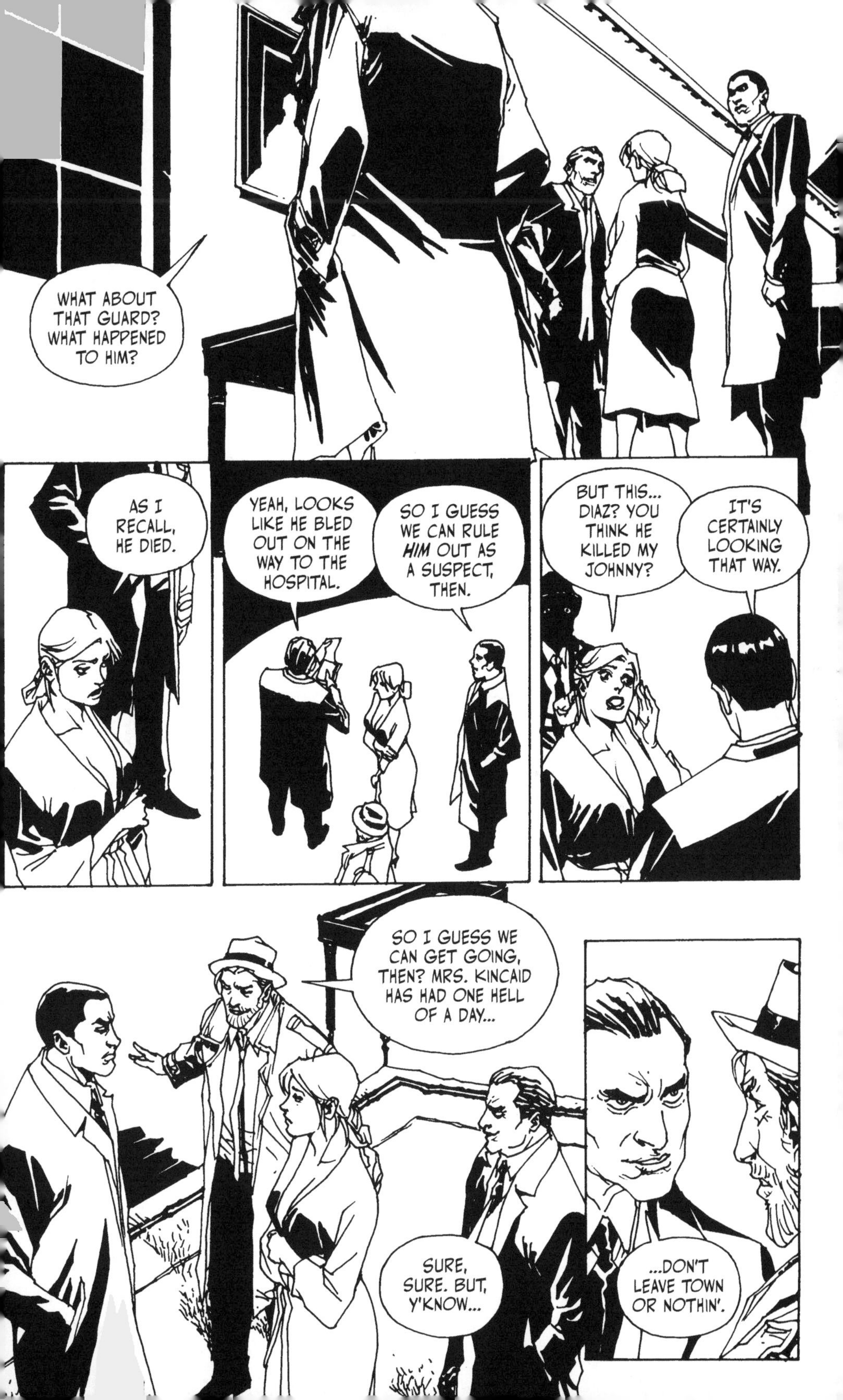
WHAT ABOUT THAT GUARD? WHAT HAPPENED TO HIM?
AS I RECALL, HE DIED.
YEAH, LOOKS LIKE HE BLED OUT ON THE WAY TO THE HOSPITAL.
SO I GUESS WE CAN RULE HIM OUT AS A SUSPECT, THEN.
BUT THIS... DIAZ? YOU THINK HE KILLED MY JOHNNY?
IT'S CERTAINLY LOOKING THAT WAY.
SO I GUESS WE CAN GET GOING, THEN? MRS. KINCAID HAS HAD ONE HELL OF A DAY...
SURE, SURE. BUT, Y'KNOW...
...DON'T LEAVE TOWN OR NOTHIN'.

THREE

"BUT I DON'T SUPPOSE WE CAN COUNT ON THAT, CAN WE?"

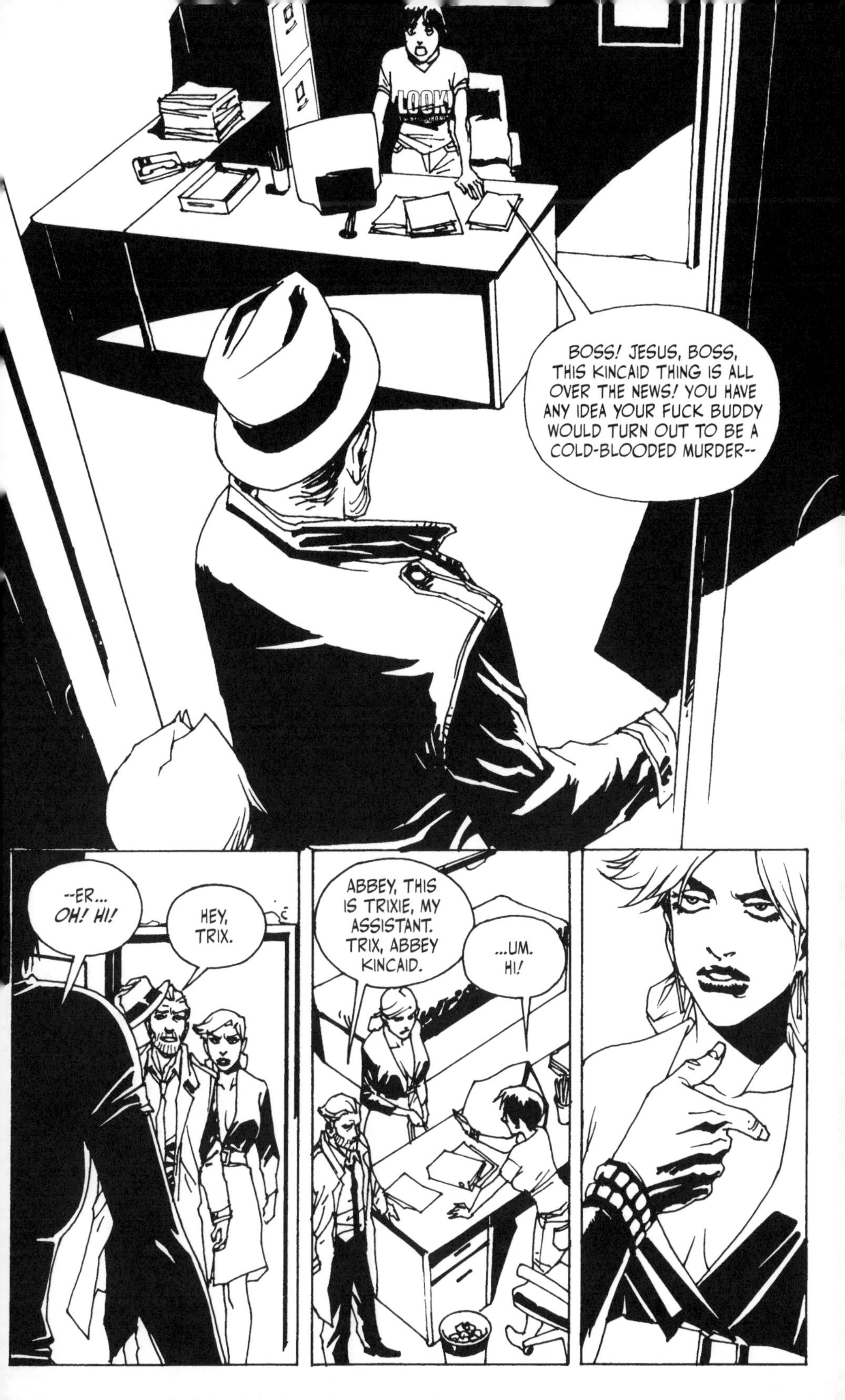
BOSS! JESUS, BOSS, THIS KINCAID THING IS ALL OVER THE NEWS! YOU HAVE ANY IDEA YOUR FUCK BUDDY WOULD TURN OUT TO BE A COLD-BLOODED MURDER--
--ER... OH! HI!
HEY, TRIX.
ABBEY, THIS IS TRIXIE, MY ASSISTANT. TRIX, ABBEY KINCAID.
...UM. HI!

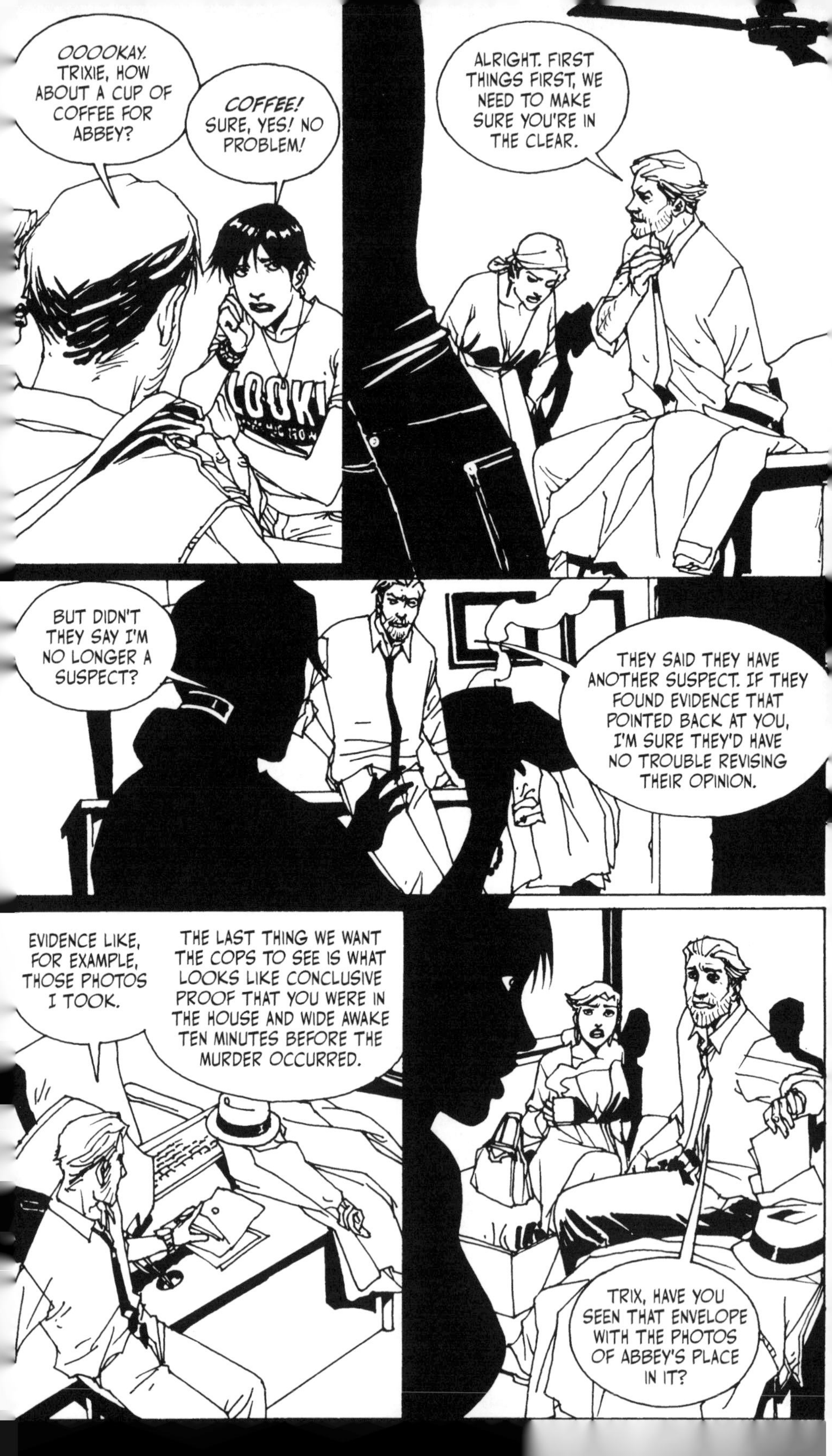
OOOOKAY. TRIXIE, HOW ABOUT A CUP OF COFFEE FOR ABBEY?
COFFEE! SURE, YES! NO PROBLEM!
LOOK!
ALRIGHT. FIRST THINGS FIRST, WE NEED TO MAKE SURE YOU'RE IN THE CLEAR.
BUT DIDN'T THEY SAY I'M NO LONGER A SUSPECT?
THEY SAID THEY HAVE ANOTHER SUSPECT. IF THEY FOUND EVIDENCE THAT POINTED BACK AT YOU, I'M SURE THEY'D HAVE NO TROUBLE REVISING THEIR OPINION.
EVIDENCE LIKE, FOR EXAMPLE, THOSE PHOTOS I TOOK.
THE LAST THING WE WANT THE COPS TO SEE IS WHAT LOOKS LIKE CONCLUSIVE PROOF THAT YOU WERE IN THE HOUSE AND WIDE AWAKE TEN MINUTES BEFORE THE MURDER OCCURRED.
TRIX, HAVE YOU SEEN THAT ENVELOPE WITH THE PHOTOS OF ABBEY'S PLACE IN IT?

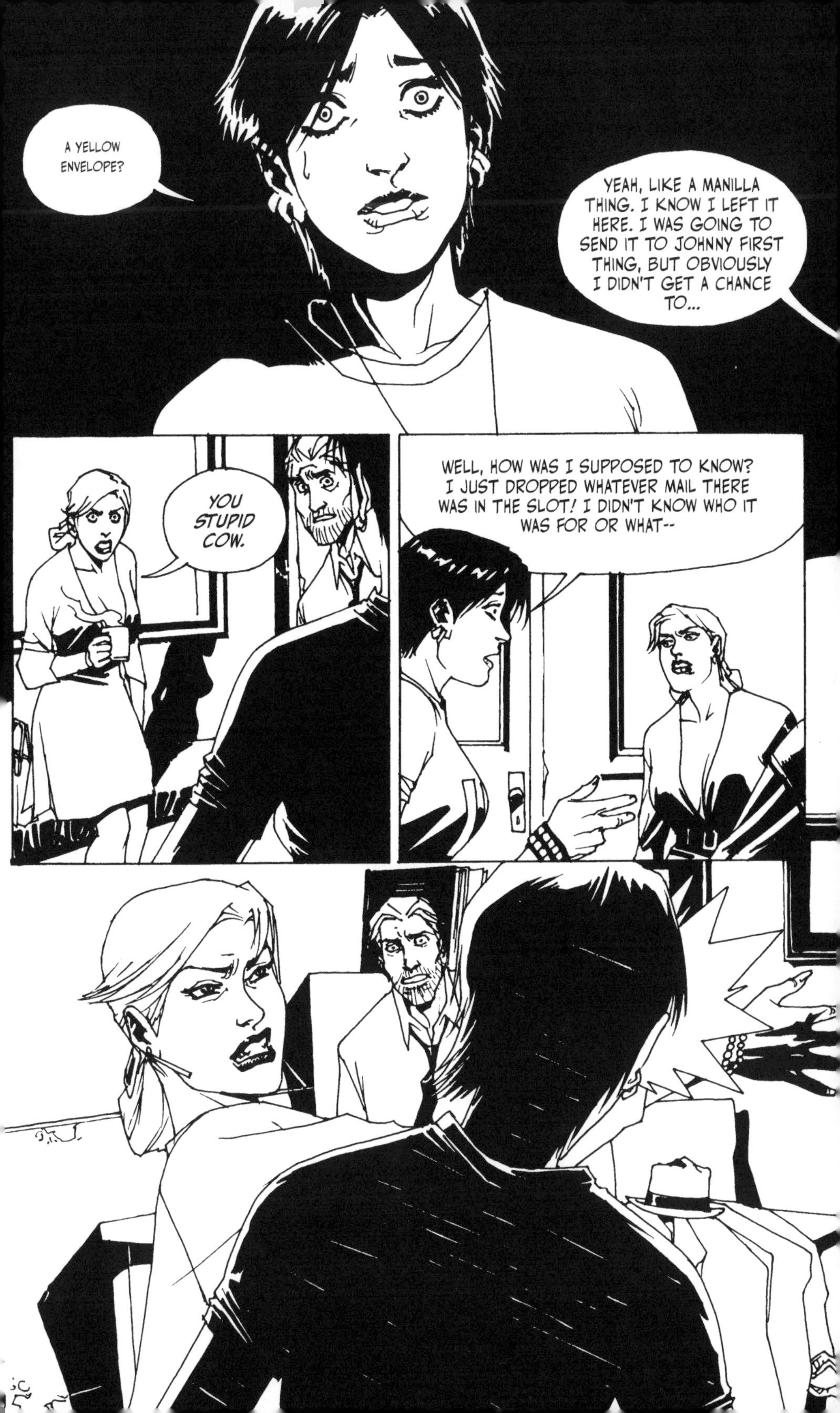
A YELLOW ENVELOPE?
YEAH, LIKE A MANILLA THING. I KNOW I LEFT IT HERE. I WAS GOING TO SEND IT TO JOHNNY FIRST THING, BUT OBVIOUSLY I DIDN'T GET A CHANCE TO...
YOU STUPID COW.
WELL, HOW WAS I SUPPOSED TO KNOW? I JUST DROPPED WHATEVER MAIL THERE WAS IN THE SLOT! I DIDN'T KNOW WHO IT WAS FOR OR WHAT--

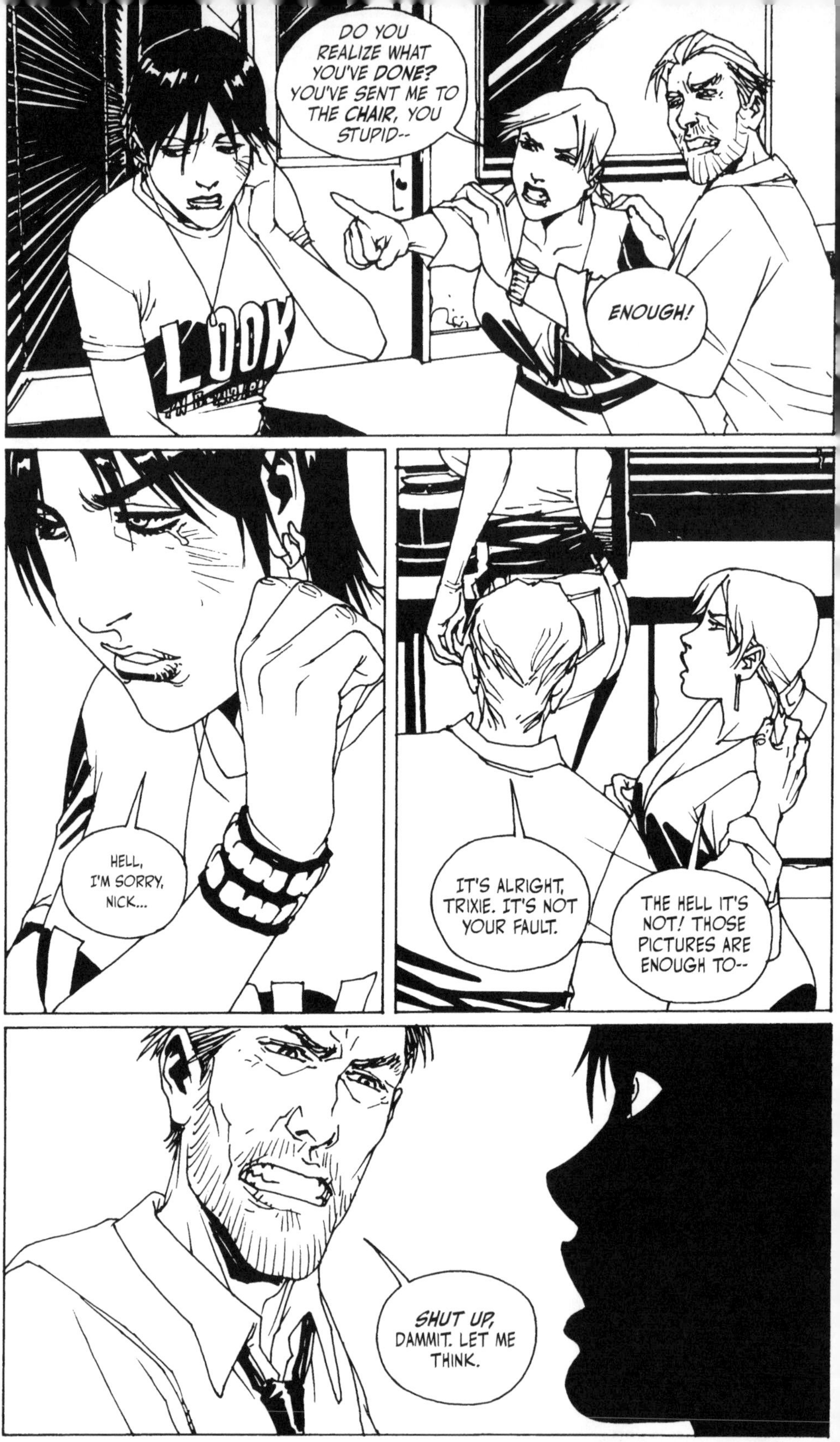
DO YOU REALIZE WHAT YOU'VE DONE? YOU'VE SENT ME TO THE CHAIR, YOU STUPID--
ENOUGH!
HELL, I'M SORRY, NICK...
IT'S ALRIGHT, TRIXIE. IT'S NOT YOUR FAULT.
THE HELL IT'S NOT! THOSE PICTURES ARE ENOUGH TO--
SHUT UP, DAMMIT. LET ME THINK.

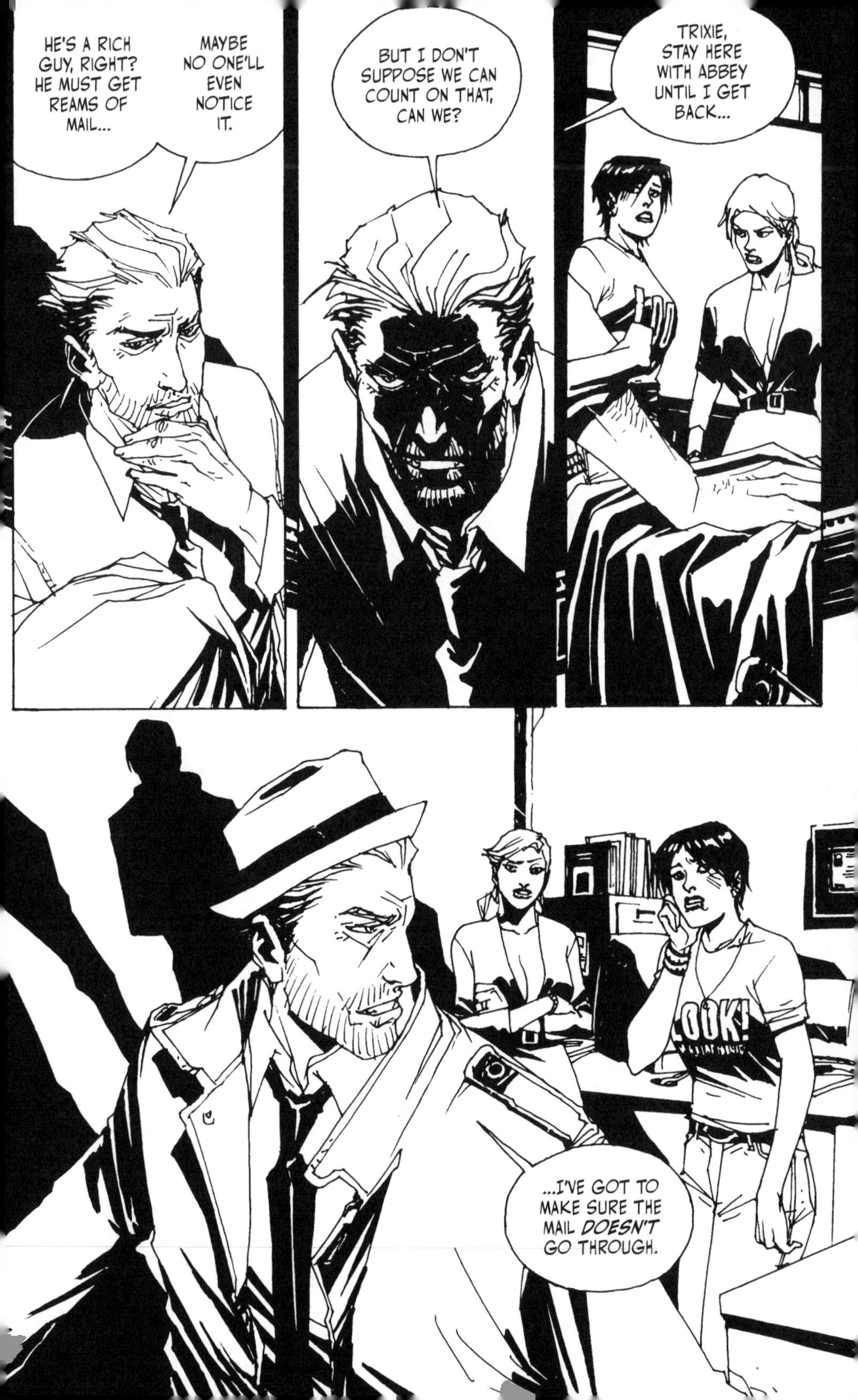
HE'S A RICH GUY, RIGHT? HE MUST GET REAMS OF MAIL...
MAYBE NO ONE'LL EVEN NOTICE IT.
BUT I DON'T SUPPOSE WE CAN COUNT ON THAT, CAN WE?
TRIXIE, STAY HERE WITH ABBEY UNTIL I GET BACK...
LOOK!
...I'VE GOT TO MAKE SURE THE MAIL *DOESN'T* GO THROUGH.

FOUR

"MR. KINCAID, OF COURSE, IS UNAVAILABLE."

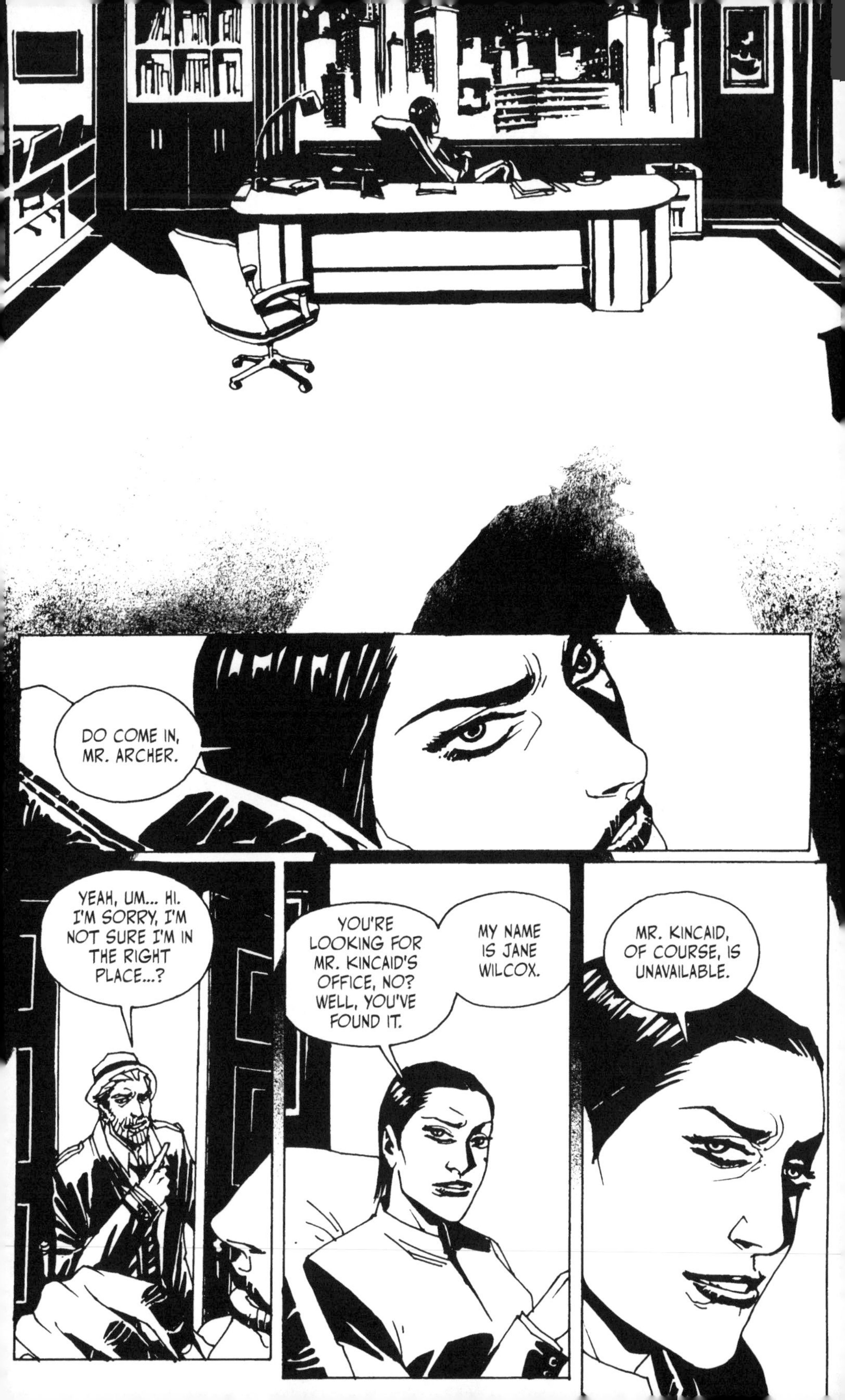
DO COME IN, MR. ARCHER.
YEAH, UM... HI. I'M SORRY, I'M NOT SURE I'M IN THE RIGHT PLACE...?
YOU'RE LOOKING FOR MR. KINCAID'S OFFICE, NO? WELL, YOU'VE FOUND IT.
MY NAME IS JANE WILCOX.
MR. KINCAID, OF COURSE, IS UNAVAILABLE.

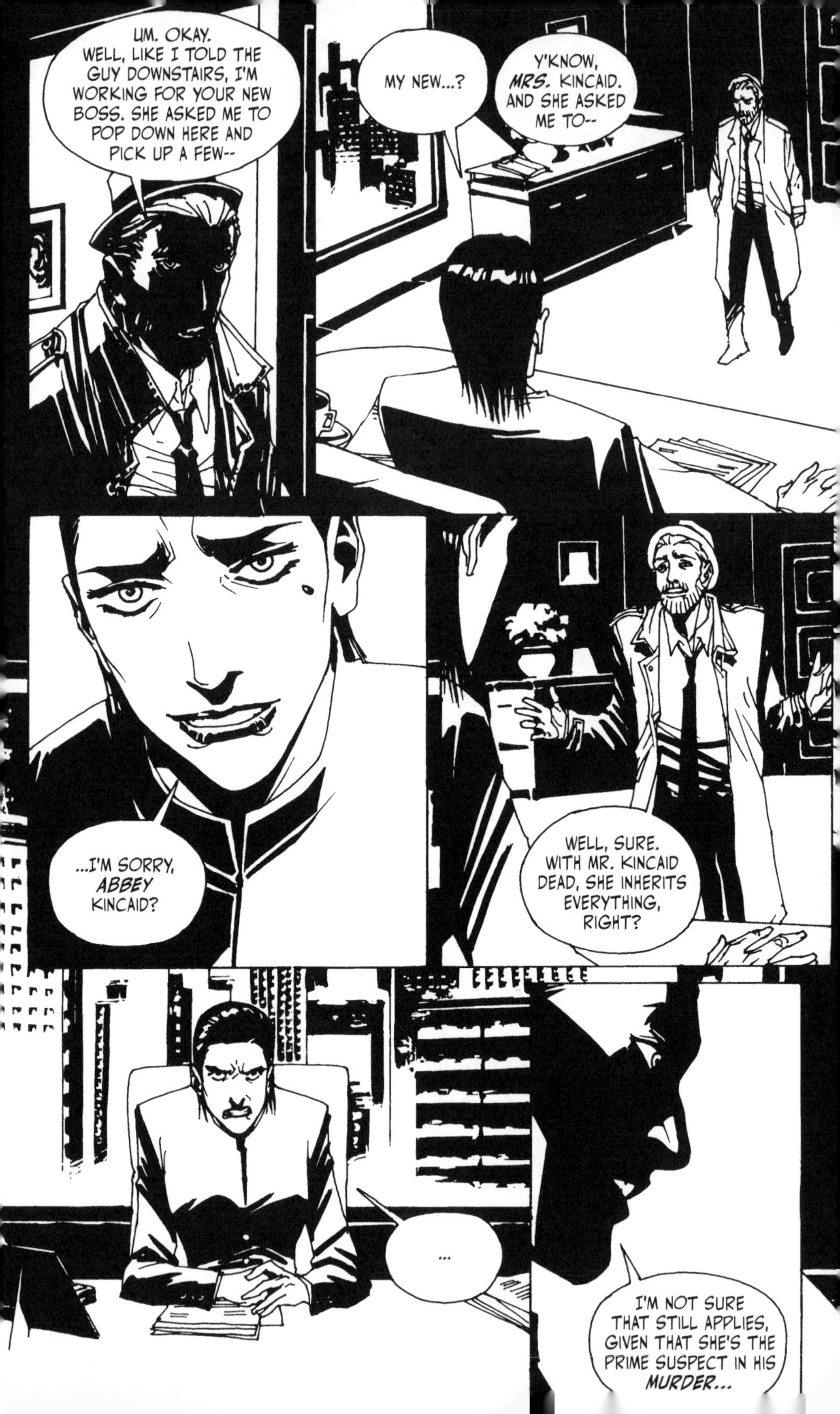
UM. OKAY. WELL, LIKE I TOLD THE GUY DOWNSTAIRS, I'M WORKING FOR YOUR NEW BOSS. SHE ASKED ME TO POP DOWN HERE AND PICK UP A FEW--
MY NEW...?
Y'KNOW, *MRS.* KINCAID. AND SHE ASKED ME TO--
...I'M SORRY, *ABBEY* KINCAID?
WELL, SURE. WITH MR. KINCAID DEAD, SHE INHERITS EVERYTHING, RIGHT?
...
I'M NOT SURE THAT STILL APPLIES, GIVEN THAT SHE'S THE PRIME SUSPECT IN HIS *MURDER*...

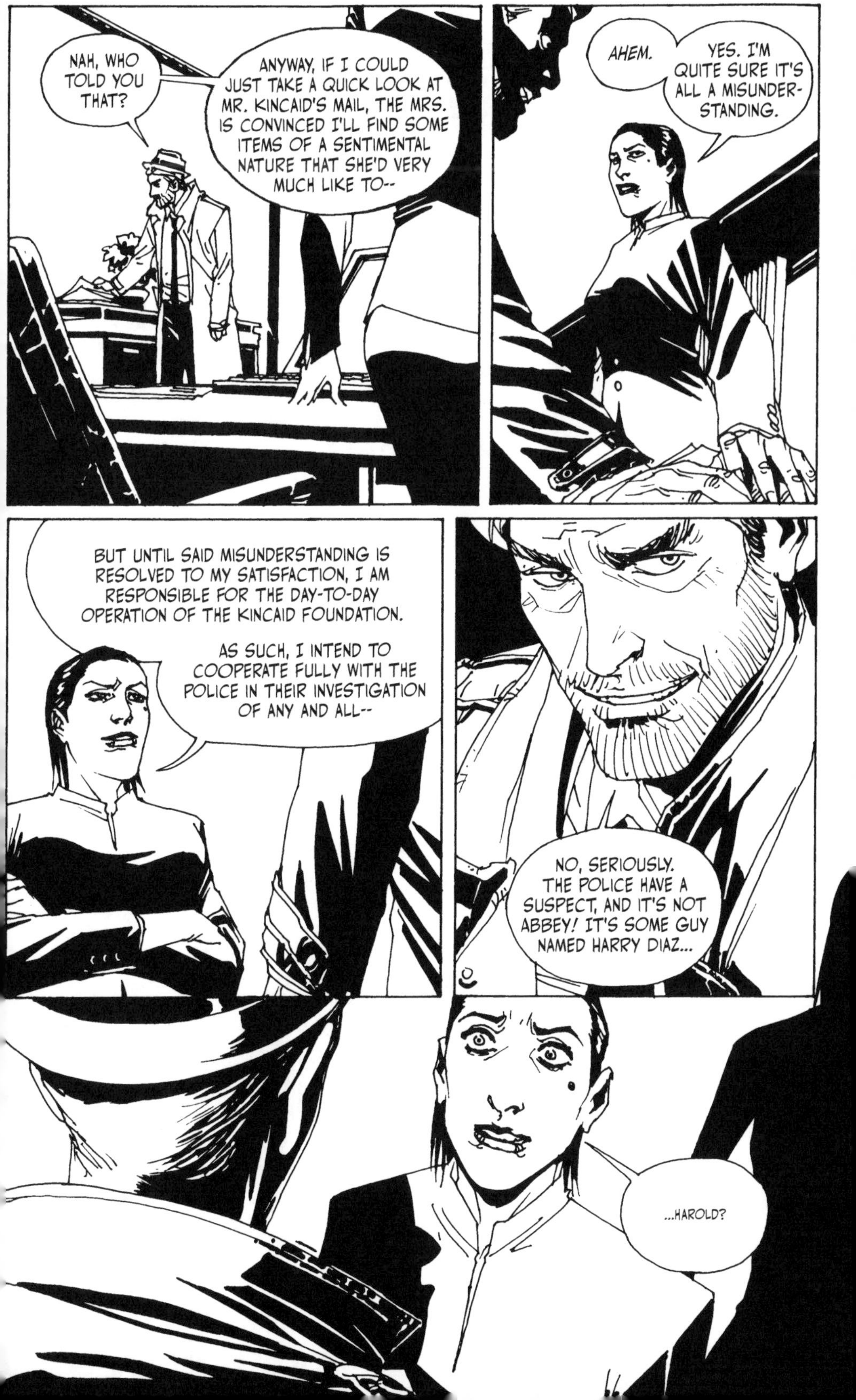
NAH, WHO TOLD YOU THAT?
ANYWAY, IF I COULD JUST TAKE A QUICK LOOK AT MR. KINCAID'S MAIL, THE MRS. IS CONVINCED I'LL FIND SOME ITEMS OF A SENTIMENTAL NATURE THAT SHE'D VERY MUCH LIKE TO--
AHEM.
YES. I'M QUITE SURE IT'S ALL A MISUNDERSTANDING.
BUT UNTIL SAID MISUNDERSTANDING IS RESOLVED TO MY SATISFACTION, I AM RESPONSIBLE FOR THE DAY-TO-DAY OPERATION OF THE KINCAID FOUNDATION.
AS SUCH, I INTEND TO COOPERATE FULLY WITH THE POLICE IN THEIR INVESTIGATION OF ANY AND ALL--
NO, SERIOUSLY. THE POLICE HAVE A SUSPECT, AND IT'S NOT ABBEY! IT'S SOME GUY NAMED HARRY DIAZ...
...HAROLD?

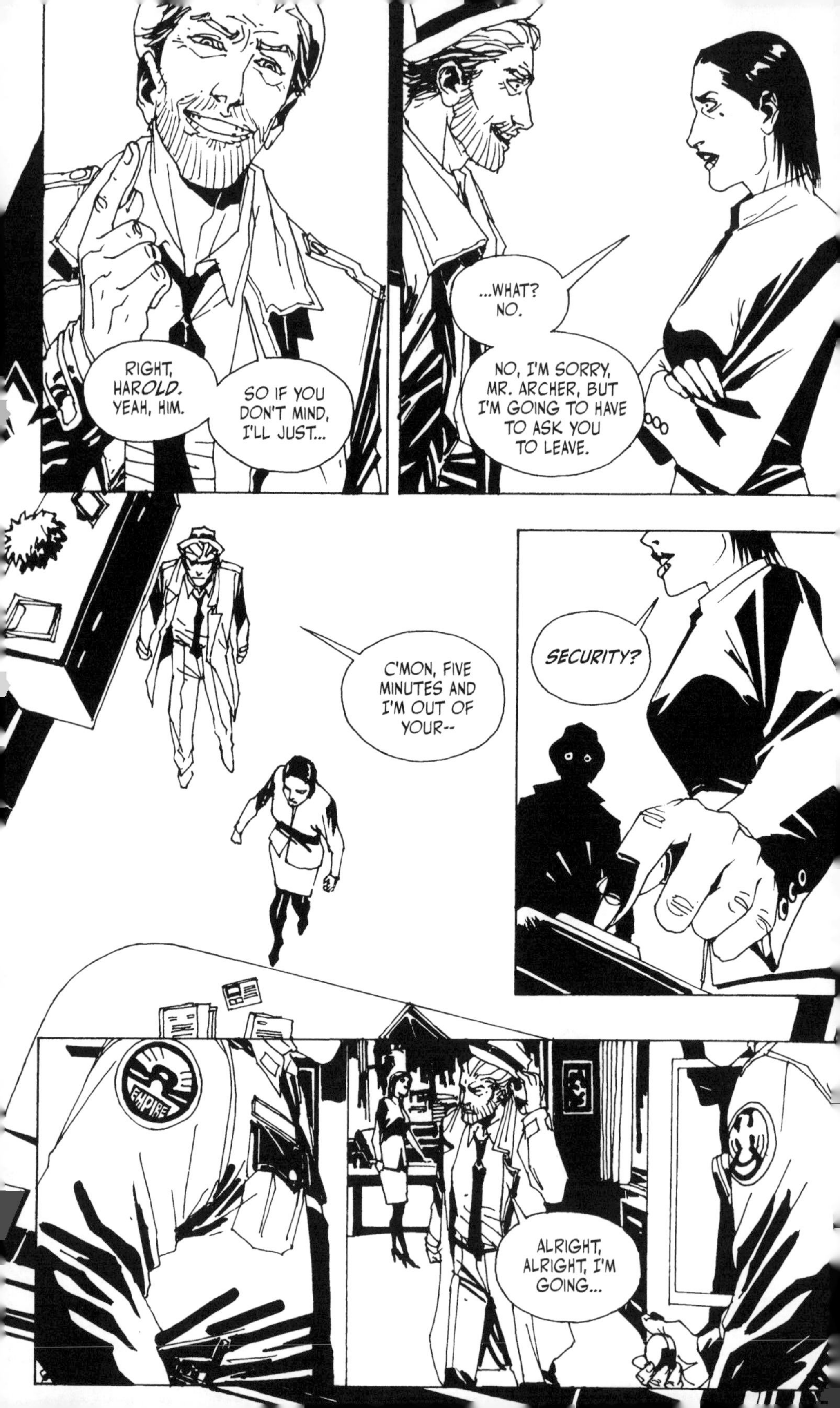
RIGHT, HAROLD. YEAH, HIM.
SO IF YOU DON'T MIND, I'LL JUST...
...WHAT? NO.
NO, I'M SORRY, MR. ARCHER, BUT I'M GOING TO HAVE TO ASK YOU TO LEAVE.
C'MON, FIVE MINUTES AND I'M OUT OF YOUR--
SECURITY?
EMPIRE
ALRIGHT, ALRIGHT, I'M GOING...

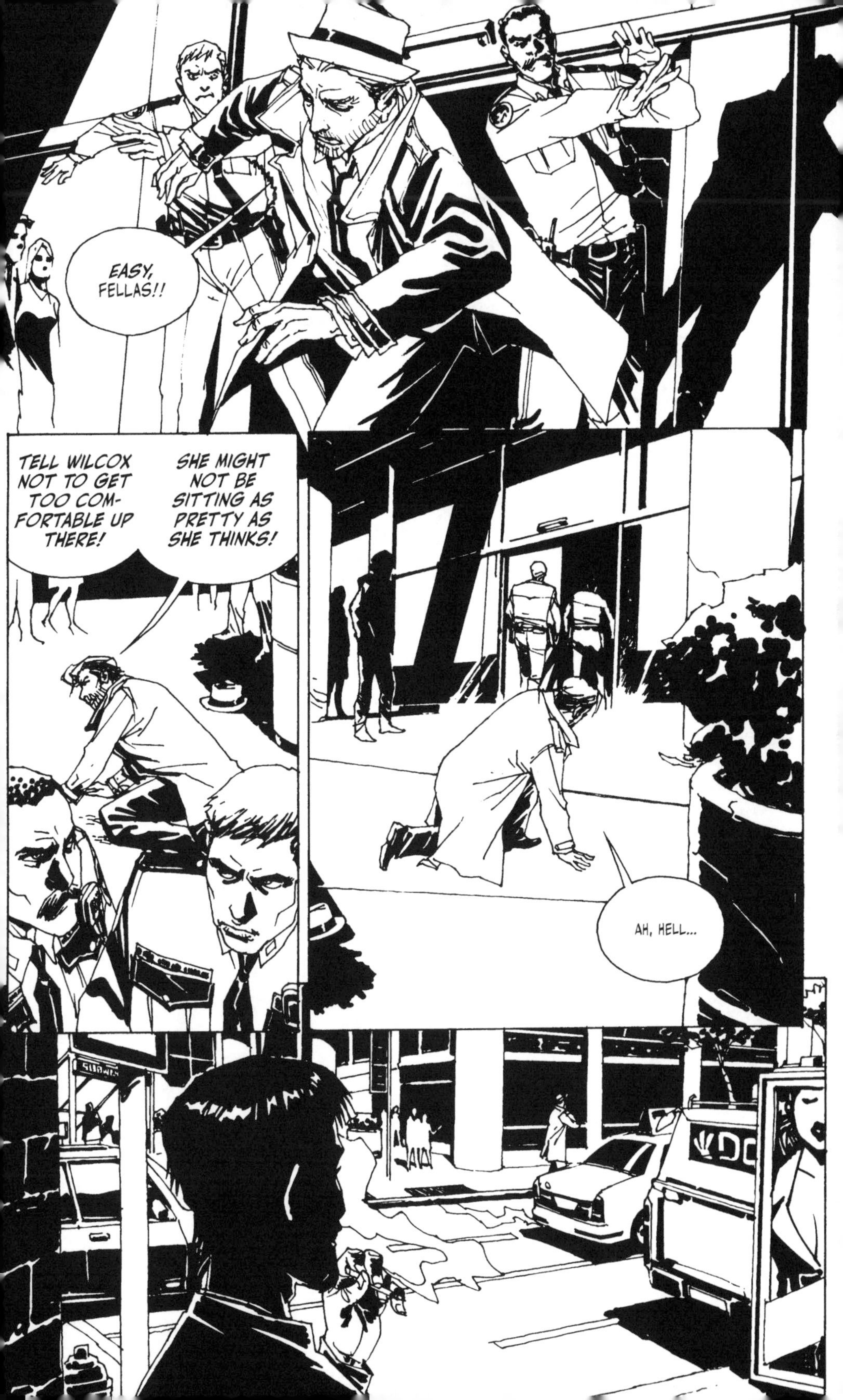
EASY, FELLAS!!
TELL WILCOX NOT TO GET TOO COMFORTABLE UP THERE!
SHE MIGHT NOT BE SITTING AS PRETTY AS SHE THINKS!
AH, HELL...

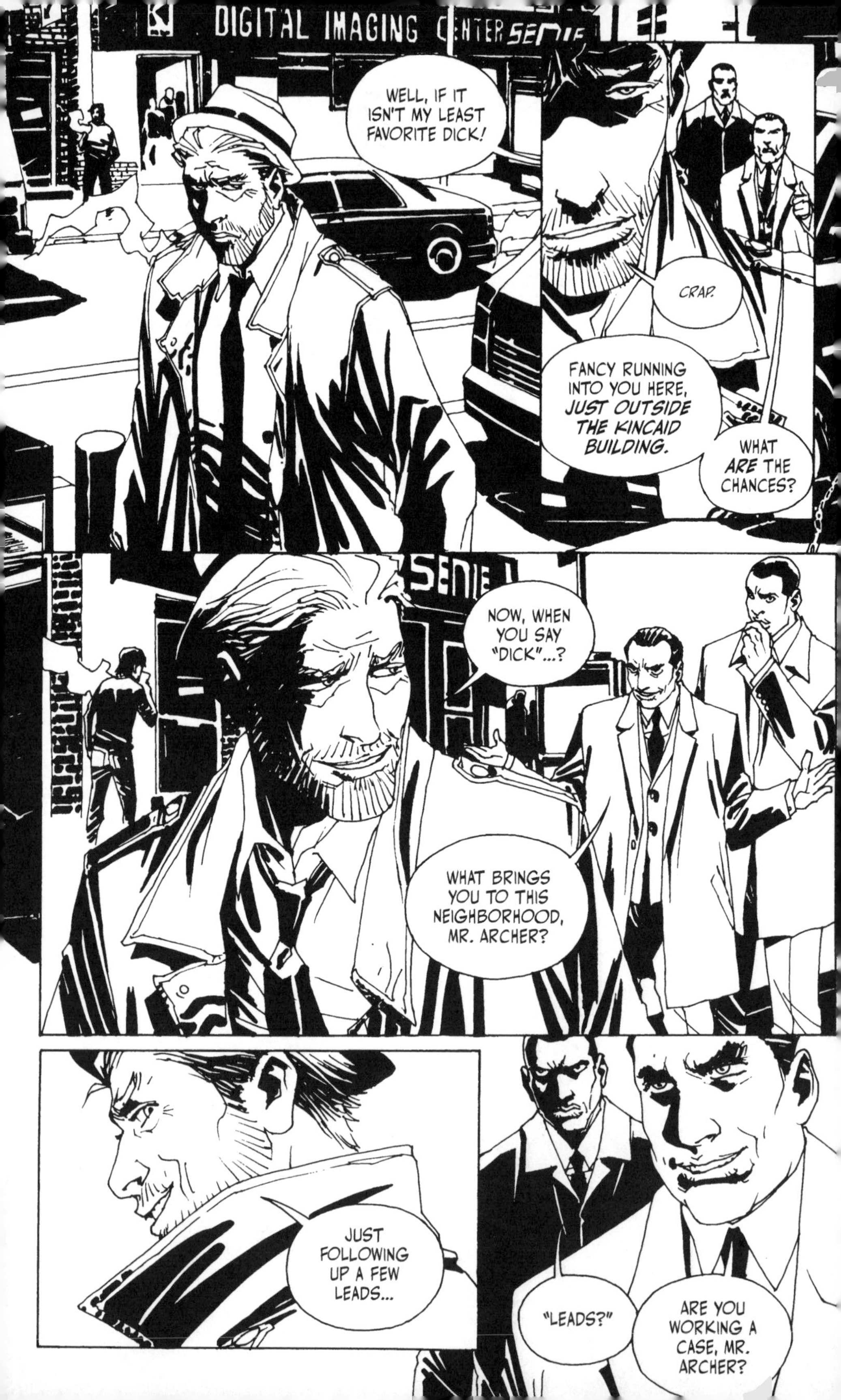
DIGITAL IMAGING CENTER
WELL, IF IT ISN'T MY LEAST FAVORITE DICK!
CRAP.
FANCY RUNNING INTO YOU HERE, *JUST OUTSIDE THE KINCAID BUILDING.*
WHAT *ARE* THE CHANCES?
NOW, WHEN YOU SAY "DICK"...?
WHAT BRINGS YOU TO THIS NEIGHBORHOOD, MR. ARCHER?
JUST FOLLOWING UP A FEW LEADS...
"LEADS?"
ARE YOU WORKING A CASE, MR. ARCHER?

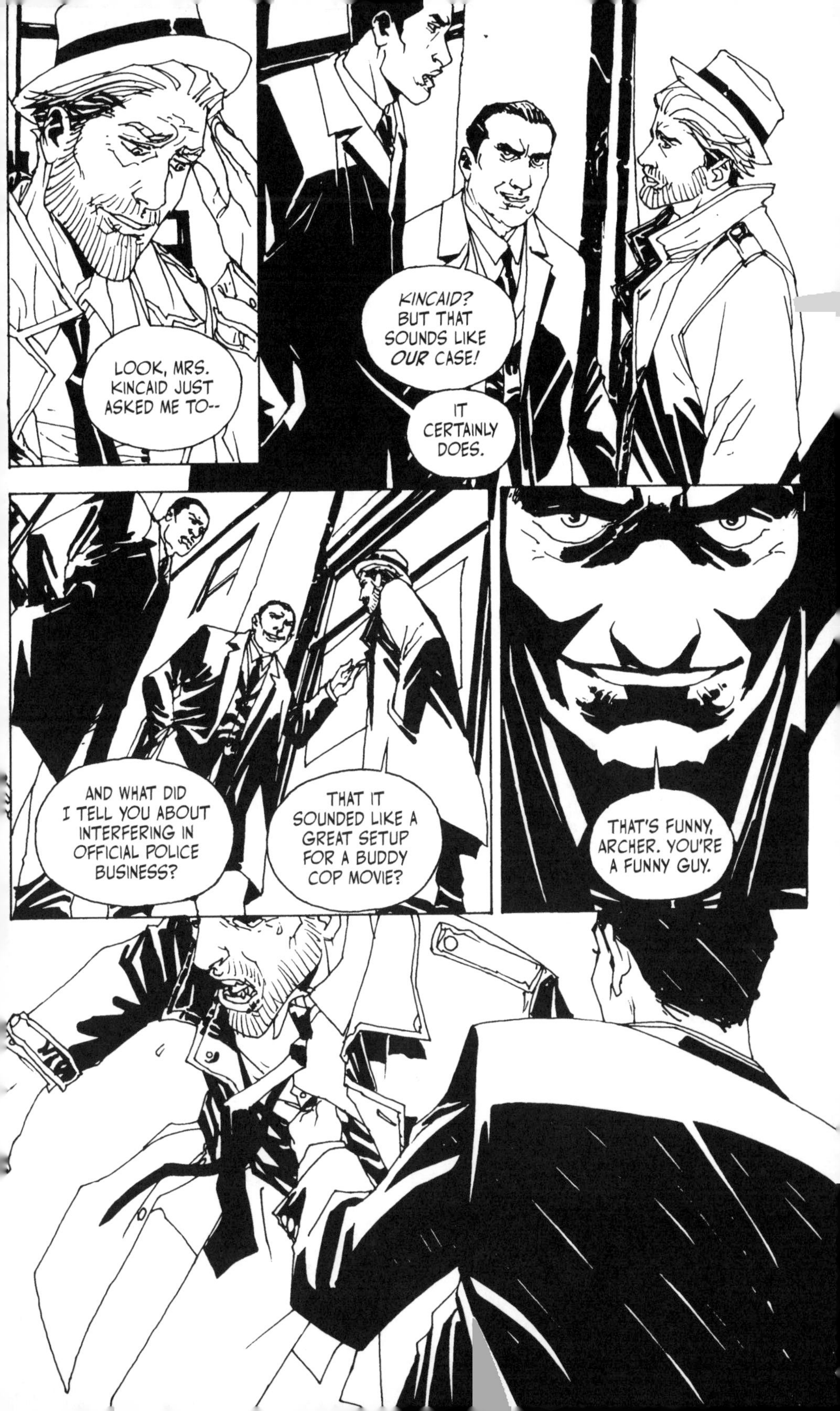
LOOK, MRS. KINCAID JUST ASKED ME TO--
KINCAID? BUT THAT SOUNDS LIKE OUR CASE!
IT CERTAINLY DOES.
AND WHAT DID I TELL YOU ABOUT INTERFERING IN OFFICIAL POLICE BUSINESS?
THAT IT SOUNDED LIKE A GREAT SETUP FOR A BUDDY COP MOVIE?
THAT'S FUNNY, ARCHER. YOU'RE A FUNNY GUY.

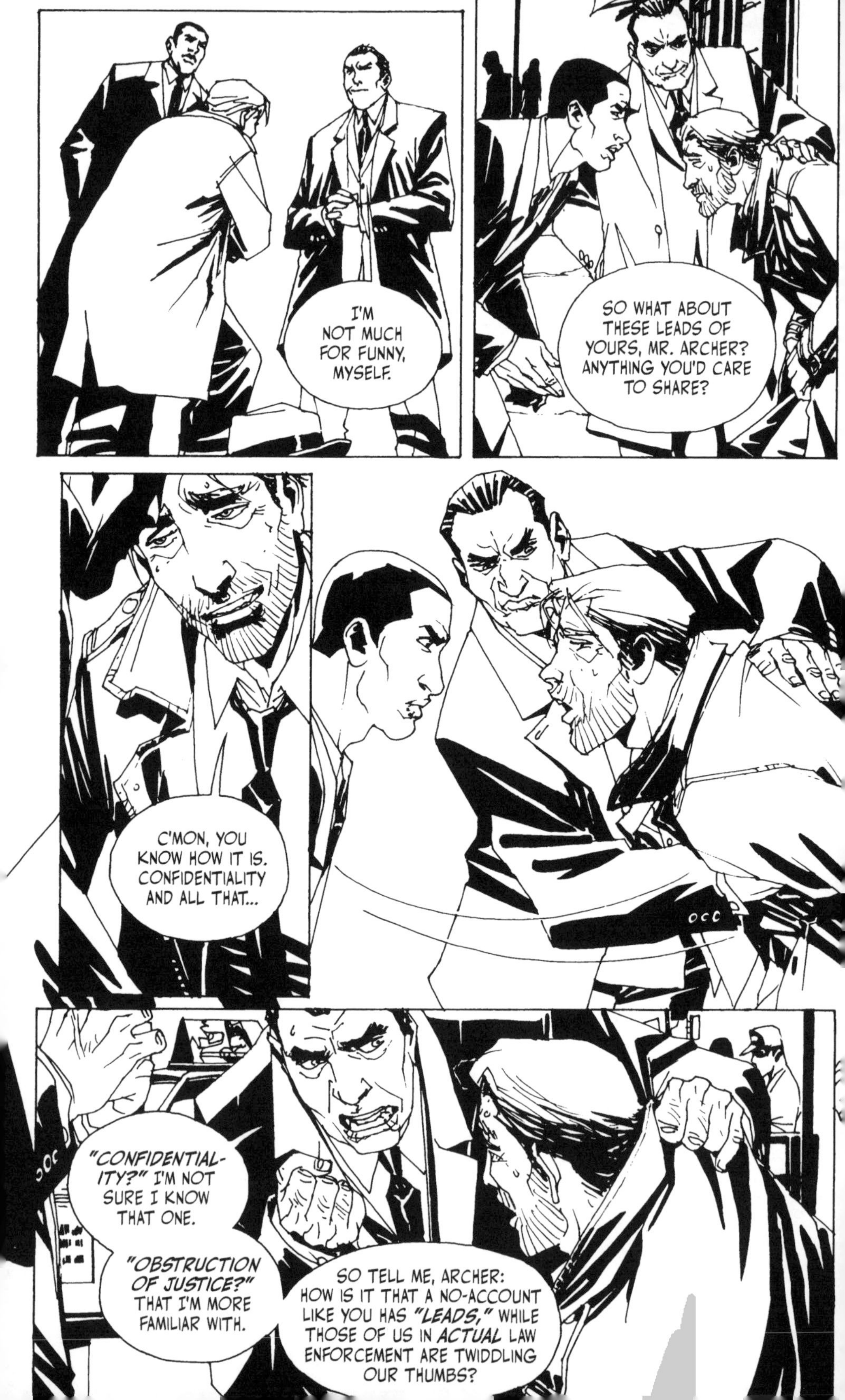
I'M NOT MUCH FOR FUNNY, MYSELF.
SO WHAT ABOUT THESE LEADS OF YOURS, MR. ARCHER? ANYTHING YOU'D CARE TO SHARE?
C'MON, YOU KNOW HOW IT IS. CONFIDENTIALITY AND ALL THAT...
"CONFIDENTIAL-ITY?" I'M NOT SURE I KNOW THAT ONE.
"OBSTRUCTION OF JUSTICE?" THAT I'M MORE FAMILIAR WITH.
SO TELL ME, ARCHER: HOW IS IT THAT A NO-ACCOUNT LIKE YOU HAS "LEADS," WHILE THOSE OF US IN ACTUAL LAW ENFORCEMENT ARE TWIDDLING OUR THUMBS?

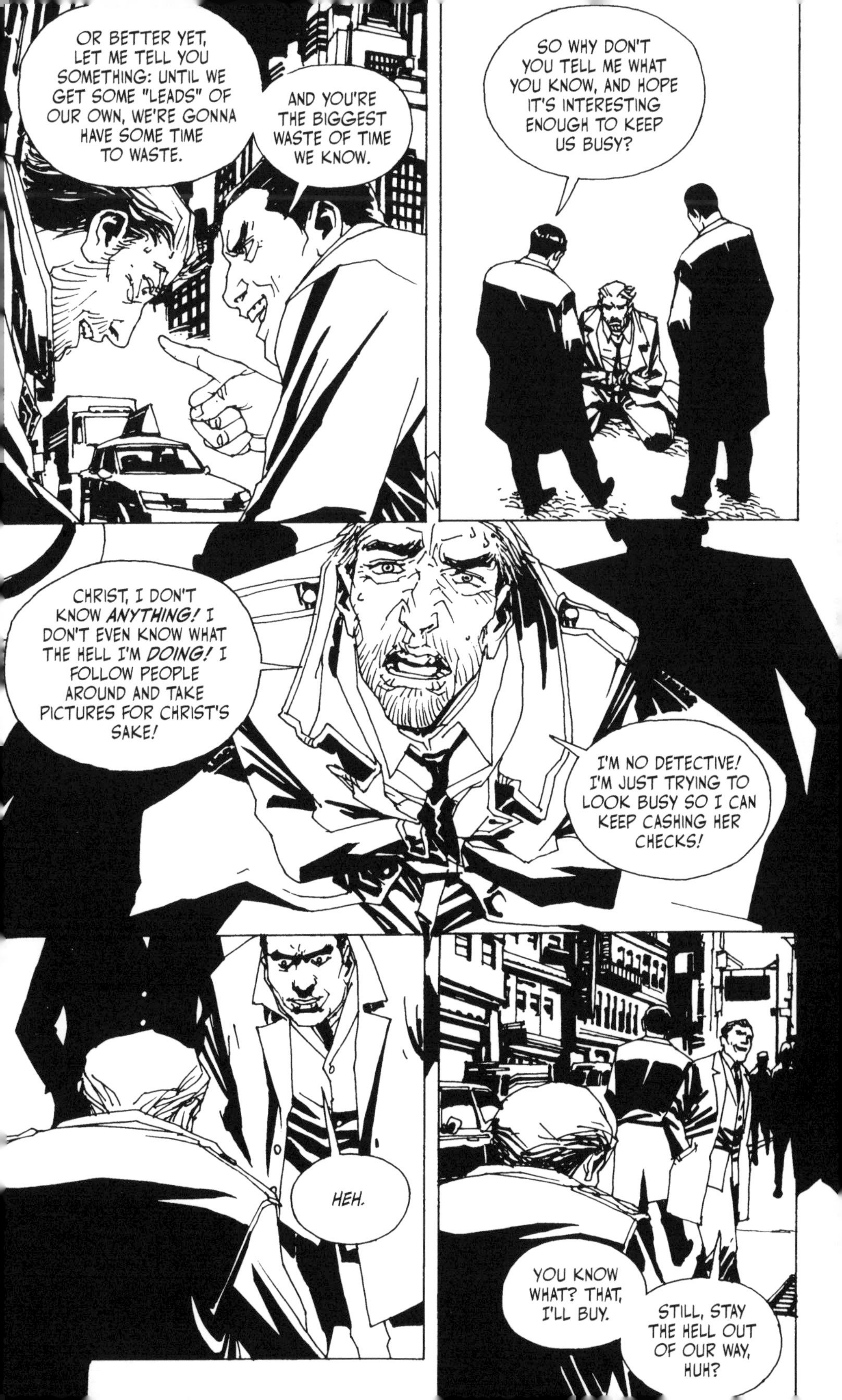
OR BETTER YET, LET ME TELL YOU SOMETHING: UNTIL WE GET SOME "LEADS" OF OUR OWN, WE'RE GONNA HAVE SOME TIME TO WASTE.
AND YOU'RE THE BIGGEST WASTE OF TIME WE KNOW.
SO WHY DON'T YOU TELL ME WHAT YOU KNOW, AND HOPE IT'S INTERESTING ENOUGH TO KEEP US BUSY?
CHRIST, I DON'T KNOW *ANYTHING!* I DON'T EVEN KNOW WHAT THE HELL I'M *DOING!* I FOLLOW PEOPLE AROUND AND TAKE PICTURES FOR CHRIST'S SAKE!
I'M NO DETECTIVE! I'M JUST TRYING TO LOOK BUSY SO I CAN KEEP CASHING HER CHECKS!
HEH.
YOU KNOW WHAT? THAT, I'LL BUY.
STILL, STAY THE HELL OUT OF OUR WAY, HUH?

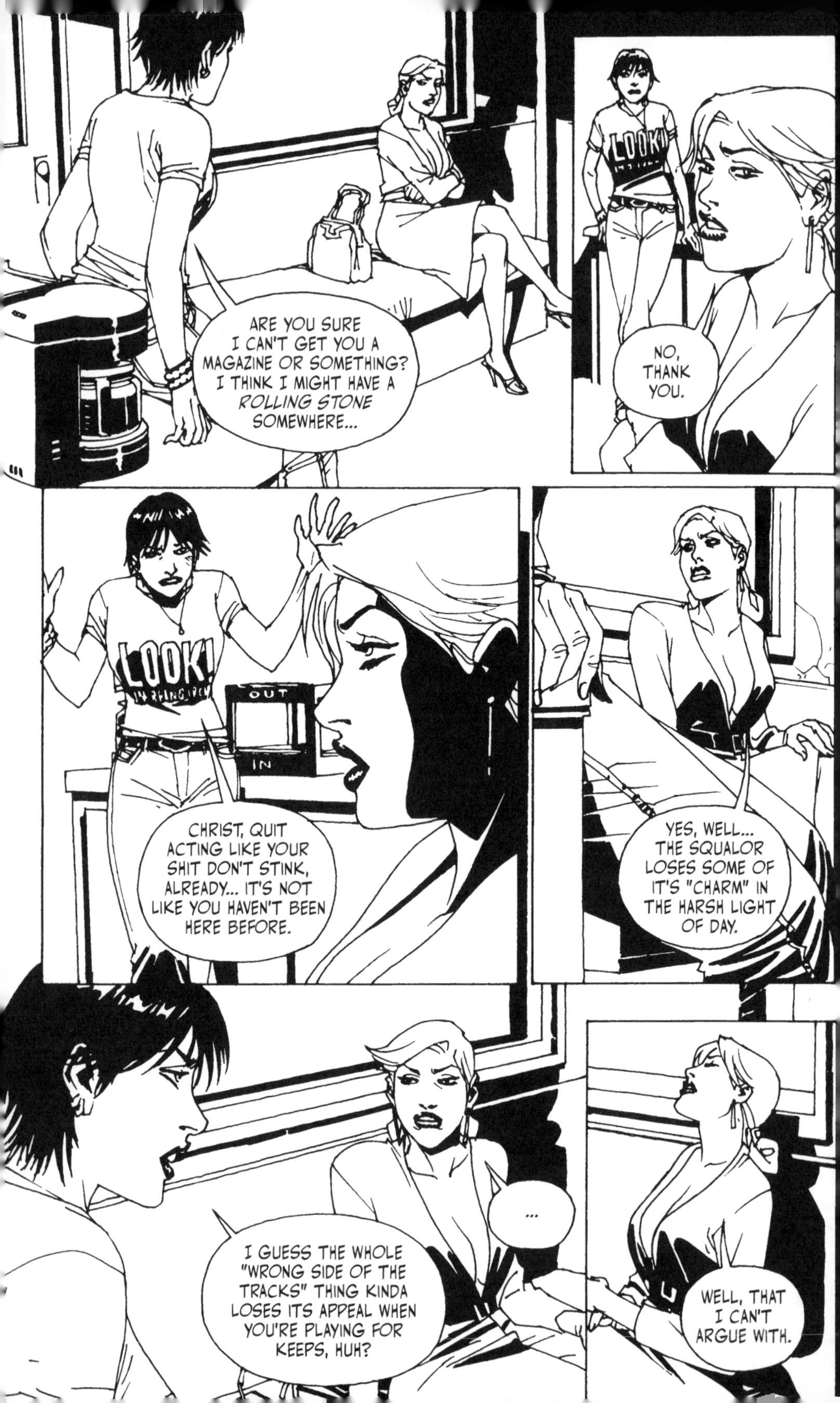
ARE YOU SURE I CAN'T GET YOU A MAGAZINE OR SOMETHING? I THINK I MIGHT HAVE A *ROLLING STONE* SOMEWHERE...
NO, THANK YOU.
LOOK!
LOOK!
OUT
IN
CHRIST, QUIT ACTING LIKE YOUR SHIT DON'T STINK, ALREADY... IT'S NOT LIKE YOU HAVEN'T BEEN HERE BEFORE.
YES, WELL... THE SQUALOR LOSES SOME OF IT'S "CHARM" IN THE HARSH LIGHT OF DAY.
I GUESS THE WHOLE "WRONG SIDE OF THE TRACKS" THING KINDA LOSES ITS APPEAL WHEN YOU'RE PLAYING FOR KEEPS, HUH?
...
WELL, THAT I CAN'T ARGUE WITH.

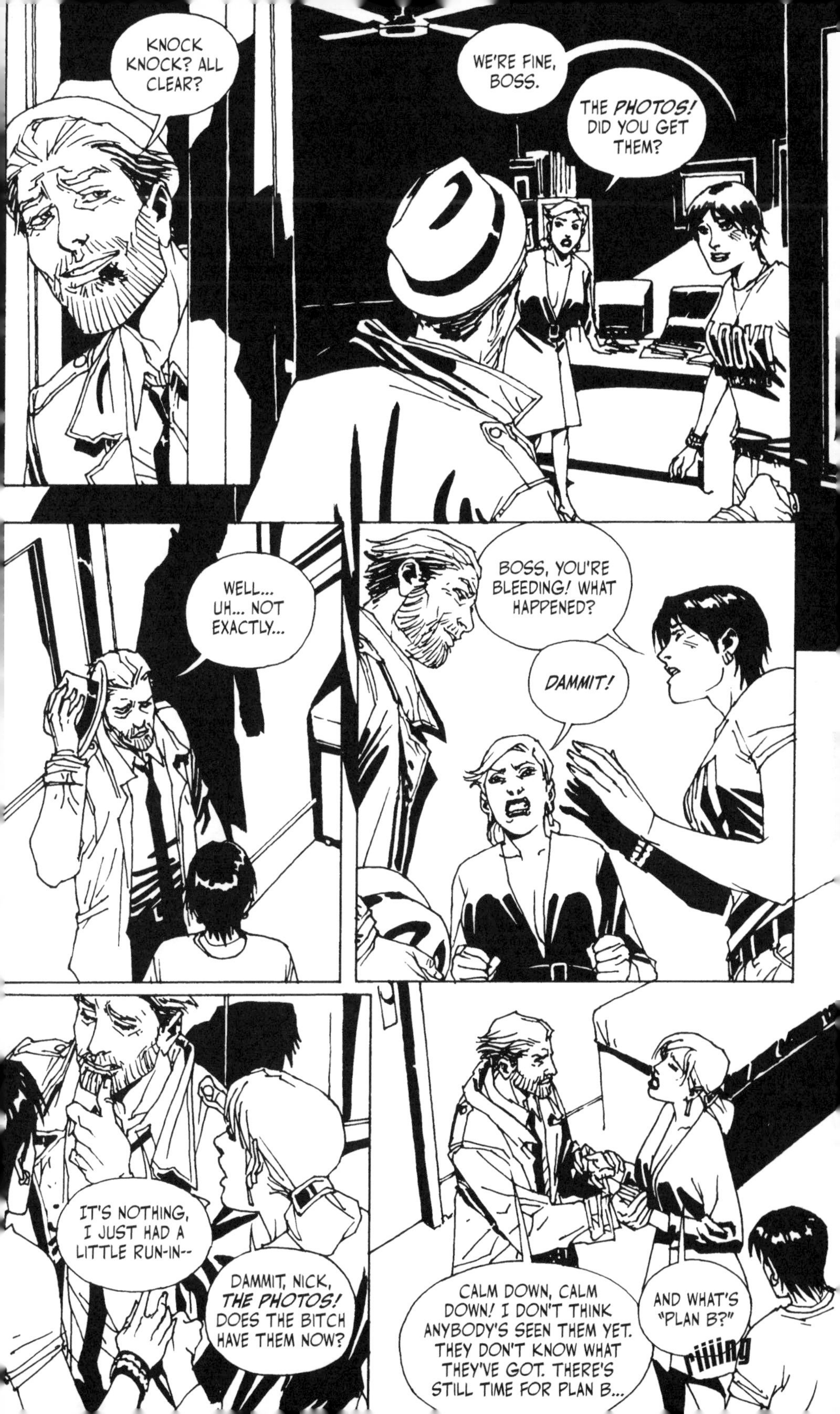
KNOCK KNOCK? ALL CLEAR?
WE'RE FINE, BOSS.
THE *PHOTOS!* DID YOU GET THEM?
WELL... UH... NOT EXACTLY...
BOSS, YOU'RE BLEEDING! WHAT HAPPENED?
DAMMIT!
IT'S NOTHING, I JUST HAD A LITTLE RUN-IN--
DAMMIT, NICK, *THE PHOTOS!* DOES THE BITCH HAVE THEM NOW?
CALM DOWN, CALM DOWN! I DON'T THINK ANYBODY'S SEEN THEM YET. THEY DON'T KNOW WHAT THEY'VE GOT. THERE'S STILL TIME FOR PLAN B...
AND WHAT'S "PLAN B?"
riiiing

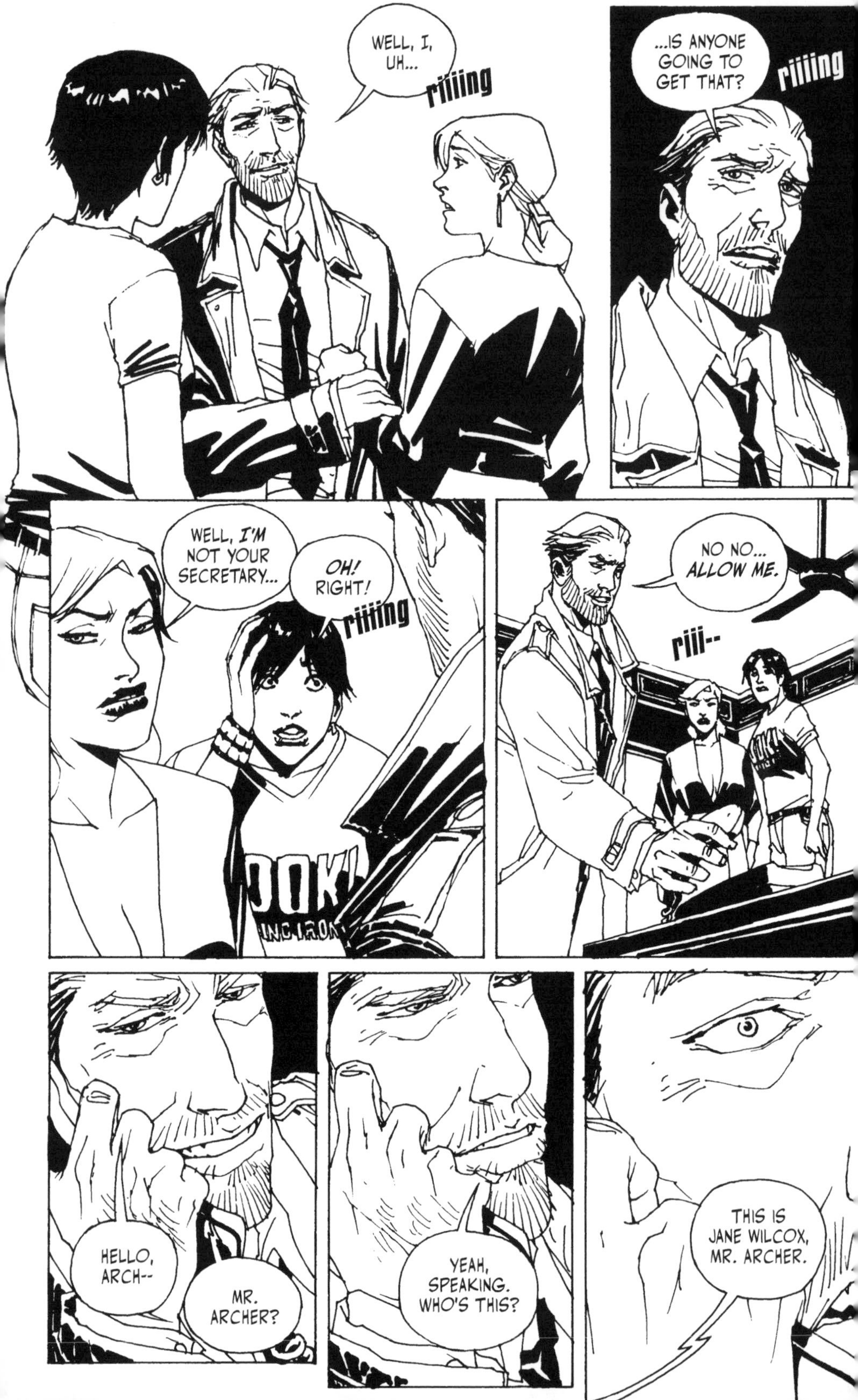
WELL, I, UH...
riiiing
...IS ANYONE GOING TO GET THAT?
riiiing
WELL, I'M NOT YOUR SECRETARY...
OH! RIGHT!
riiiing
NO NO... ALLOW ME.
riii--
HELLO, ARCH--
MR. ARCHER?
YEAH, SPEAKING. WHO'S THIS?
THIS IS JANE WILCOX, MR. ARCHER.

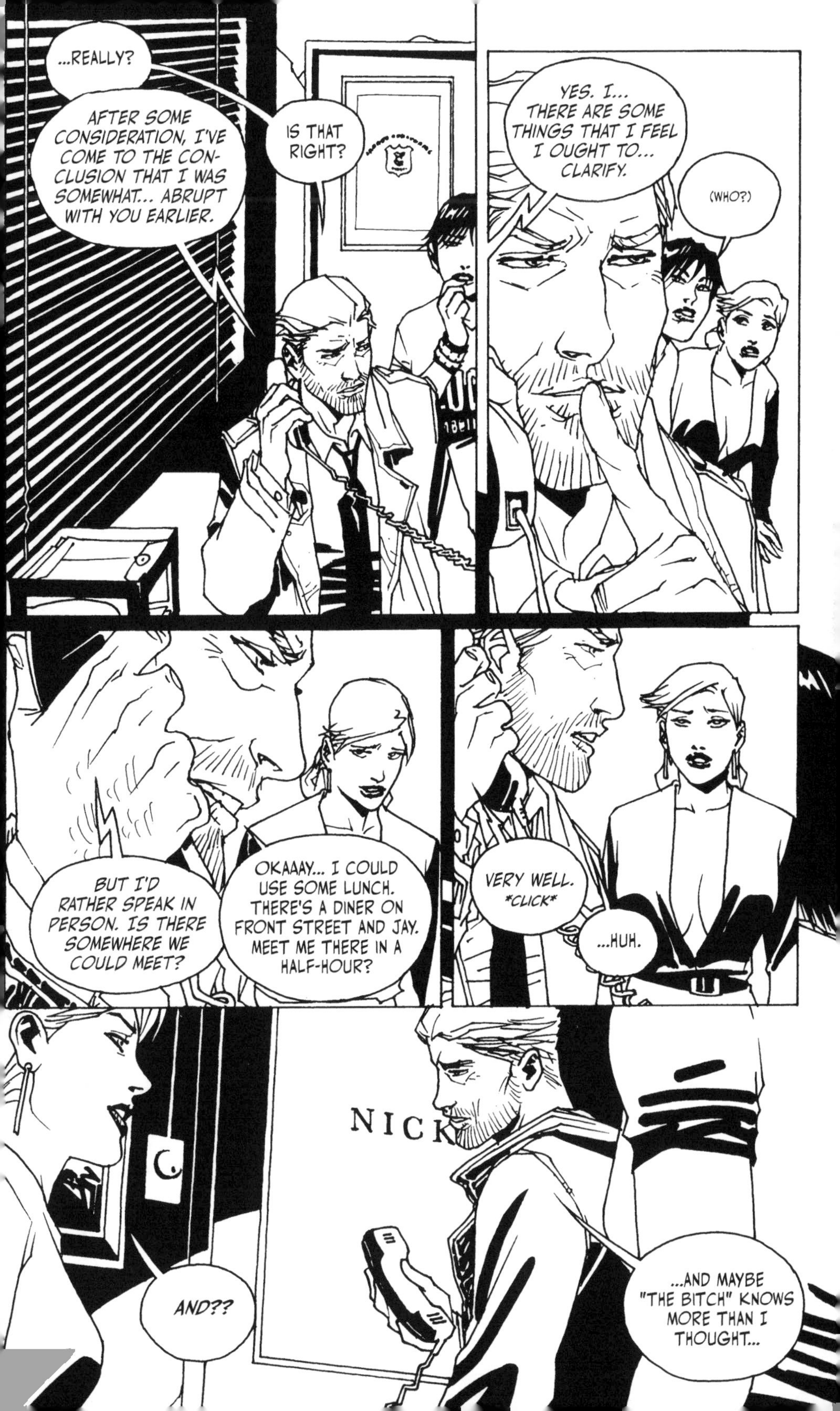

...REALLY?
AFTER SOME CONSIDERATION, I'VE COME TO THE CON-CLUSION THAT I WAS SOMEWHAT... ABRUPT WITH YOU EARLIER.
IS THAT RIGHT?
YES. I... THERE ARE SOME THINGS THAT I FEEL I OUGHT TO... CLARIFY.
(WHO?)
BUT I'D RATHER SPEAK IN PERSON. IS THERE SOMEWHERE WE COULD MEET?
OKAAAY... I COULD USE SOME LUNCH. THERE'S A DINER ON FRONT STREET AND JAY. MEET ME THERE IN A HALF-HOUR?
VERY WELL. *CLICK*
...HUH.
NICK
AND??
...AND MAYBE "THE BITCH" KNOWS MORE THAN I THOUGHT...

FIVE "LET ME GUESS...
I SHOULD SEE THE OTHER GUY?"

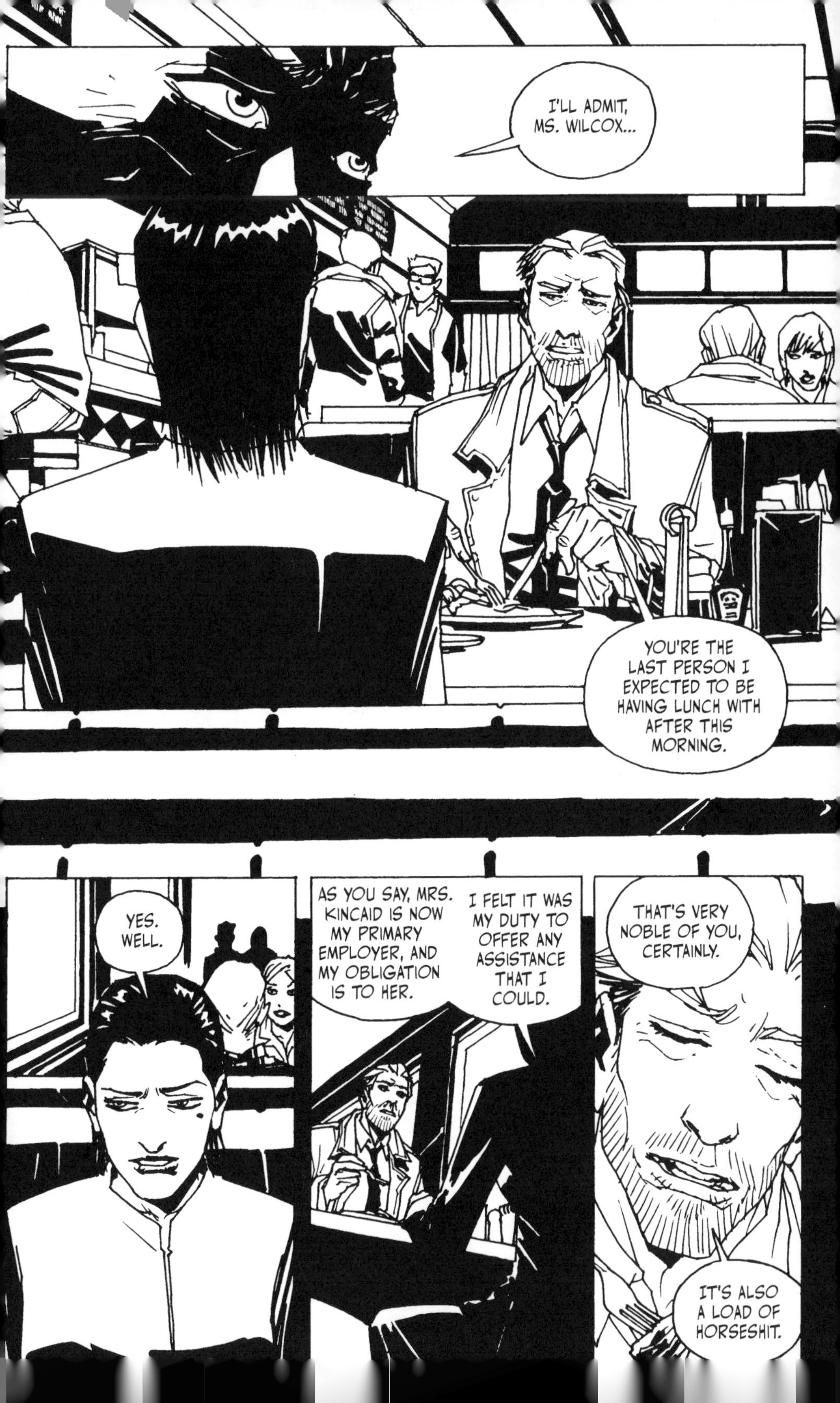
I'LL ADMIT, MS. WILCOX...
YOU'RE THE LAST PERSON I EXPECTED TO BE HAVING LUNCH WITH AFTER THIS MORNING.
YES. WELL.
AS YOU SAY, MRS. KINCAID IS NOW MY PRIMARY EMPLOYER, AND MY OBLIGATION IS TO HER.
I FELT IT WAS MY DUTY TO OFFER ANY ASSISTANCE THAT I COULD.
THAT'S VERY NOBLE OF YOU, CERTAINLY.
IT'S ALSO A LOAD OF HORSESHIT.

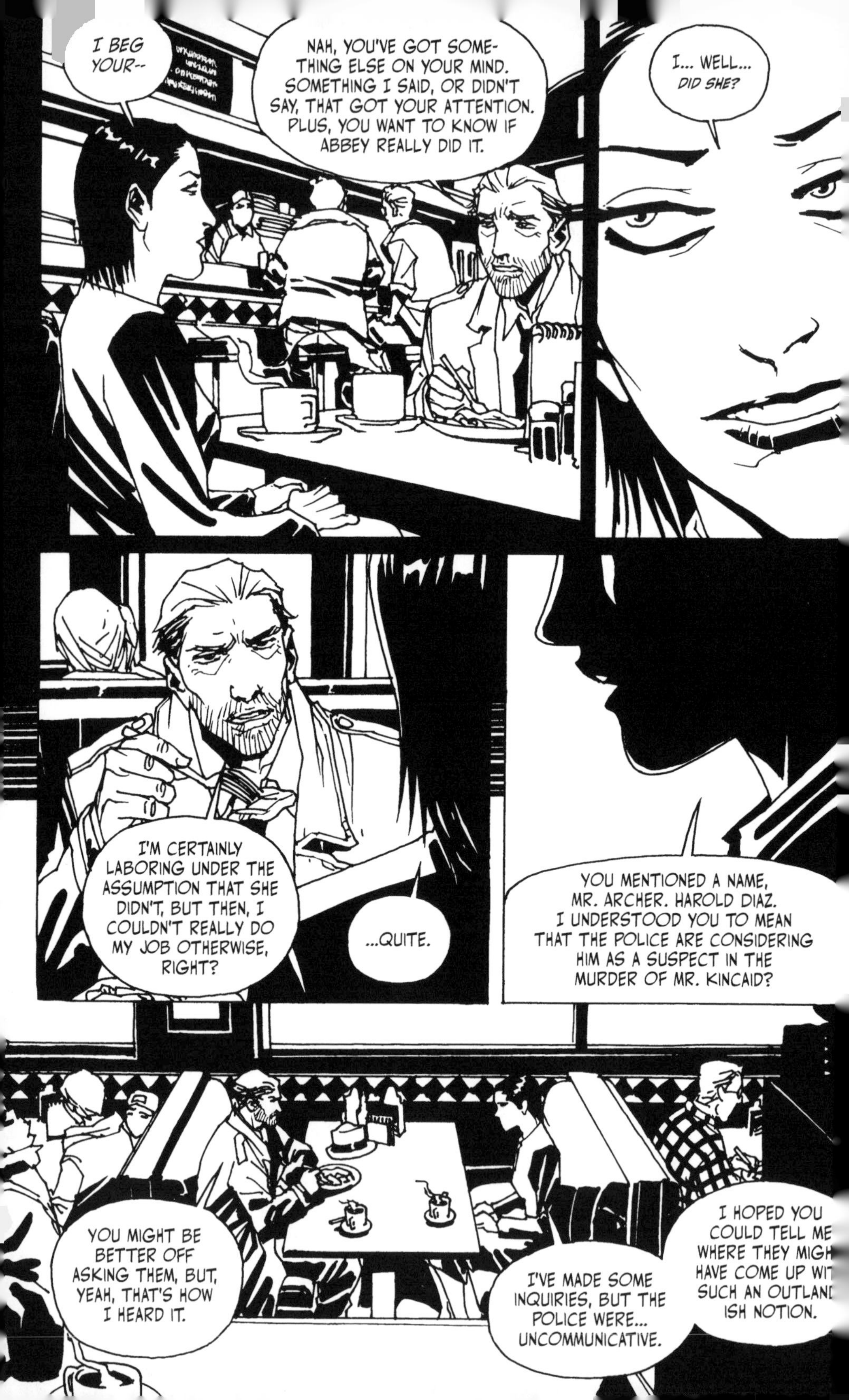
I BEG YOUR--
NAH, YOU'VE GOT SOMETHING ELSE ON YOUR MIND. SOMETHING I SAID, OR DIDN'T SAY, THAT GOT YOUR ATTENTION. PLUS, YOU WANT TO KNOW IF ABBEY REALLY DID IT.
I... WELL... DID SHE?
I'M CERTAINLY LABORING UNDER THE ASSUMPTION THAT SHE DIDN'T, BUT THEN, I COULDN'T REALLY DO MY JOB OTHERWISE, RIGHT?
...QUITE.
YOU MENTIONED A NAME, MR. ARCHER. HAROLD DIAZ. I UNDERSTOOD YOU TO MEAN THAT THE POLICE ARE CONSIDERING HIM AS A SUSPECT IN THE MURDER OF MR. KINCAID?
YOU MIGHT BE BETTER OFF ASKING THEM, BUT, YEAH, THAT'S HOW I HEARD IT.
I'VE MADE SOME INQUIRIES, BUT THE POLICE WERE... UNCOMMUNICATIVE.
I HOPED YOU COULD TELL ME WHERE THEY MIGH HAVE COME UP WIT SUCH AN OUTLAND ISH NOTION.

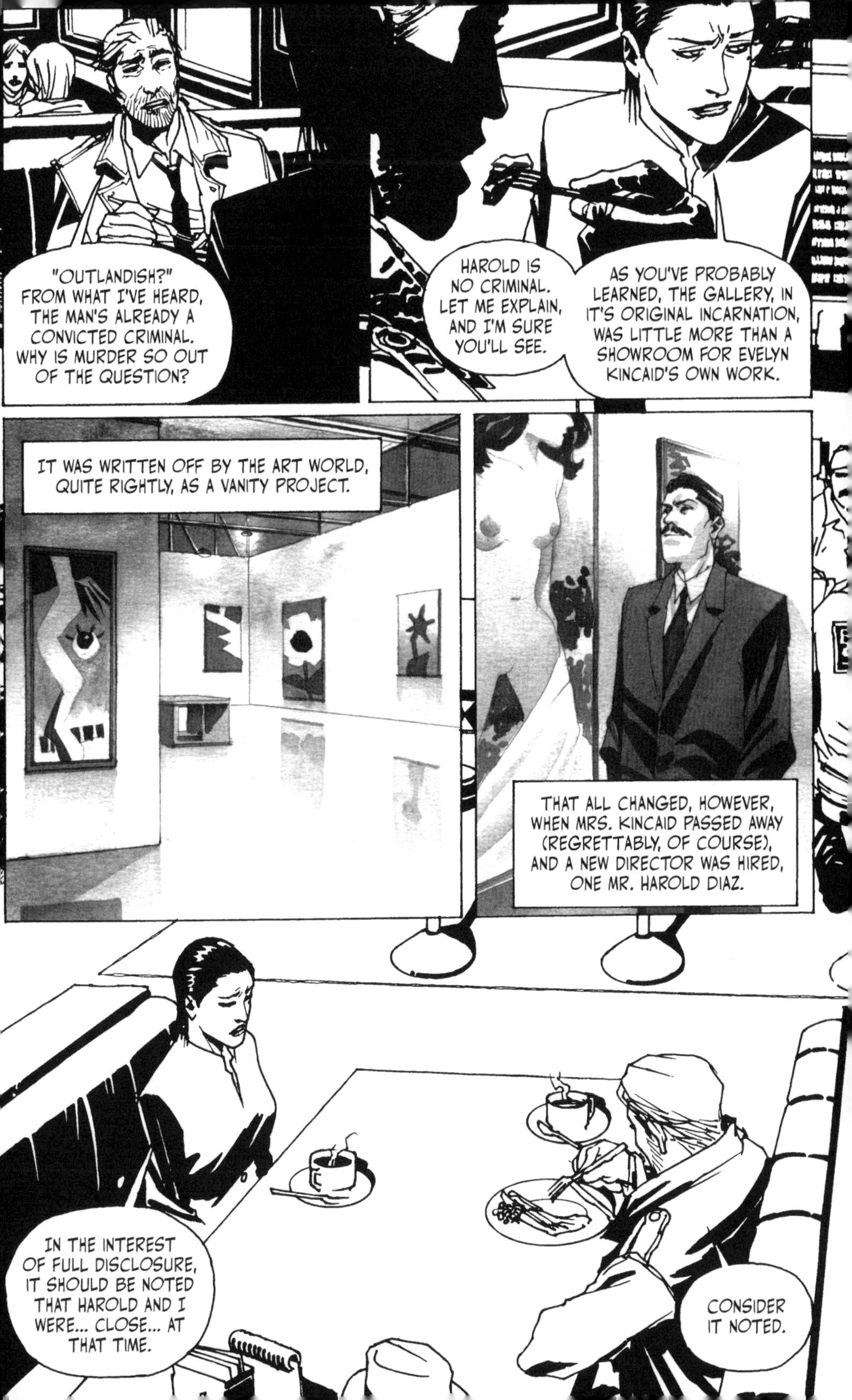
"OUTLANDISH?" FROM WHAT I'VE HEARD, THE MAN'S ALREADY A CONVICTED CRIMINAL. WHY IS MURDER SO OUT OF THE QUESTION?
HAROLD IS NO CRIMINAL. LET ME EXPLAIN, AND I'M SURE YOU'LL SEE.
AS YOU'VE PROBABLY LEARNED, THE GALLERY, IN IT'S ORIGINAL INCARNATION, WAS LITTLE MORE THAN A SHOWROOM FOR EVELYN KINCAID'S OWN WORK.
IT WAS WRITTEN OFF BY THE ART WORLD, QUITE RIGHTLY, AS A VANITY PROJECT.
THAT ALL CHANGED, HOWEVER, WHEN MRS. KINCAID PASSED AWAY (REGRETTABLY, OF COURSE), AND A NEW DIRECTOR WAS HIRED, ONE MR. HAROLD DIAZ.
IN THE INTEREST OF FULL DISCLOSURE, IT SHOULD BE NOTED THAT HAROLD AND I WERE... CLOSE... AT THAT TIME.
CONSIDER IT NOTED.

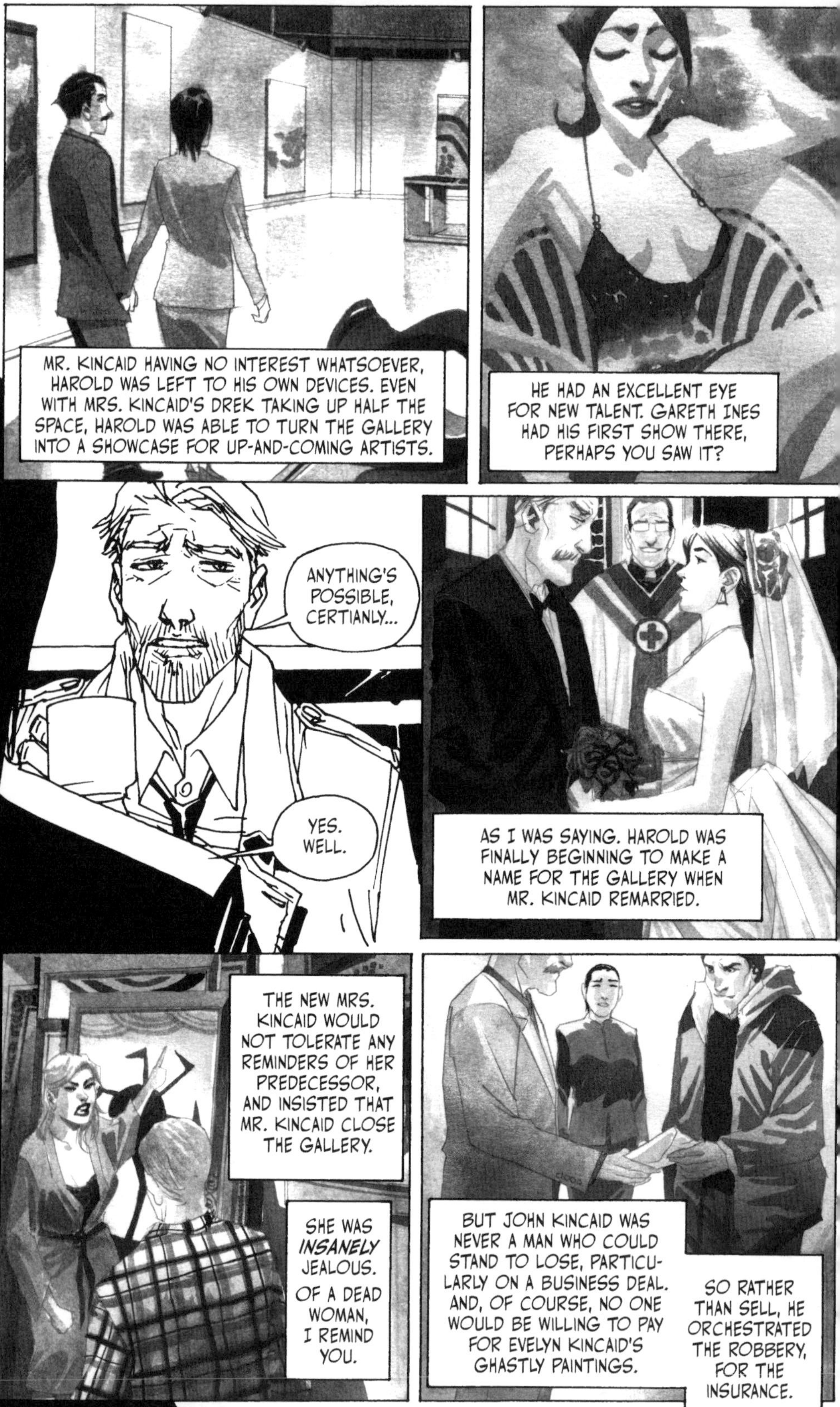
MR. KINCAID HAVING NO INTEREST WHATSOEVER, HAROLD WAS LEFT TO HIS OWN DEVICES. EVEN WITH MRS. KINCAID'S DREK TAKING UP HALF THE SPACE, HAROLD WAS ABLE TO TURN THE GALLERY INTO A SHOWCASE FOR UP-AND-COMING ARTISTS.
HE HAD AN EXCELLENT EYE FOR NEW TALENT. GARETH INES HAD HIS FIRST SHOW THERE, PERHAPS YOU SAW IT?
ANYTHING'S POSSIBLE, CERTIANLY...
YES. WELL.
AS I WAS SAYING. HAROLD WAS FINALLY BEGINNING TO MAKE A NAME FOR THE GALLERY WHEN MR. KINCAID REMARRIED.
THE NEW MRS. KINCAID WOULD NOT TOLERATE ANY REMINDERS OF HER PREDECESSOR, AND INSISTED THAT MR. KINCAID CLOSE THE GALLERY.
SHE WAS *INSANELY* JEALOUS.
OF A DEAD WOMAN, I REMIND YOU.
BUT JOHN KINCAID WAS NEVER A MAN WHO COULD STAND TO LOSE, PARTICU-LARLY ON A BUSINESS DEAL. AND, OF COURSE, NO ONE WOULD BE WILLING TO PAY FOR EVELYN KINCAID'S GHASTLY PAINTINGS.
SO RATHER THAN SELL, HE ORCHESTRATED THE ROBBERY, FOR THE INSURANCE.

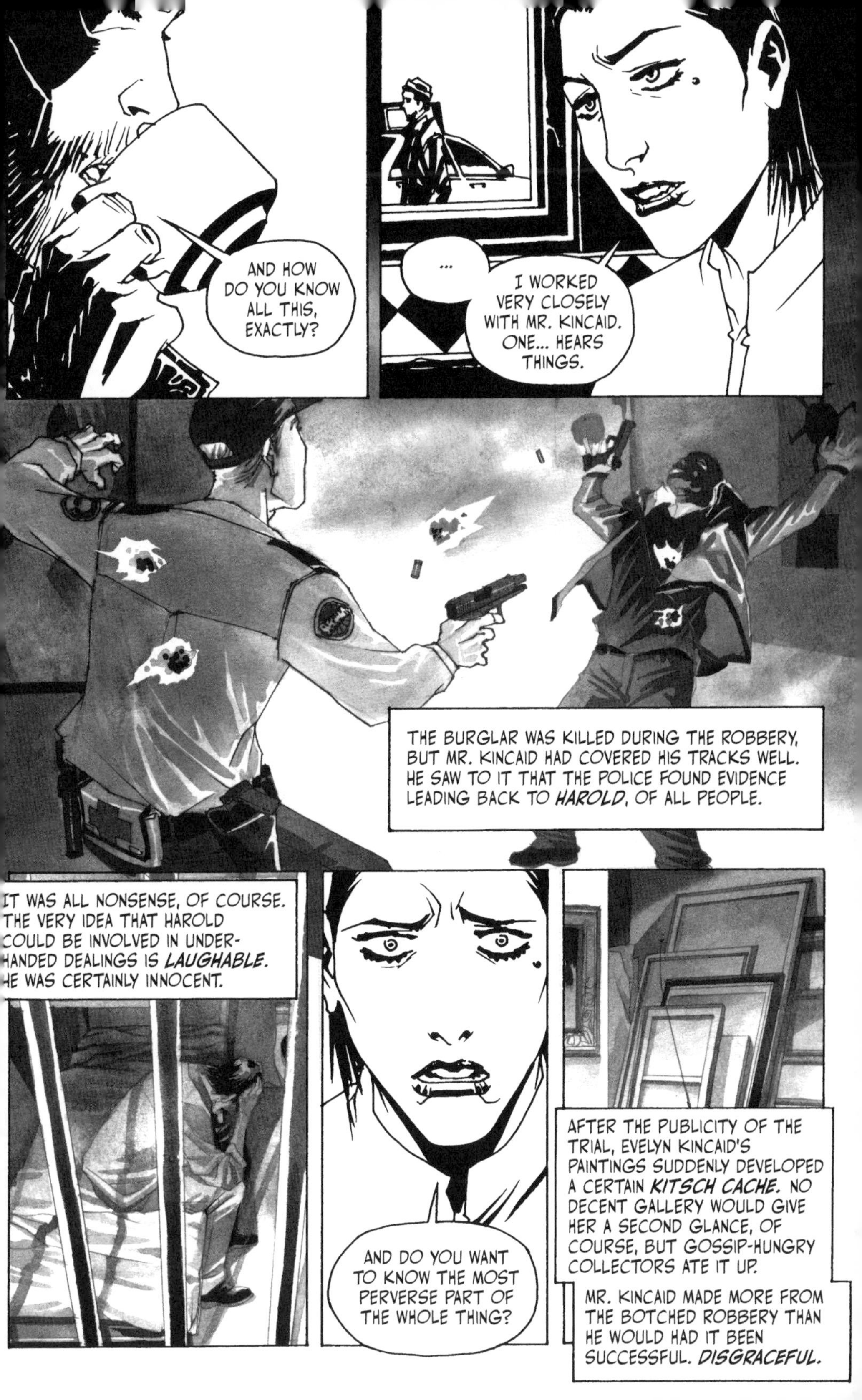
AND HOW DO YOU KNOW ALL THIS, EXACTLY?
...
I WORKED VERY CLOSELY WITH MR. KINCAID. ONE... HEARS THINGS.
THE BURGLAR WAS KILLED DURING THE ROBBERY, BUT MR. KINCAID HAD COVERED HIS TRACKS WELL. HE SAW TO IT THAT THE POLICE FOUND EVIDENCE LEADING BACK TO HAROLD, OF ALL PEOPLE.
IT WAS ALL NONSENSE, OF COURSE. THE VERY IDEA THAT HAROLD COULD BE INVOLVED IN UNDER-HANDED DEALINGS IS LAUGHABLE. HE WAS CERTAINLY INNOCENT.
AND DO YOU WANT TO KNOW THE MOST PERVERSE PART OF THE WHOLE THING?
AFTER THE PUBLICITY OF THE TRIAL, EVELYN KINCAID'S PAINTINGS SUDDENLY DEVELOPED A CERTAIN KITSCH CACHE. NO DECENT GALLERY WOULD GIVE HER A SECOND GLANCE, OF COURSE, BUT GOSSIP-HUNGRY COLLECTORS ATE IT UP.
MR. KINCAID MADE MORE FROM THE BOTCHED ROBBERY THAN HE WOULD HAD IT BEEN SUCCESSFUL. DISGRACEFUL.

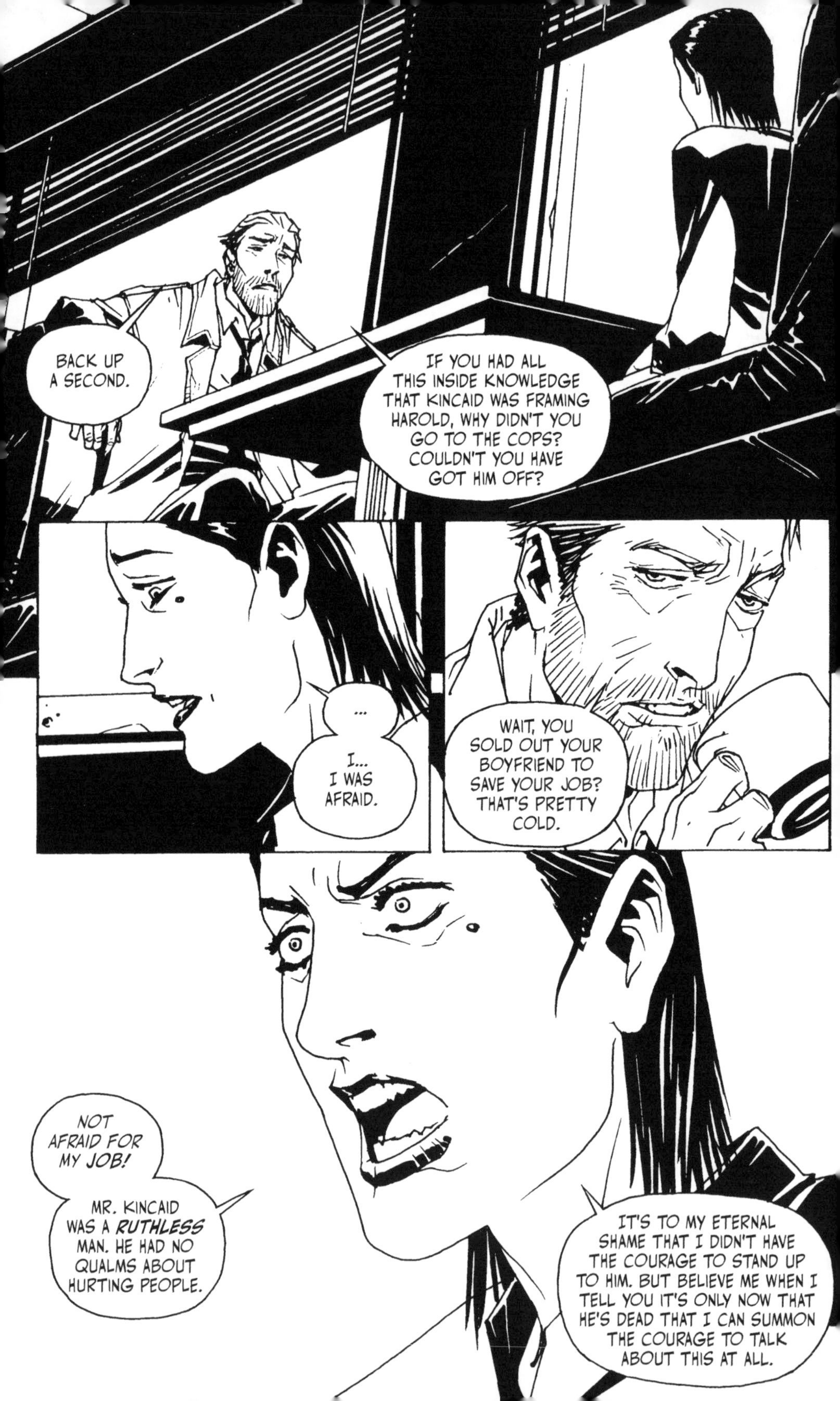
BACK UP A SECOND.
IF YOU HAD ALL THIS INSIDE KNOWLEDGE THAT KINCAID WAS FRAMING HAROLD, WHY DIDN'T YOU GO TO THE COPS? COULDN'T YOU HAVE GOT HIM OFF?
...
I... I WAS AFRAID.
WAIT, YOU SOLD OUT YOUR BOYFRIEND TO SAVE YOUR JOB? THAT'S PRETTY COLD.
NOT AFRAID FOR MY *JOB!*
MR. KINCAID WAS A ***RUTHLESS*** MAN. HE HAD NO QUALMS ABOUT HURTING PEOPLE.
IT'S TO MY ETERNAL SHAME THAT I DIDN'T HAVE THE COURAGE TO STAND UP TO HIM. BUT BELIEVE ME WHEN I TELL YOU IT'S ONLY NOW THAT HE'S DEAD THAT I CAN SUMMON THE COURAGE TO TALK ABOUT THIS AT ALL.

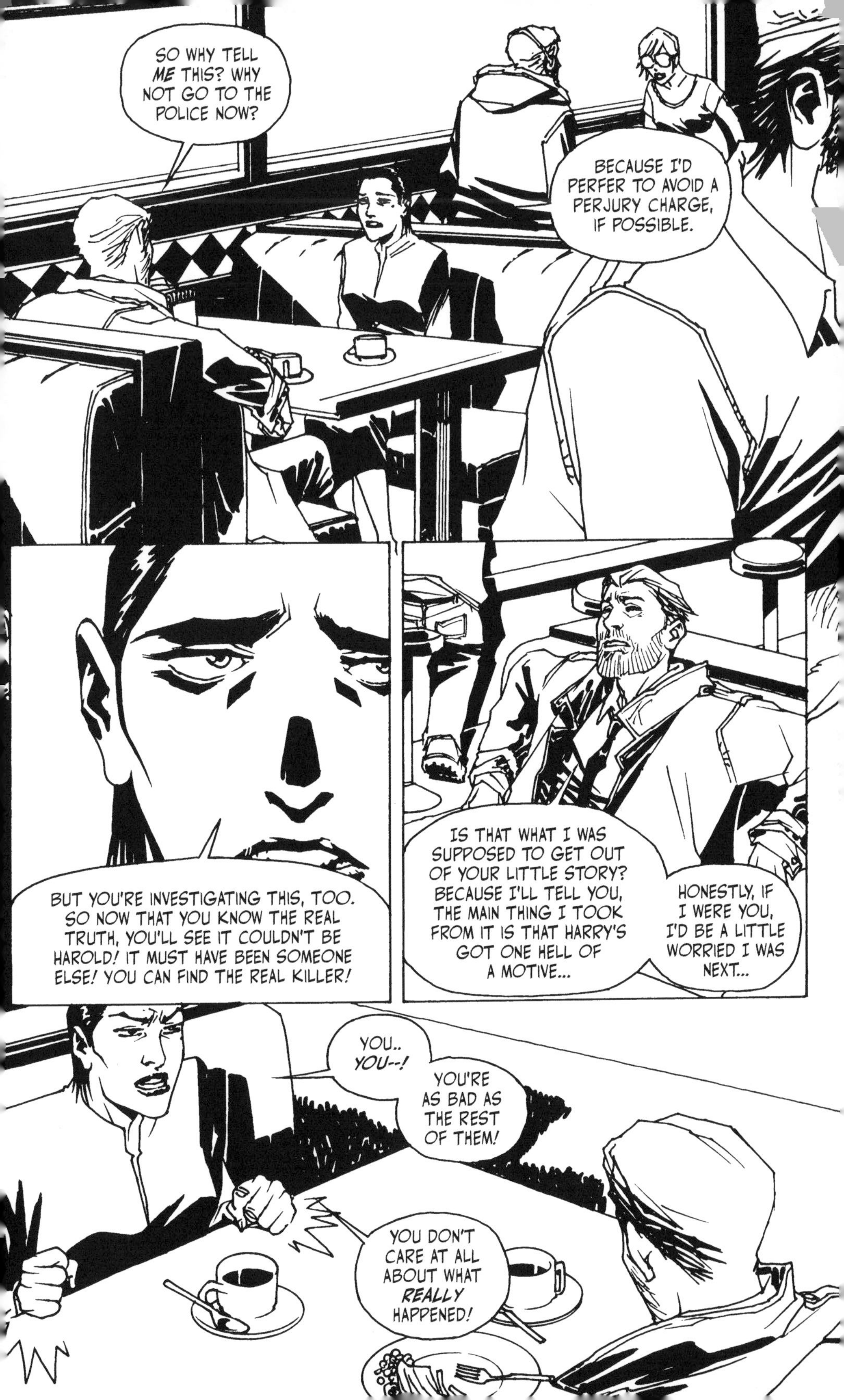
SO WHY TELL *ME* THIS? WHY NOT GO TO THE POLICE NOW?
BECAUSE I'D PERFER TO AVOID A PERJURY CHARGE, IF POSSIBLE.
BUT YOU'RE INVESTIGATING THIS, TOO. SO NOW THAT YOU KNOW THE REAL TRUTH, YOU'LL SEE IT COULDN'T BE HAROLD! IT MUST HAVE BEEN SOMEONE ELSE! YOU CAN FIND THE REAL KILLER!
IS THAT WHAT I WAS SUPPOSED TO GET OUT OF YOUR LITTLE STORY? BECAUSE I'LL TELL YOU, THE MAIN THING I TOOK FROM IT IS THAT HARRY'S GOT ONE HELL OF A MOTIVE...
HONESTLY, IF I WERE YOU, I'D BE A LITTLE WORRIED I WAS NEXT...
YOU.. *YOU--!*
YOU'RE AS BAD AS THE REST OF THEM!
YOU DON'T CARE AT ALL ABOUT WHAT *REALLY* HAPPENED!

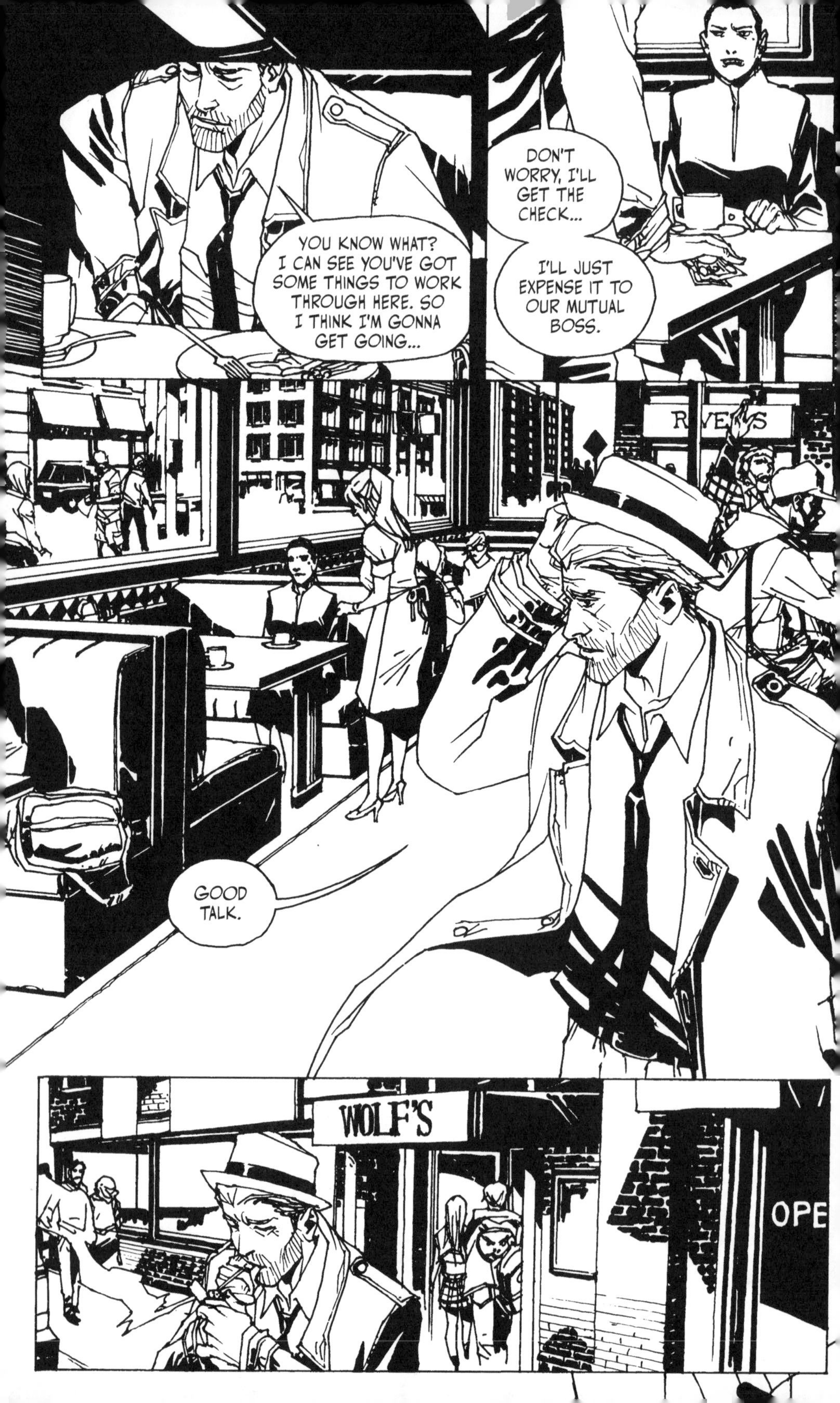
YOU KNOW WHAT? I CAN SEE YOU'VE GOT SOME THINGS TO WORK THROUGH HERE. SO I THINK I'M GONNA GET GOING...
DON'T WORRY, I'LL GET THE CHECK...
I'LL JUST EXPENSE IT TO OUR MUTUAL BOSS.
GOOD TALK.
WOLF'S
OPE

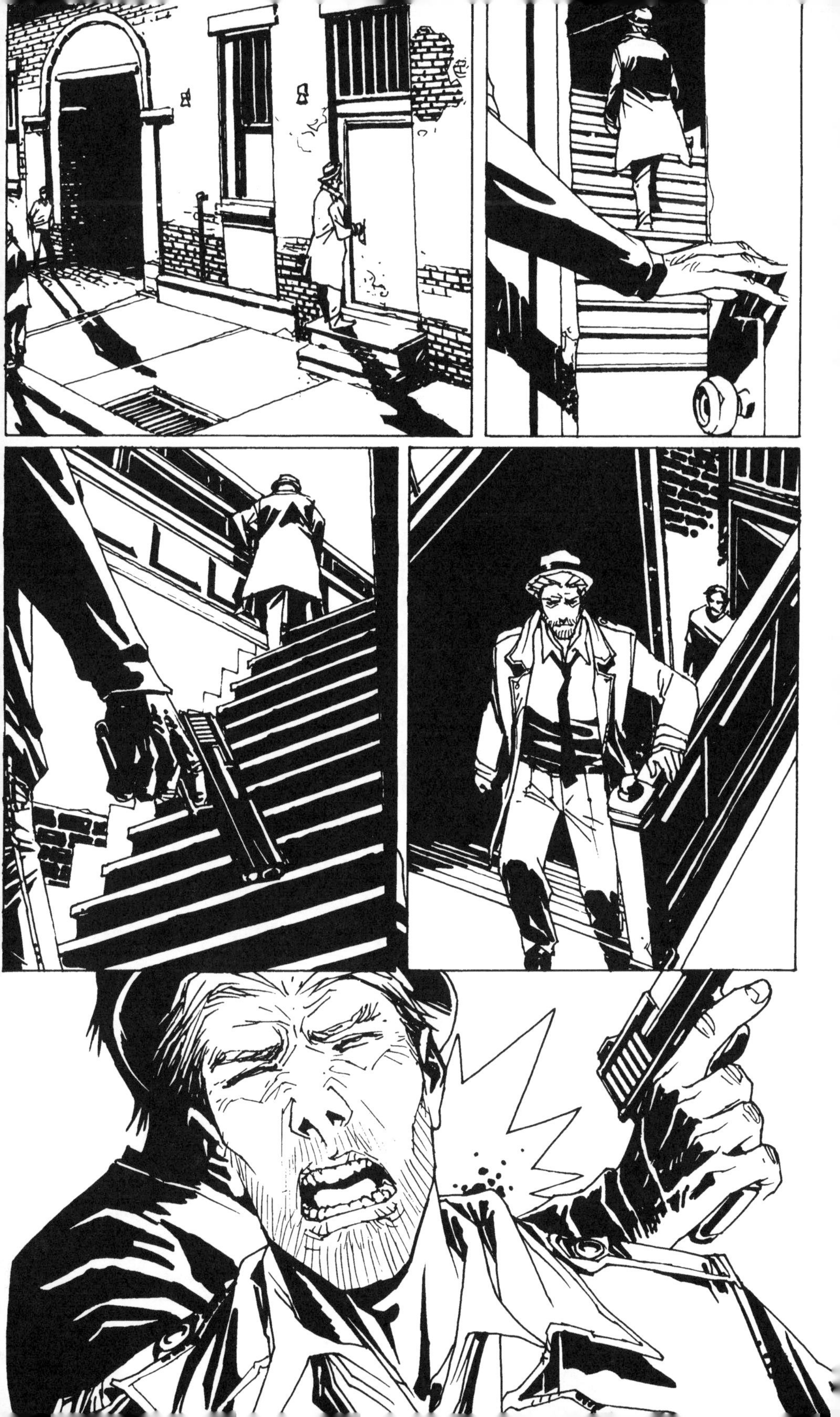

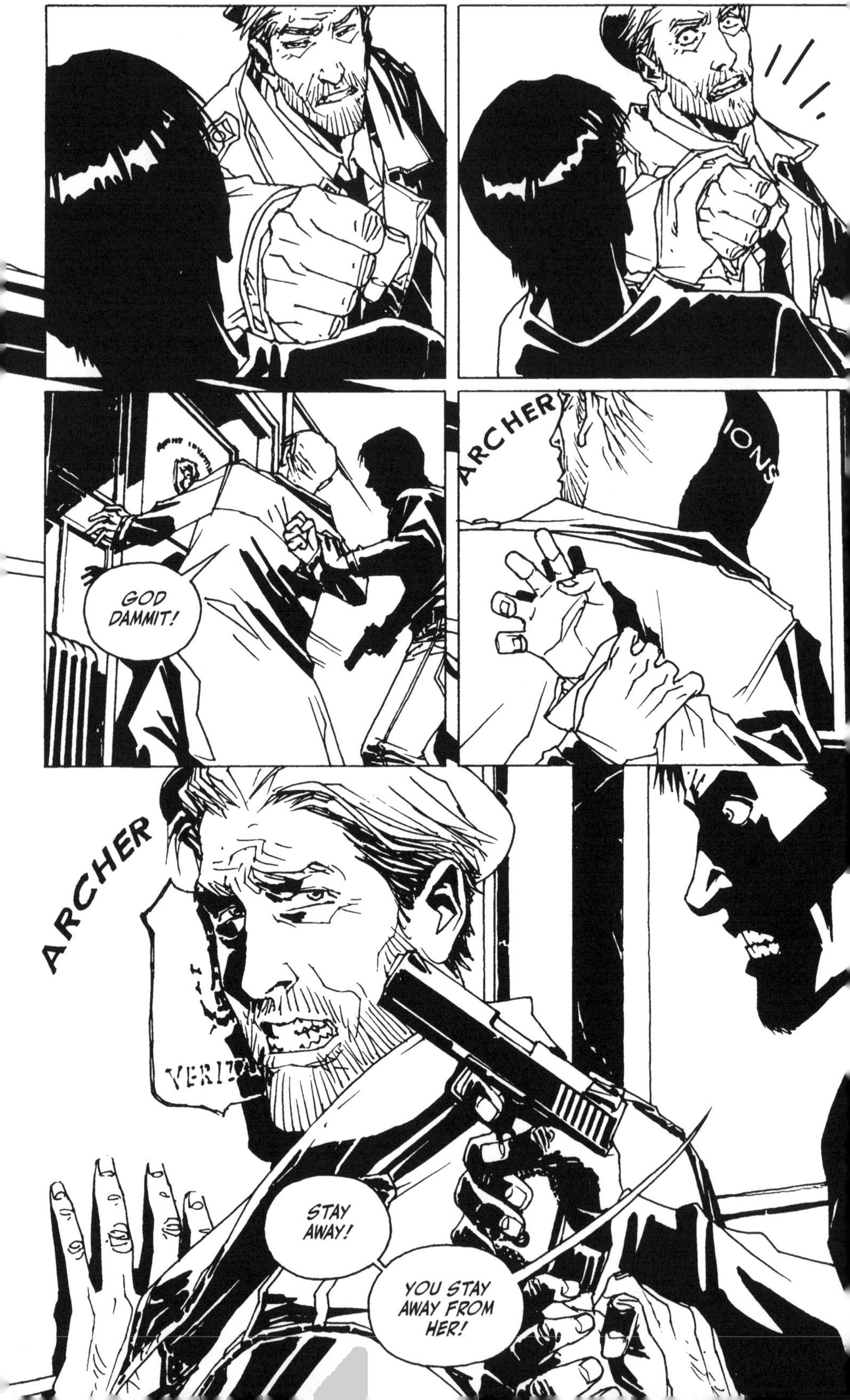
GOD DAMMIT!
ARCHER
IONS
ARCHER
VERIT
STAY AWAY!
YOU STAY AWAY FROM HER!

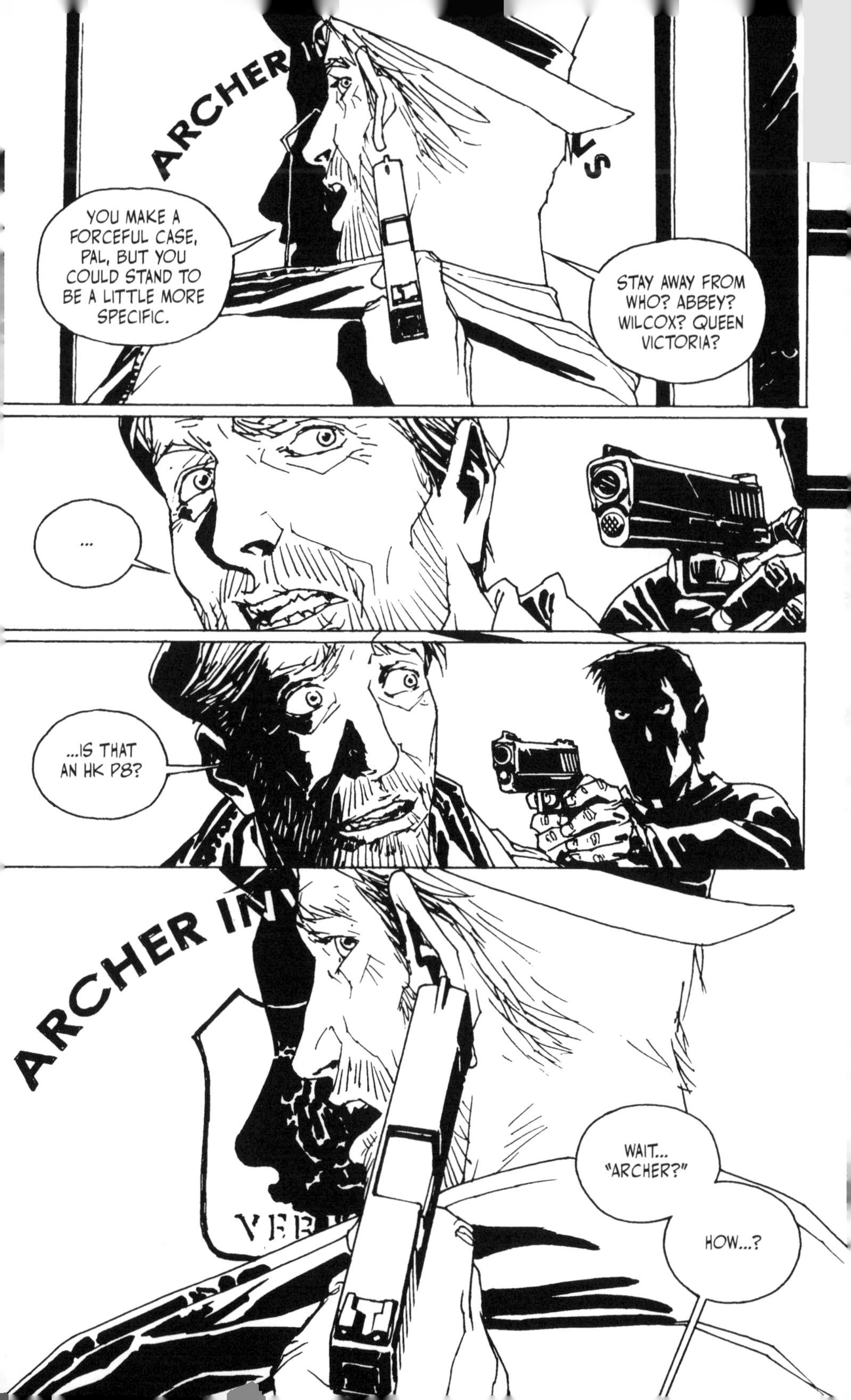
ARCHER
YOU MAKE A FORCEFUL CASE, PAL, BUT YOU COULD STAND TO BE A LITTLE MORE SPECIFIC.
STAY AWAY FROM WHO? ABBEY? WILCOX? QUEEN VICTORIA?
...
...IS THAT AN HK P8?
ARCHER IN
WAIT... "ARCHER?"
HOW...?

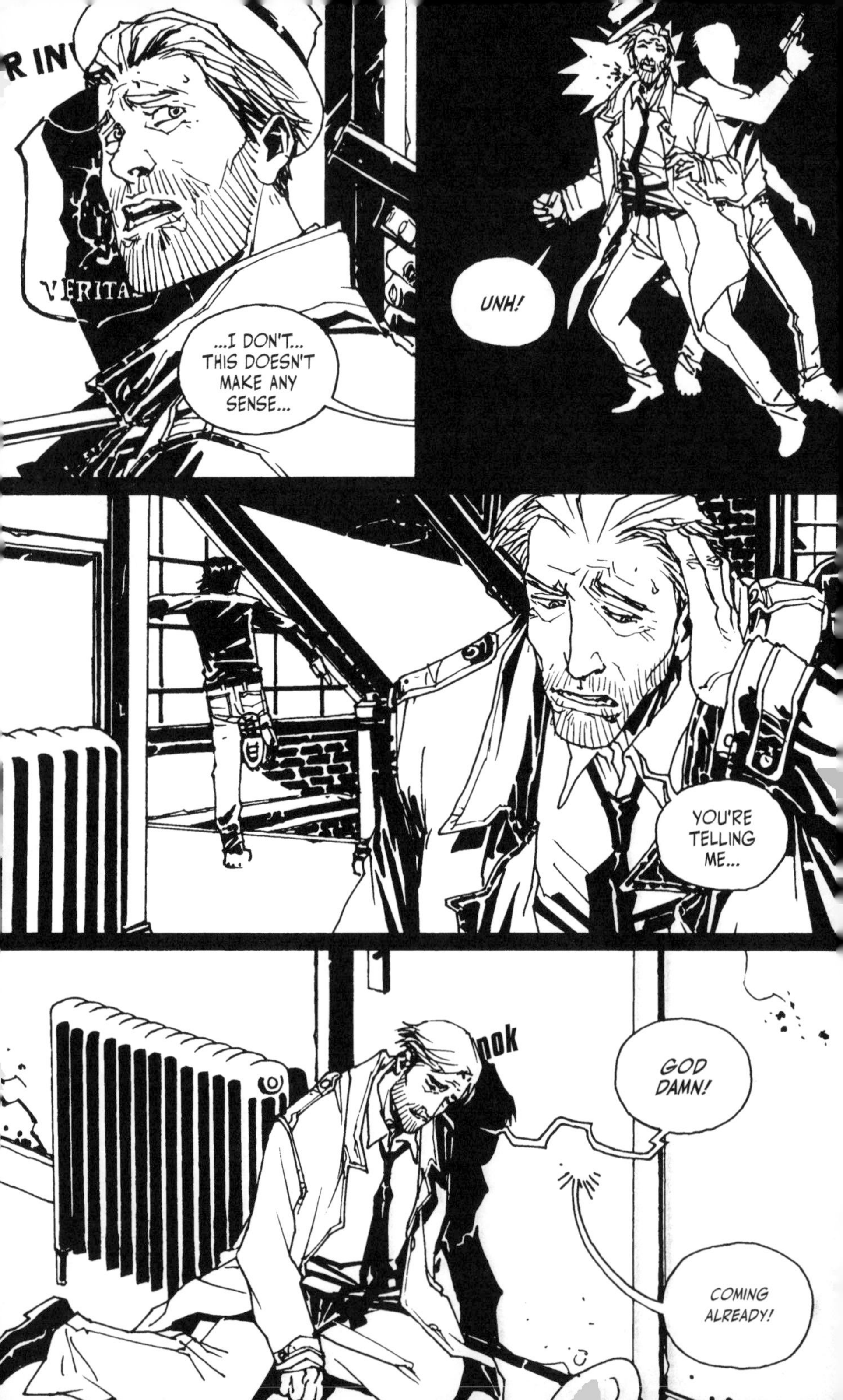
R IN
VERITA
...I DON'T... THIS DOESN'T MAKE ANY SENSE...
UNH!
YOU'RE TELLING ME...
nok
GOD DAMN!
COMING ALREADY!

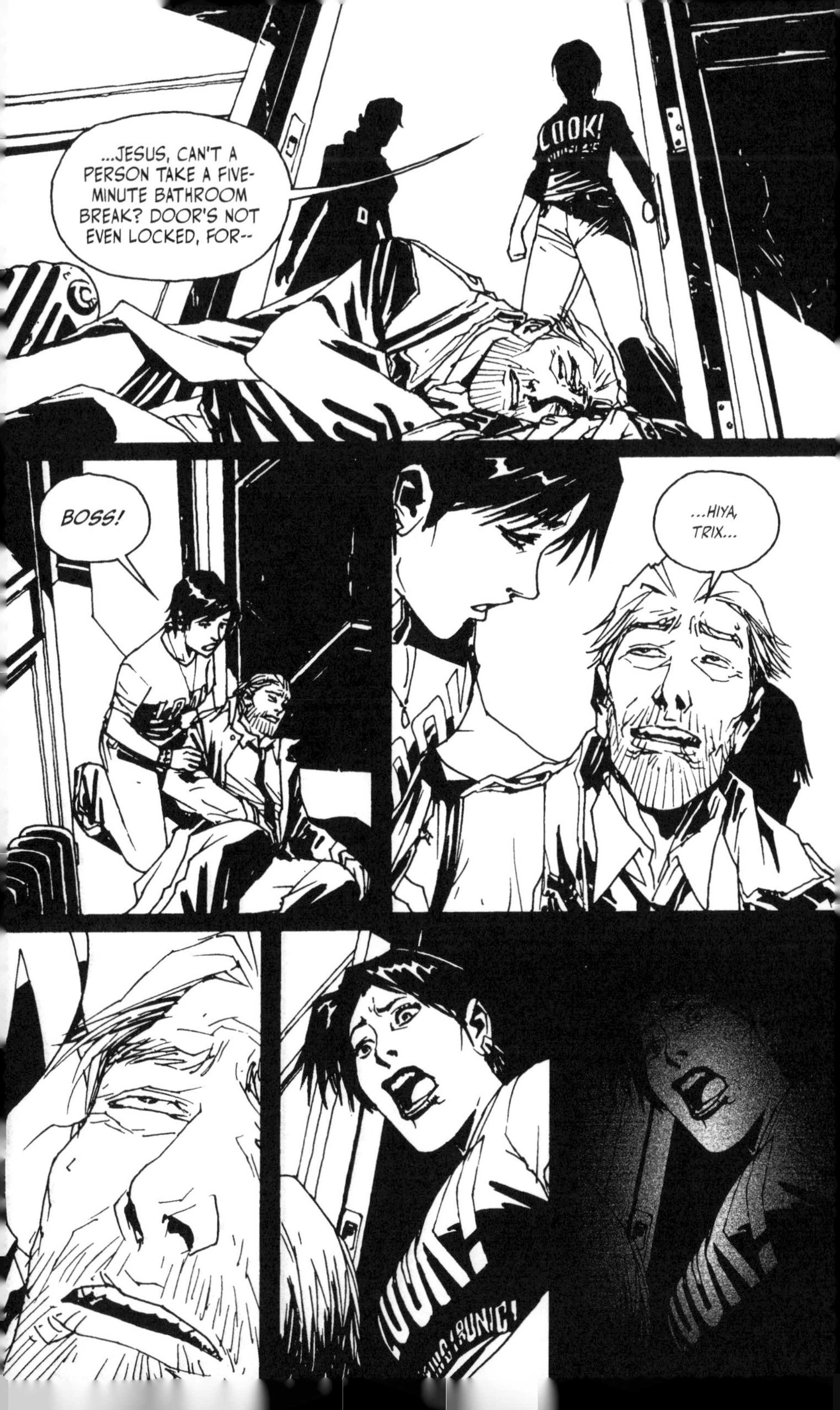
...JESUS, CAN'T A PERSON TAKE A FIVE-MINUTE BATHROOM BREAK? DOOR'S NOT EVEN LOCKED, FOR--
LOOK!
BOSS!
...HIYA, TRIX...
LOOK!
LOOK!

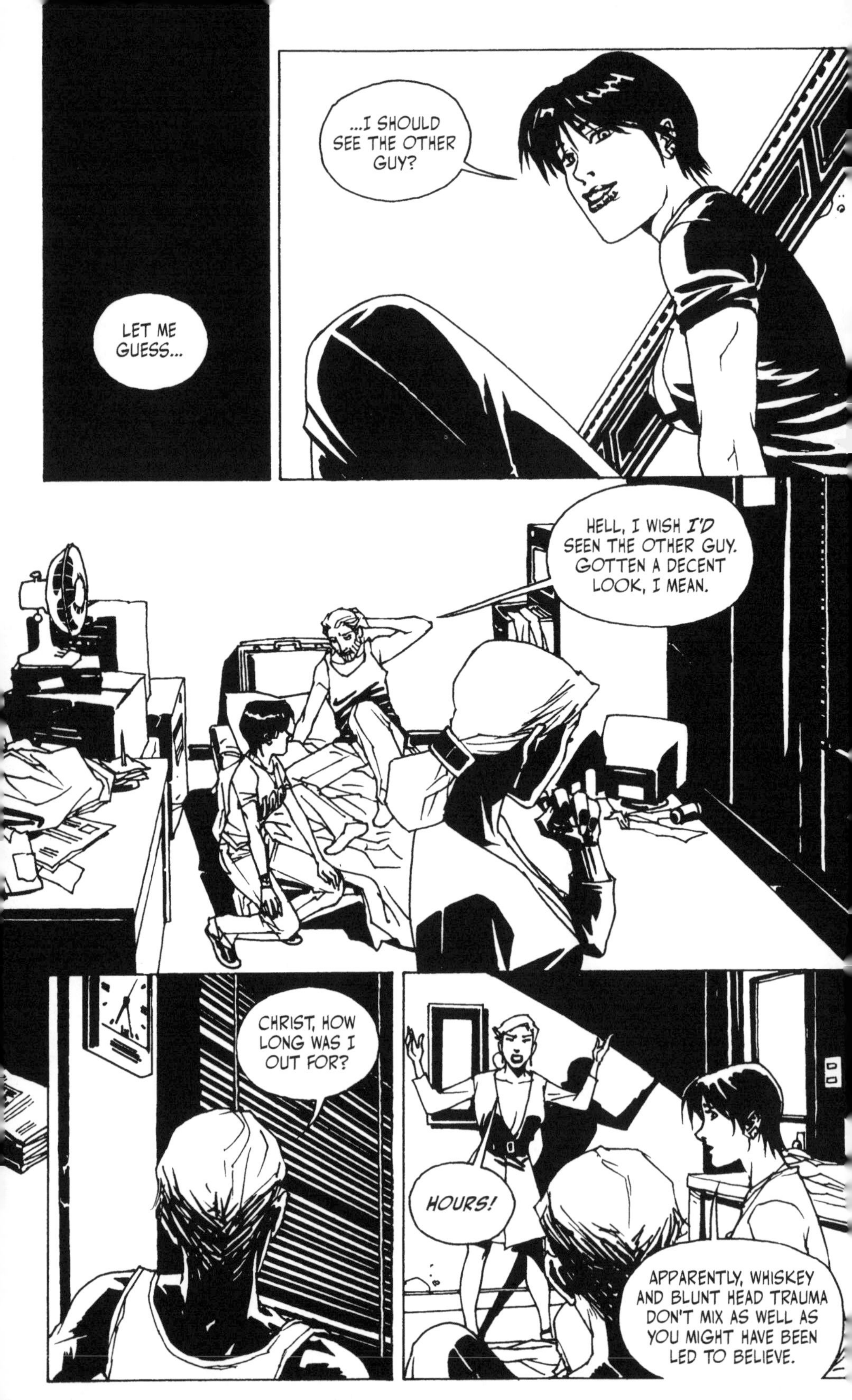
LET ME GUESS...
...I SHOULD SEE THE OTHER GUY?
HELL, I WISH I'D SEEN THE OTHER GUY. GOTTEN A DECENT LOOK, I MEAN.
CHRIST, HOW LONG WAS I OUT FOR?
HOURS!
APPARENTLY, WHISKEY AND BLUNT HEAD TRAUMA DON'T MIX AS WELL AS YOU MIGHT HAVE BEEN LED TO BELIEVE.

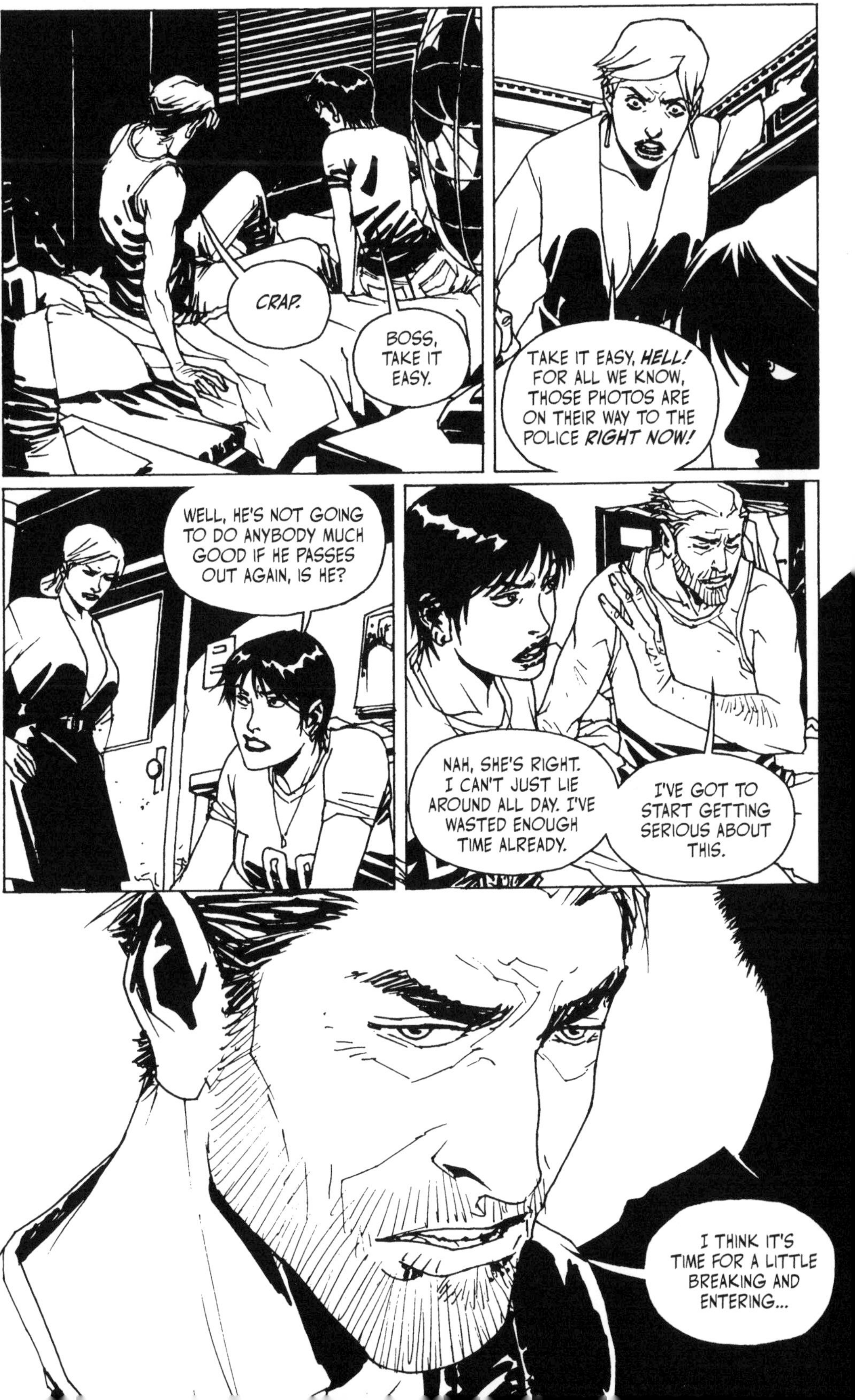
CRAP.
BOSS, TAKE IT EASY.
TAKE IT EASY, HELL! FOR ALL WE KNOW, THOSE PHOTOS ARE ON THEIR WAY TO THE POLICE RIGHT NOW!
WELL, HE'S NOT GOING TO DO ANYBODY MUCH GOOD IF HE PASSES OUT AGAIN, IS HE?
NAH, SHE'S RIGHT. I CAN'T JUST LIE AROUND ALL DAY. I'VE WASTED ENOUGH TIME ALREADY.
I'VE GOT TO START GETTING SERIOUS ABOUT THIS.
I THINK IT'S TIME FOR A LITTLE BREAKING AND ENTERING...

SIX "EVEN IF THIS TIME HE *DOES* DESERVE IT?"

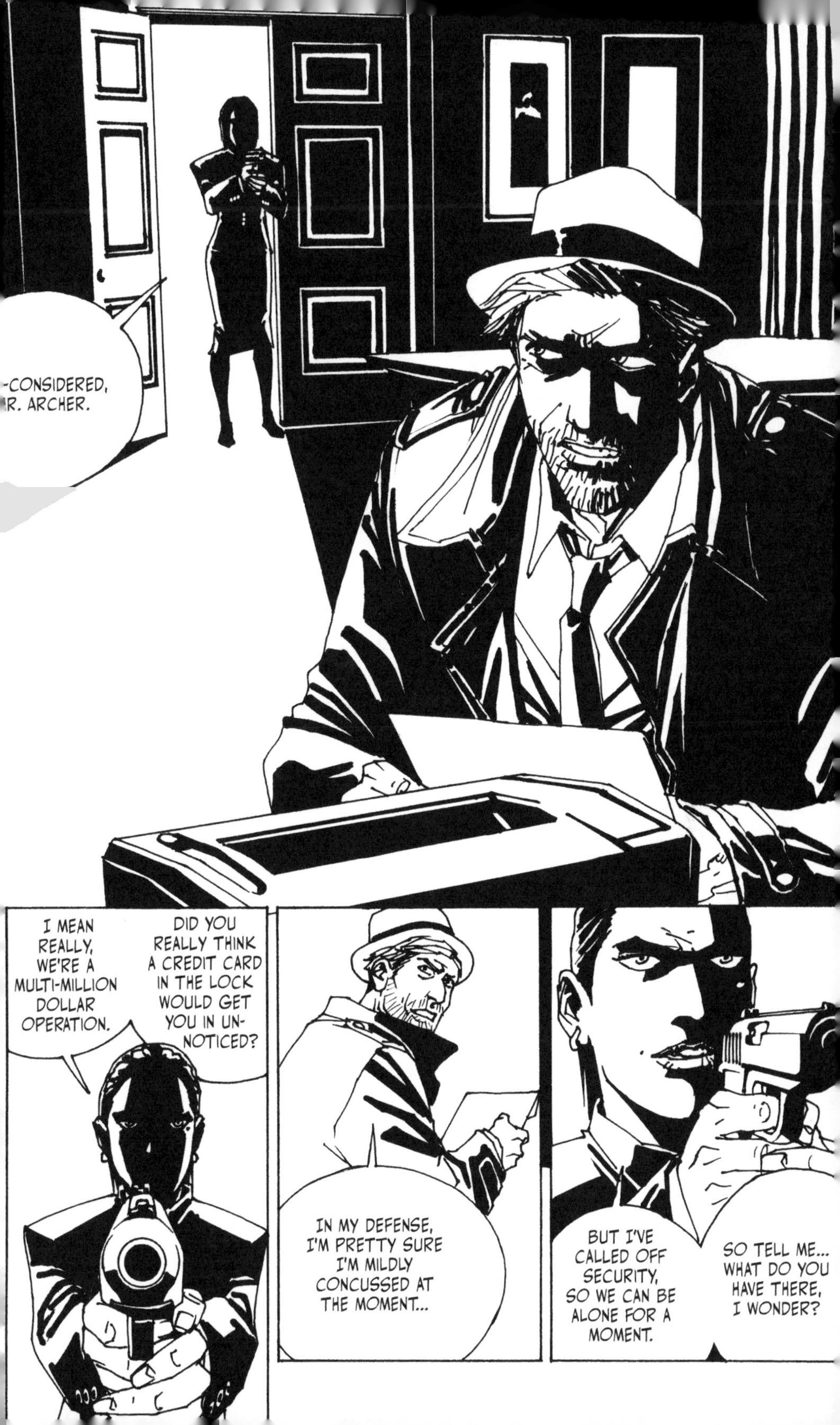
-CONSIDERED,
R. ARCHER.
I MEAN REALLY, WE'RE A MULTI-MILLION DOLLAR OPERATION.
DID YOU REALLY THINK A CREDIT CARD IN THE LOCK WOULD GET YOU IN UN-NOTICED?
IN MY DEFENSE, I'M PRETTY SURE I'M MILDLY CONCUSSED AT THE MOMENT...
BUT I'VE CALLED OFF SECURITY, SO WE CAN BE ALONE FOR A MOMENT.
SO TELL ME... WHAT DO YOU HAVE THERE, I WONDER?

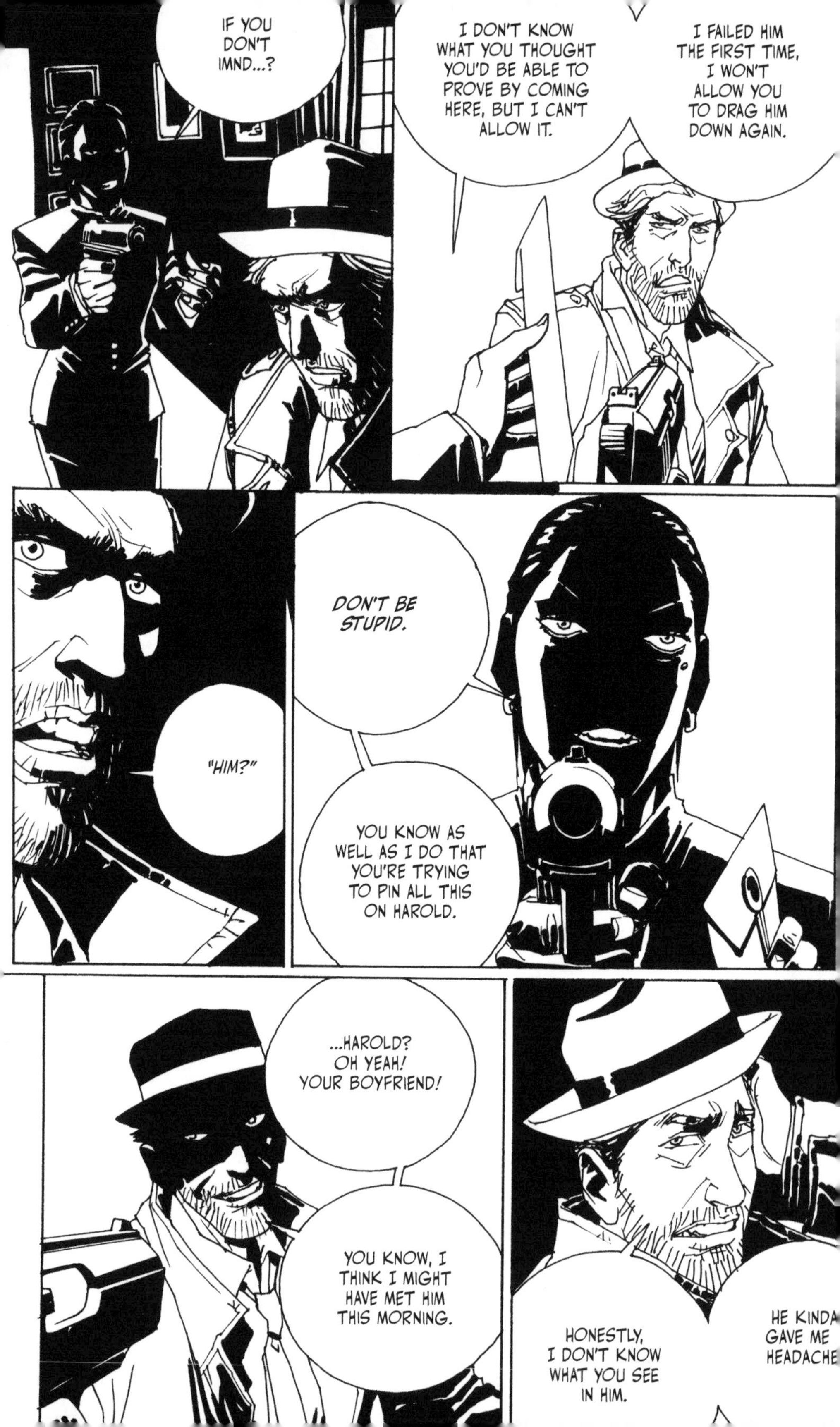
IF YOU DON'T IMND...?
I DON'T KNOW WHAT YOU THOUGHT YOU'D BE ABLE TO PROVE BY COMING HERE, BUT I CAN'T ALLOW IT.
I FAILED HIM THE FIRST TIME, I WON'T ALLOW YOU TO DRAG HIM DOWN AGAIN.
"HIM?"
DON'T BE STUPID.
YOU KNOW AS WELL AS I DO THAT YOU'RE TRYING TO PIN ALL THIS ON HAROLD.
...HAROLD? OH YEAH! YOUR BOYFRIEND!
YOU KNOW, I THINK I MIGHT HAVE MET HIM THIS MORNING.
HONESTLY, I DON'T KNOW WHAT YOU SEE IN HIM.
HE KINDA GAVE ME HEADACHE

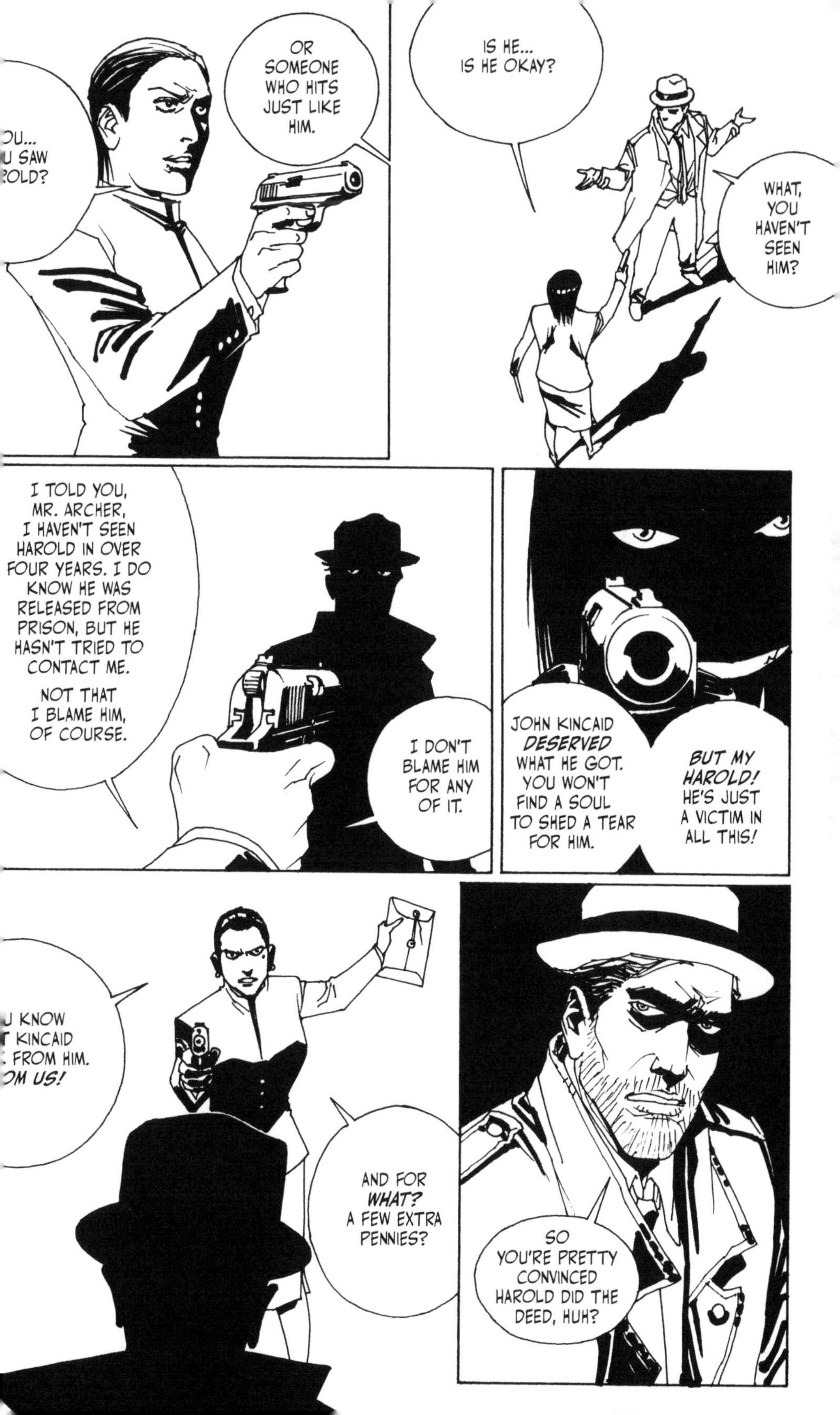

OU...
U SAW
ROLD?
OR SOMEONE WHO HITS JUST LIKE HIM.
IS HE... IS HE OKAY?
WHAT, YOU HAVEN'T SEEN HIM?
I TOLD YOU, MR. ARCHER, I HAVEN'T SEEN HAROLD IN OVER FOUR YEARS. I DO KNOW HE WAS RELEASED FROM PRISON, BUT HE HASN'T TRIED TO CONTACT ME.
NOT THAT I BLAME HIM, OF COURSE.
I DON'T BLAME HIM FOR ANY OF IT.
JOHN KINCAID *DESERVED* WHAT HE GOT. YOU WON'T FIND A SOUL TO SHED A TEAR FOR HIM.
BUT MY HAROLD! HE'S JUST A VICTIM IN ALL THIS!
U KNOW
T KINCAID
FROM HIM.
OM US!
AND FOR *WHAT?* A FEW EXTRA PENNIES?
SO YOU'RE PRETTY CONVINCED HAROLD DID THE DEED, HUH?

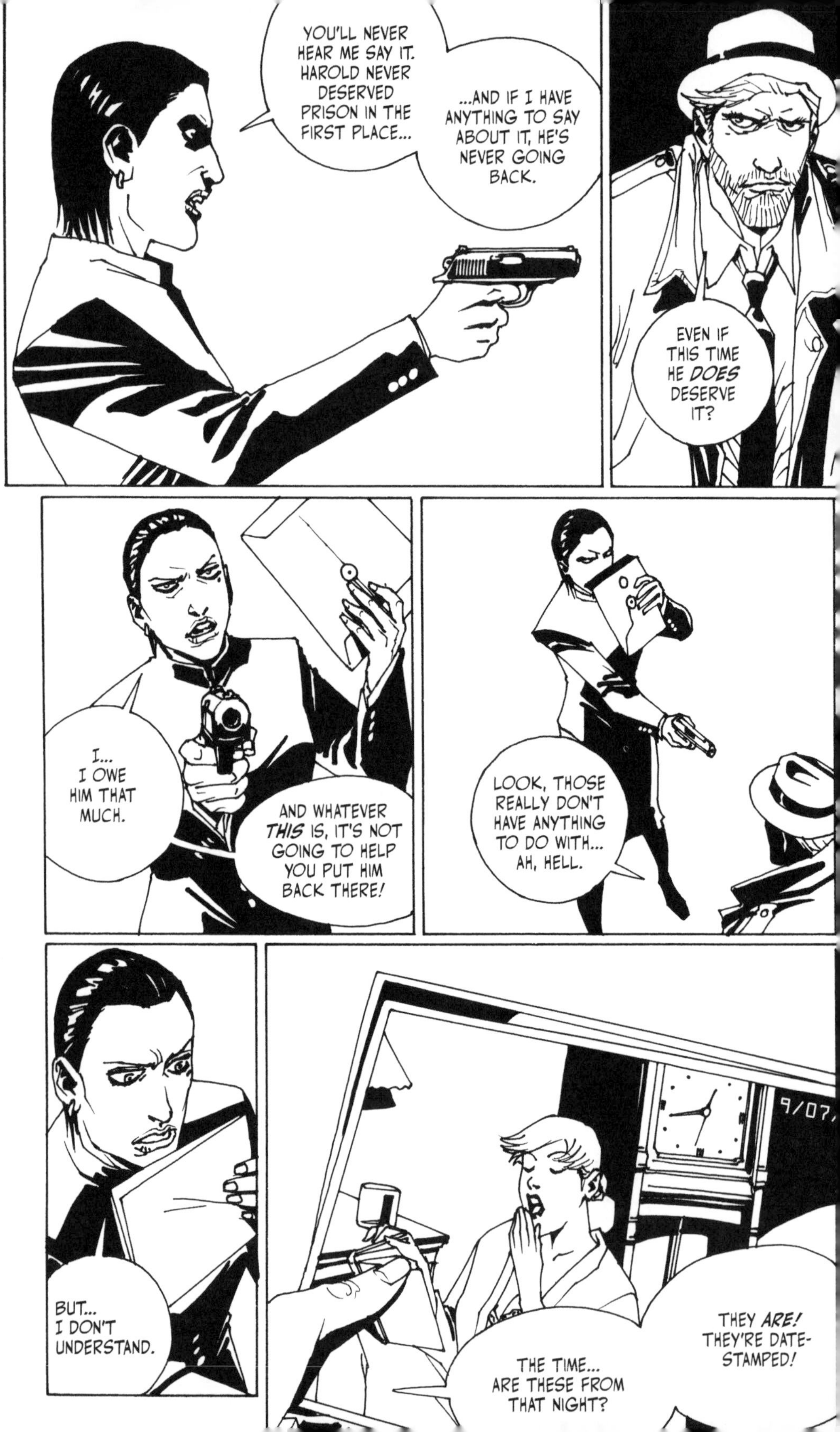
YOU'LL NEVER HEAR ME SAY IT. HAROLD NEVER DESERVED PRISON IN THE FIRST PLACE...
...AND IF I HAVE ANYTHING TO SAY ABOUT IT, HE'S NEVER GOING BACK.
EVEN IF THIS TIME HE *DOES* DESERVE IT?
I... I OWE HIM THAT MUCH.
AND WHATEVER *THIS* IS, IT'S NOT GOING TO HELP YOU PUT HIM BACK THERE!
LOOK, THOSE REALLY DON'T HAVE ANYTHING TO DO WITH... AH, HELL.
BUT... I DON'T UNDERSTAND.
THE TIME... ARE THESE FROM THAT NIGHT?
THEY *ARE!* THEY'RE DATE-STAMPED!

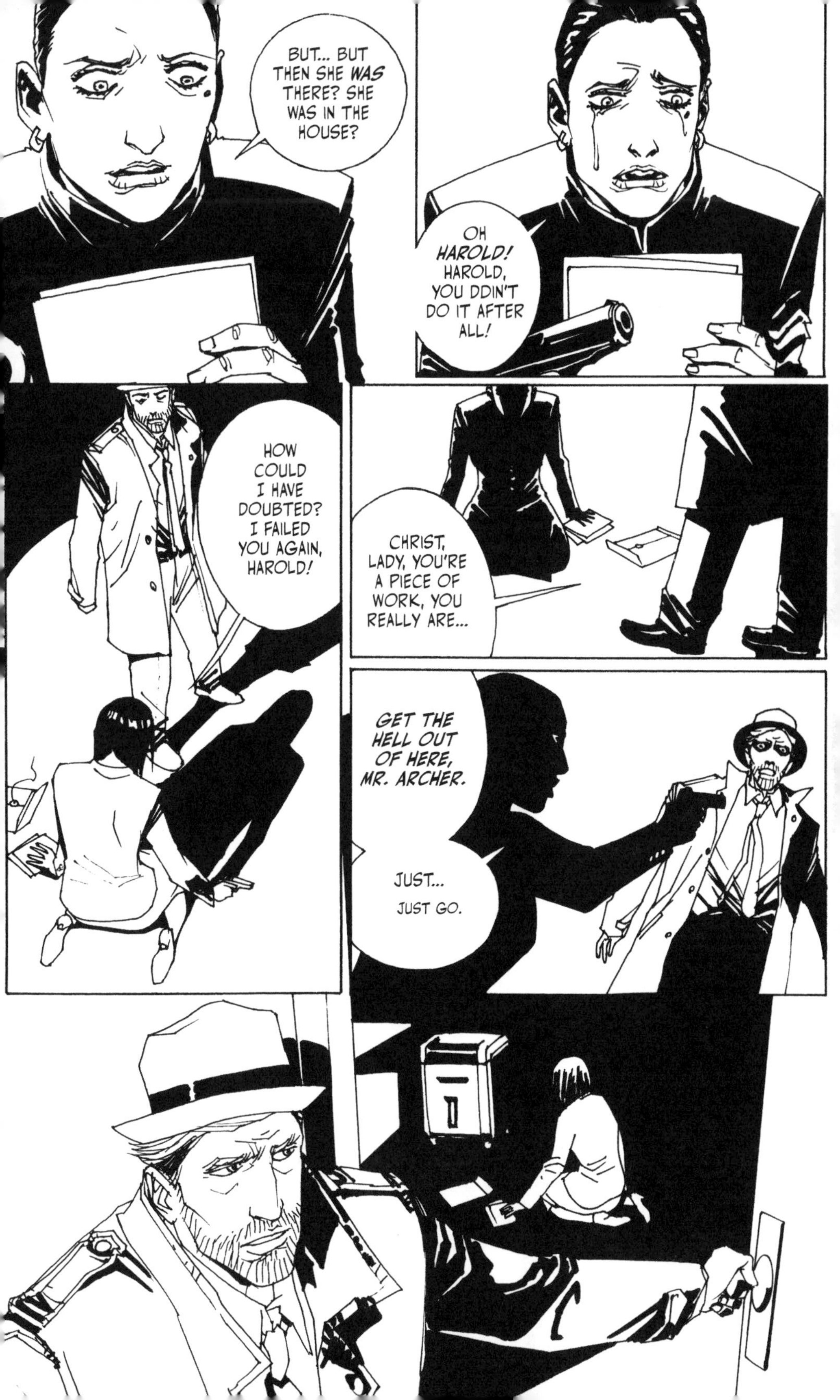

BUT... BUT THEN SHE *WAS* THERE? SHE WAS IN THE HOUSE?
OH *HAROLD!* HAROLD, YOU DDIN'T DO IT AFTER ALL!
HOW COULD I HAVE DOUBTED? I FAILED YOU AGAIN, HAROLD!
CHRIST, LADY, YOU'RE A PIECE OF WORK, YOU REALLY ARE...
GET THE HELL OUT OF HERE, MR. ARCHER.
JUST... JUST GO.

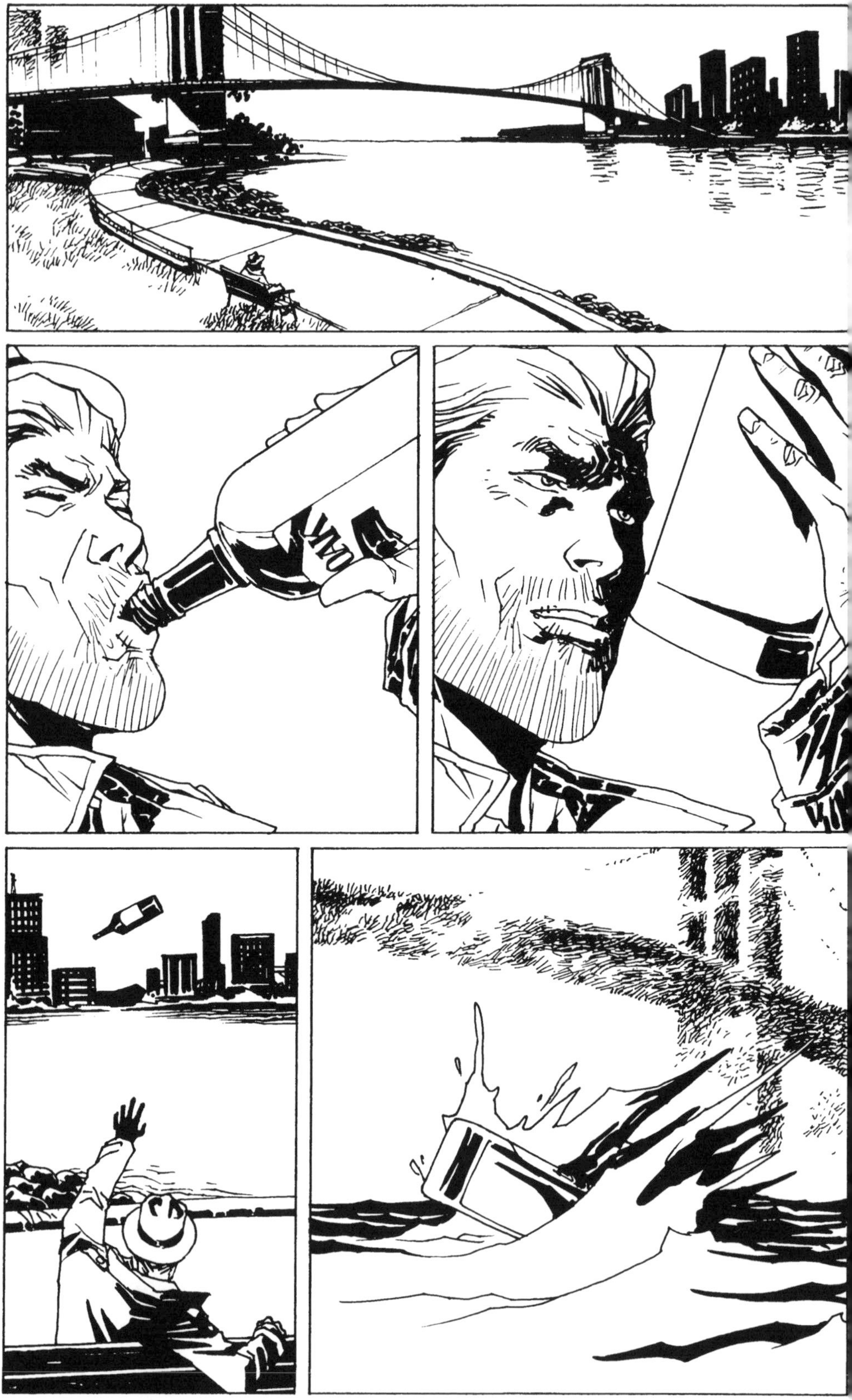

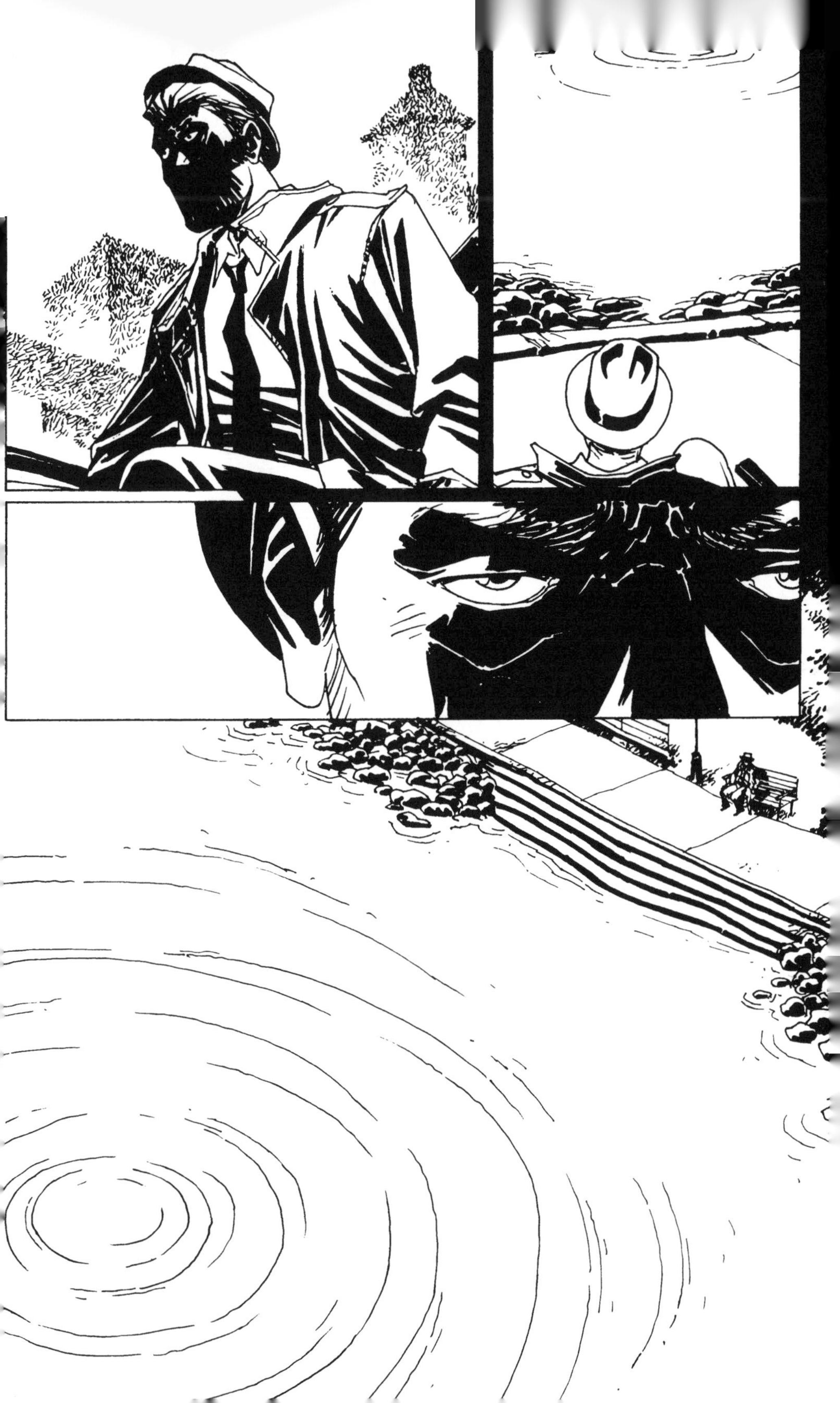

SEVEN

"THAT'S ALRIGHT, SUGARPLUM. I WOULDN'T KNOW WHAT TO SAY TO THAT, EITHER."

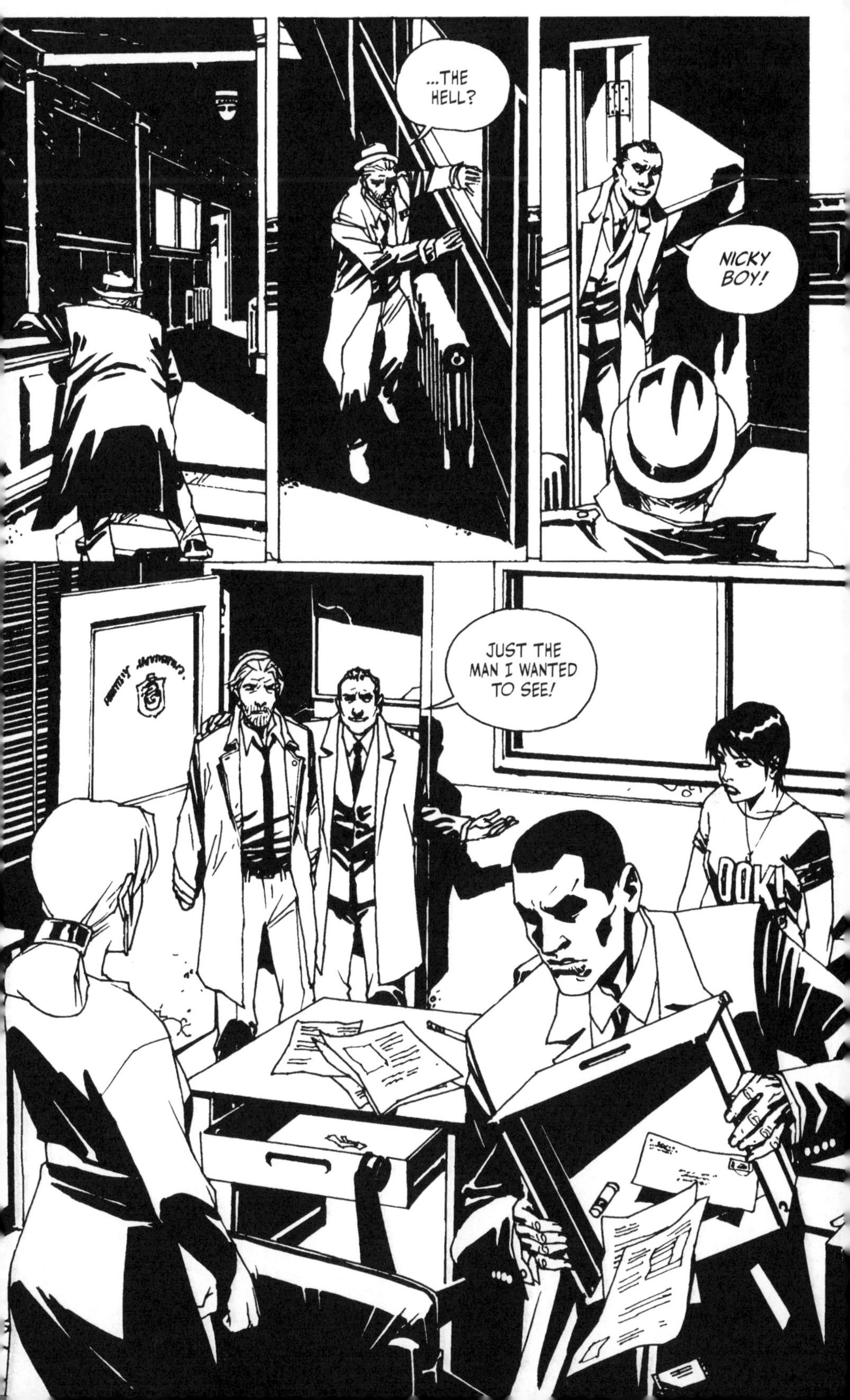
...THE HELL?
NICKY BOY!
JUST THE MAN I WANTED TO SEE!

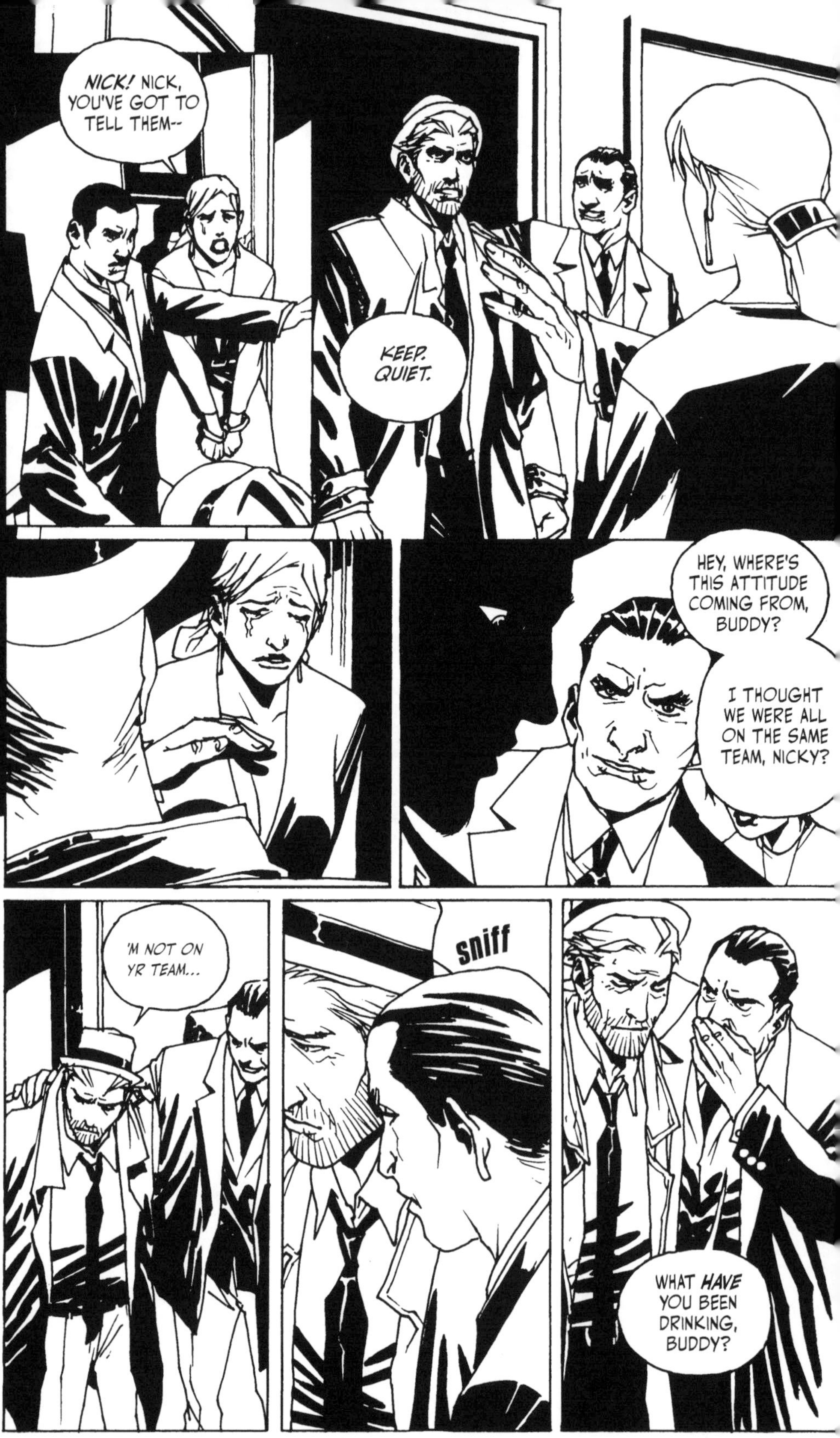

NICK! NICK, YOU'VE GOT TO TELL THEM--
KEEP. QUIET.
HEY, WHERE'S THIS ATTITUDE COMING FROM, BUDDY?
I THOUGHT WE WERE ALL ON THE SAME TEAM, NICKY?
'M NOT ON YR TEAM...
Sniff
WHAT HAVE YOU BEEN DRINKING, BUDDY?

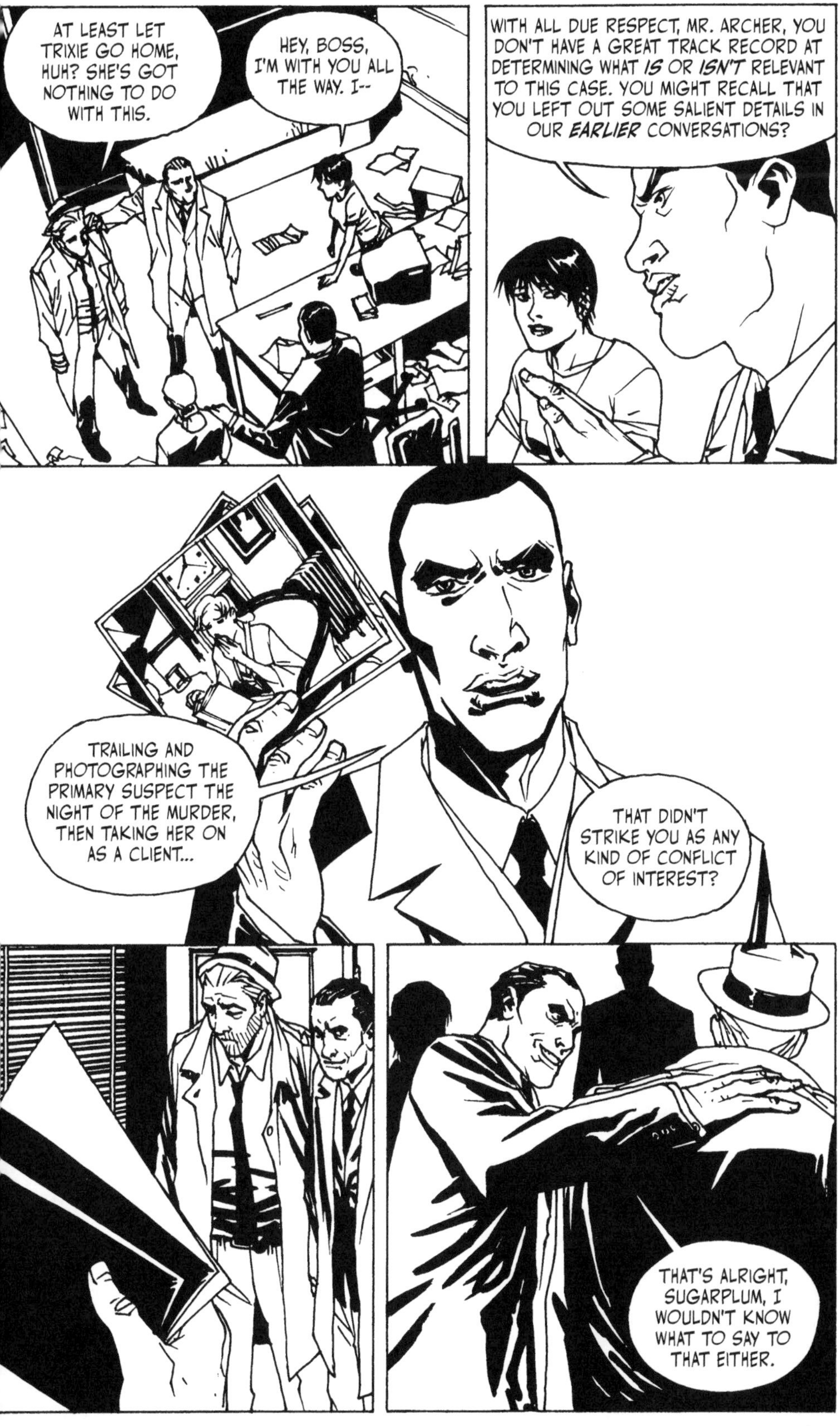
AT LEAST LET TRIXIE GO HOME, HUH? SHE'S GOT NOTHING TO DO WITH THIS.
HEY, BOSS, I'M WITH YOU ALL THE WAY. I--
WITH ALL DUE RESPECT, MR. ARCHER, YOU DON'T HAVE A GREAT TRACK RECORD AT DETERMINING WHAT *IS* OR *ISN'T* RELEVANT TO THIS CASE. YOU MIGHT RECALL THAT YOU LEFT OUT SOME SALIENT DETAILS IN OUR *EARLIER* CONVERSATIONS?
TRAILING AND PHOTOGRAPHING THE PRIMARY SUSPECT THE NIGHT OF THE MURDER, THEN TAKING HER ON AS A CLIENT...
THAT DIDN'T STRIKE YOU AS ANY KIND OF CONFLICT OF INTEREST?
THAT'S ALRIGHT, SUGARPLUM, I WOULDN'T KNOW WHAT TO SAY TO THAT EITHER.

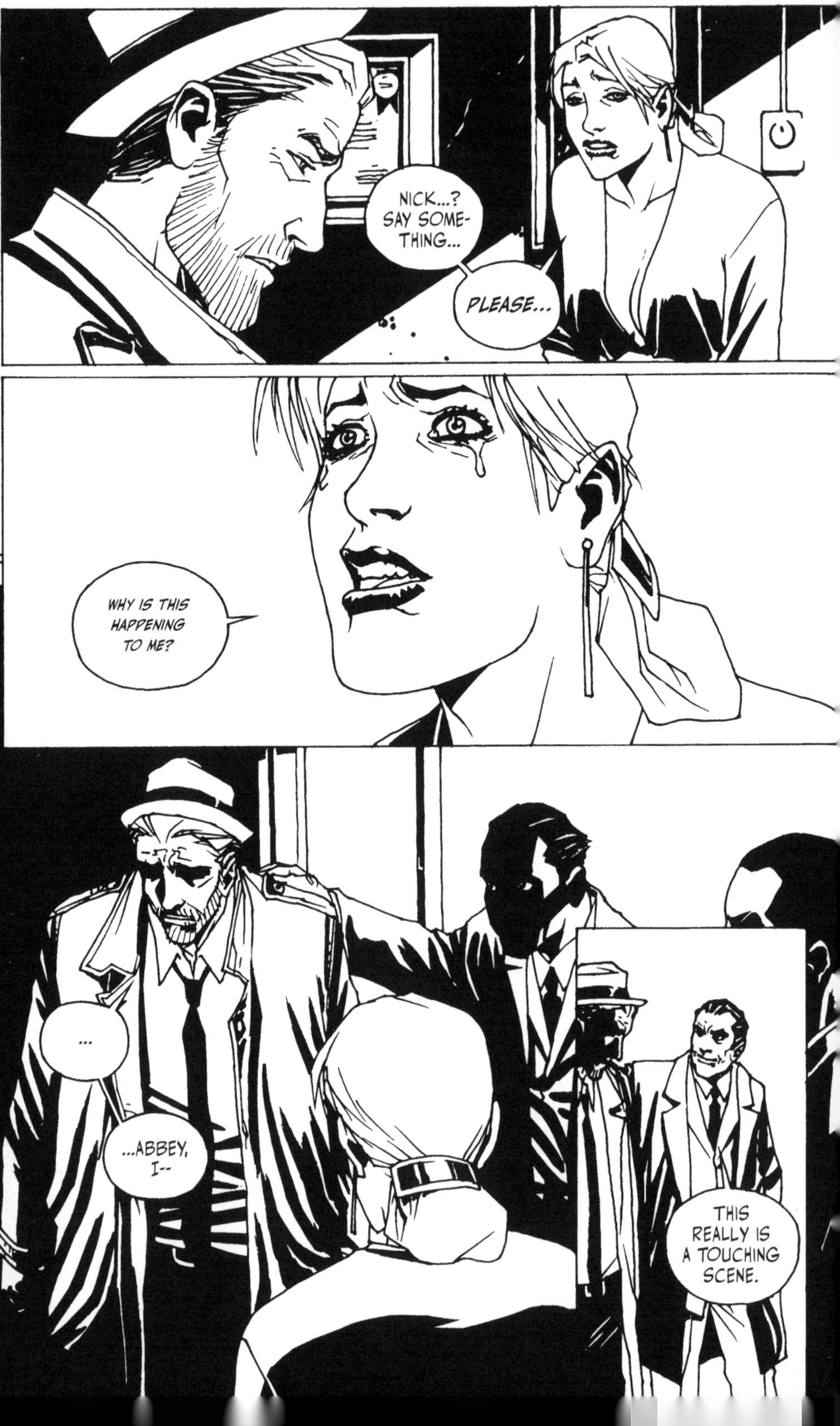

NICK...? SAY SOME-THING...
PLEASE...
WHY IS THIS HAPPENING TO ME?
...
...ABBEY, I--
THIS REALLY IS A TOUCHING SCENE.

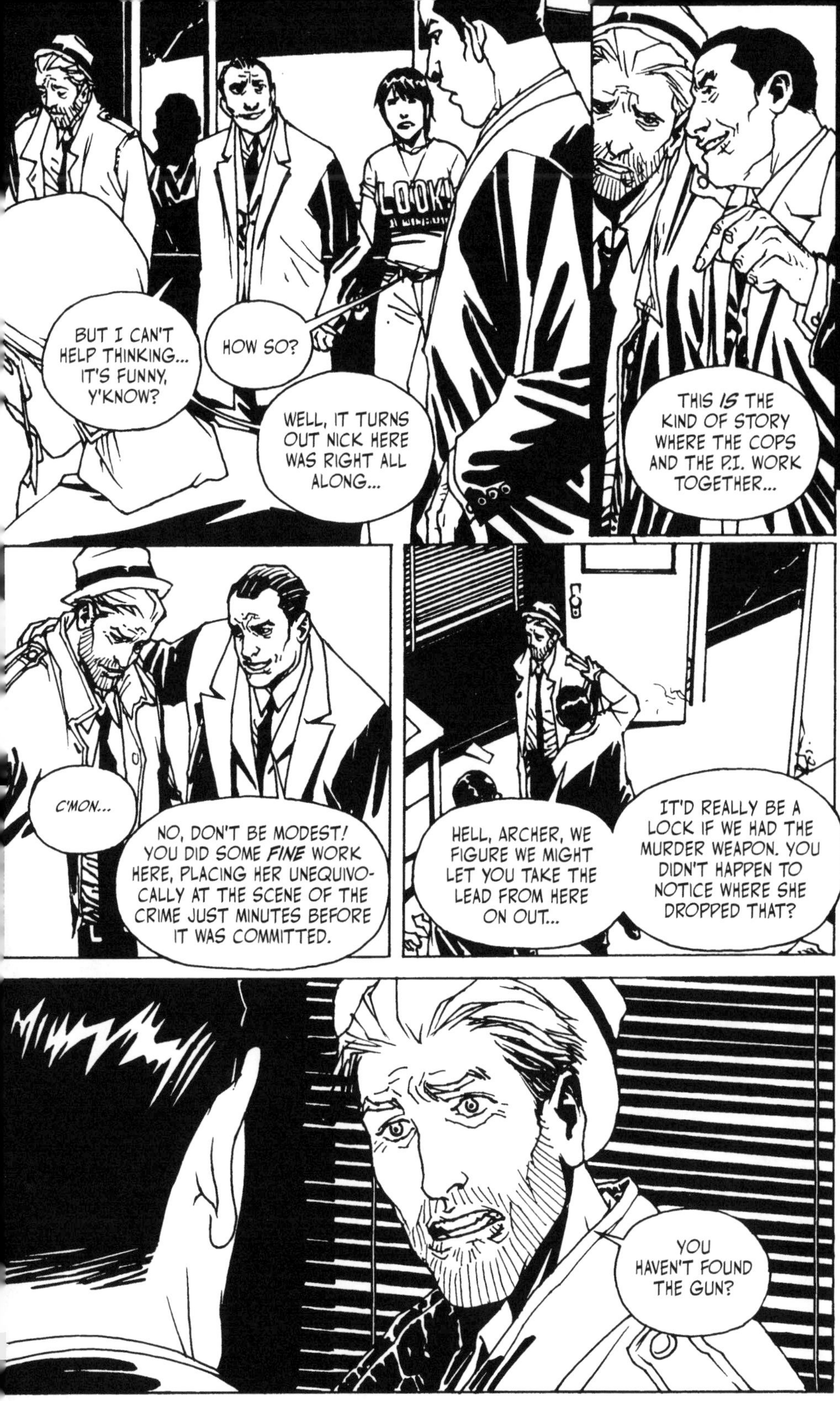
BUT I CAN'T HELP THINKING... IT'S FUNNY, Y'KNOW?
HOW SO?
WELL, IT TURNS OUT NICK HERE WAS RIGHT ALL ALONG...
THIS *IS* THE KIND OF STORY WHERE THE COPS AND THE P.I. WORK TOGETHER...
C'MON...
NO, DON'T BE MODEST! YOU DID SOME *FINE* WORK HERE, PLACING HER UNEQUIVOCALLY AT THE SCENE OF THE CRIME JUST MINUTES BEFORE IT WAS COMMITTED.
HELL, ARCHER, WE FIGURE WE MIGHT LET YOU TAKE THE LEAD FROM HERE ON OUT...
IT'D REALLY BE A LOCK IF WE HAD THE MURDER WEAPON. YOU DIDN'T HAPPEN TO NOTICE WHERE SHE DROPPED THAT?
YOU HAVEN'T FOUND THE GUN?

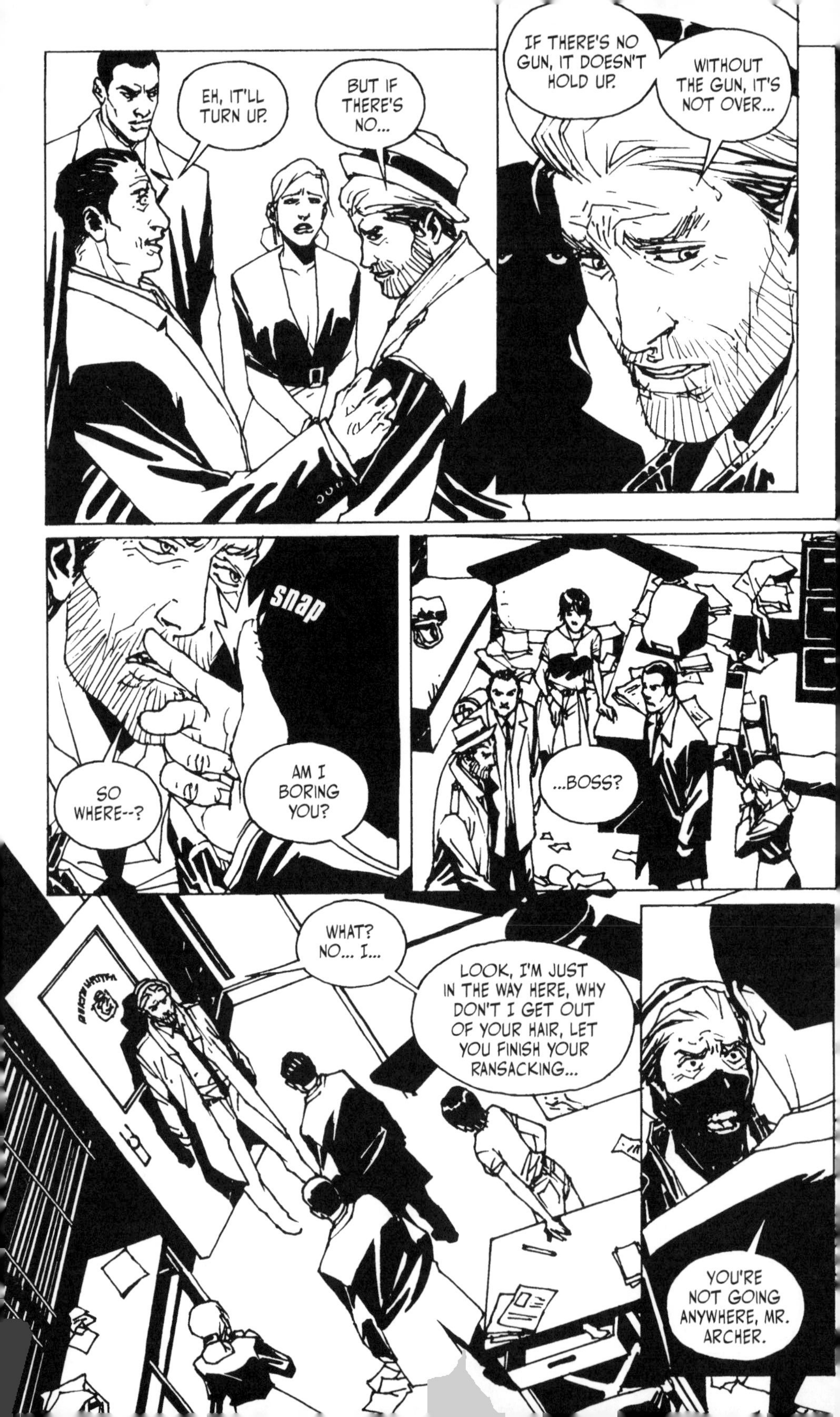
EH, IT'LL TURN UP.
BUT IF THERE'S NO...
IF THERE'S NO GUN, IT DOESN'T HOLD UP.
WITHOUT THE GUN, IT'S NOT OVER...
snap
SO WHERE--?
AM I BORING YOU?
...BOSS?
WHAT? NO... I...
LOOK, I'M JUST IN THE WAY HERE, WHY DON'T I GET OUT OF YOUR HAIR, LET YOU FINISH YOUR RANSACKING...
YOU'RE NOT GOING ANYWHERE, MR. ARCHER.

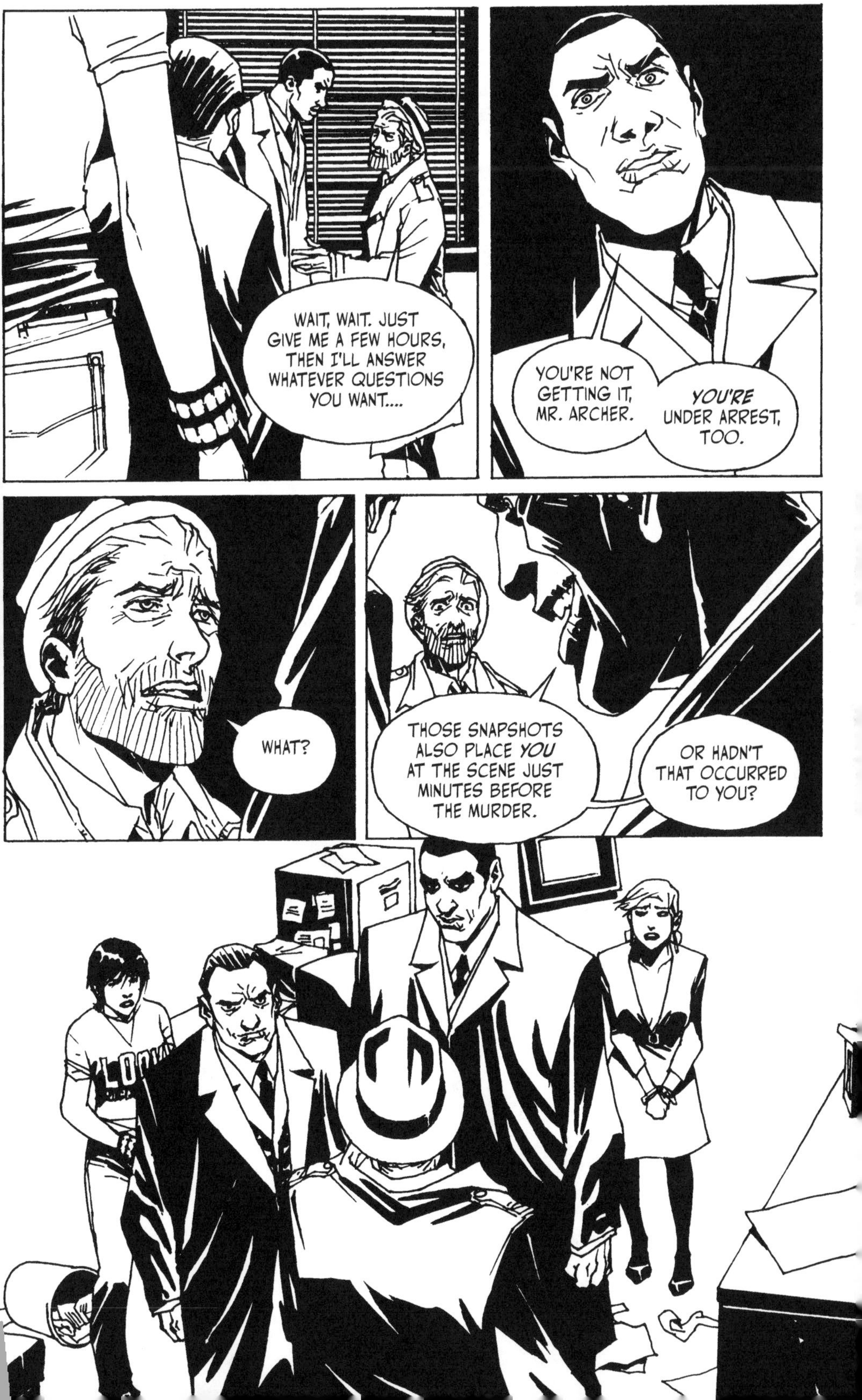
WAIT, WAIT. JUST GIVE ME A FEW HOURS, THEN I'LL ANSWER WHATEVER QUESTIONS YOU WANT....
YOU'RE NOT GETTING IT, MR. ARCHER.
YOU'RE UNDER ARREST, TOO.
WHAT?
THOSE SNAPSHOTS ALSO PLACE *YOU* AT THE SCENE JUST MINUTES BEFORE THE MURDER.
OR HADN'T THAT OCCURRED TO YOU?

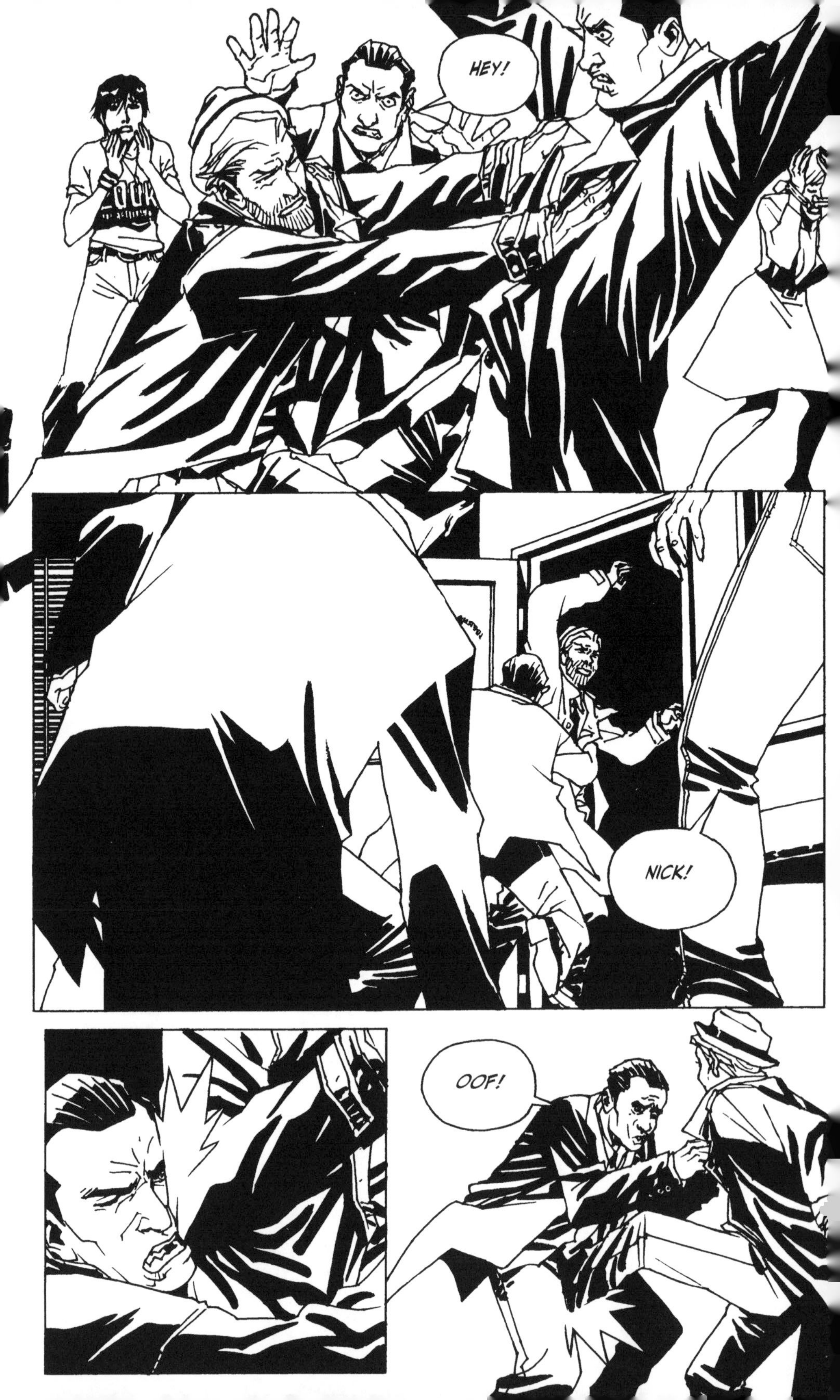
HEY!
NICK!
OOF!

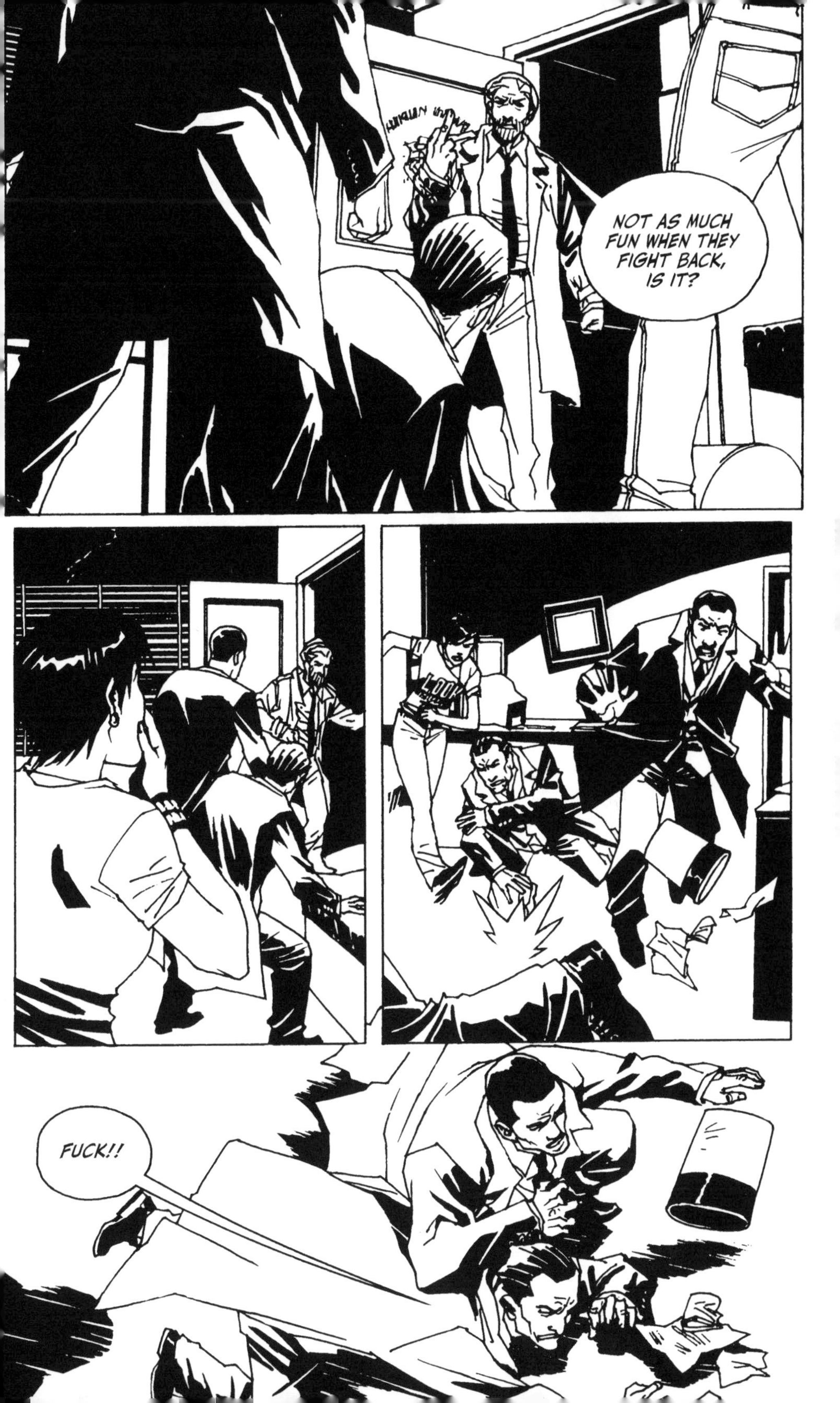
NOT AS MUCH FUN WHEN THEY FIGHT BACK, IS IT?
FUCK!!

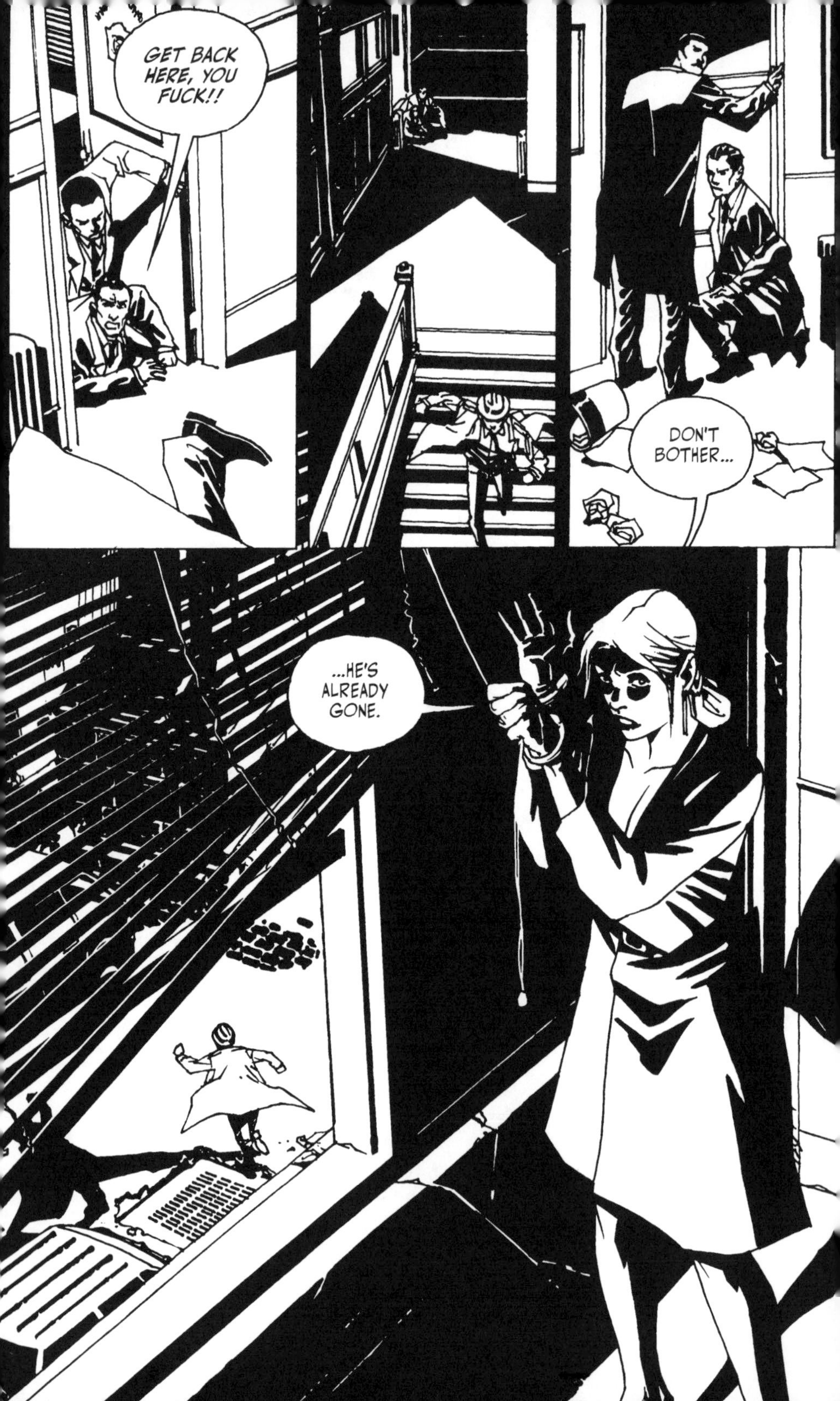
GET BACK HERE, YOU FUCK!!
DON'T BOTHER...
...HE'S ALREADY GONE.

EIGHT "THIS IS ALL PRETTY GODDAMN FUNNY."

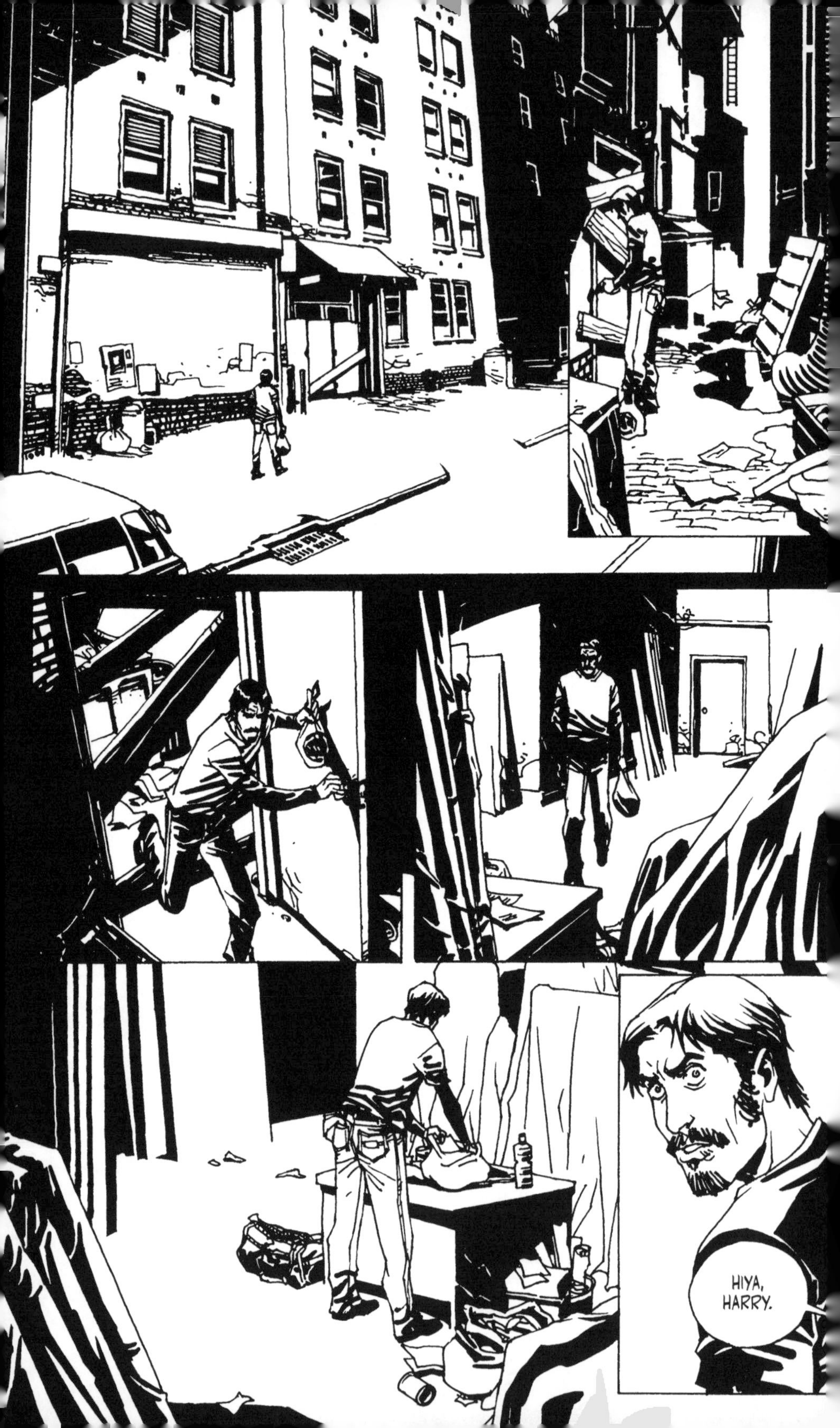

HIYA, HARRY.

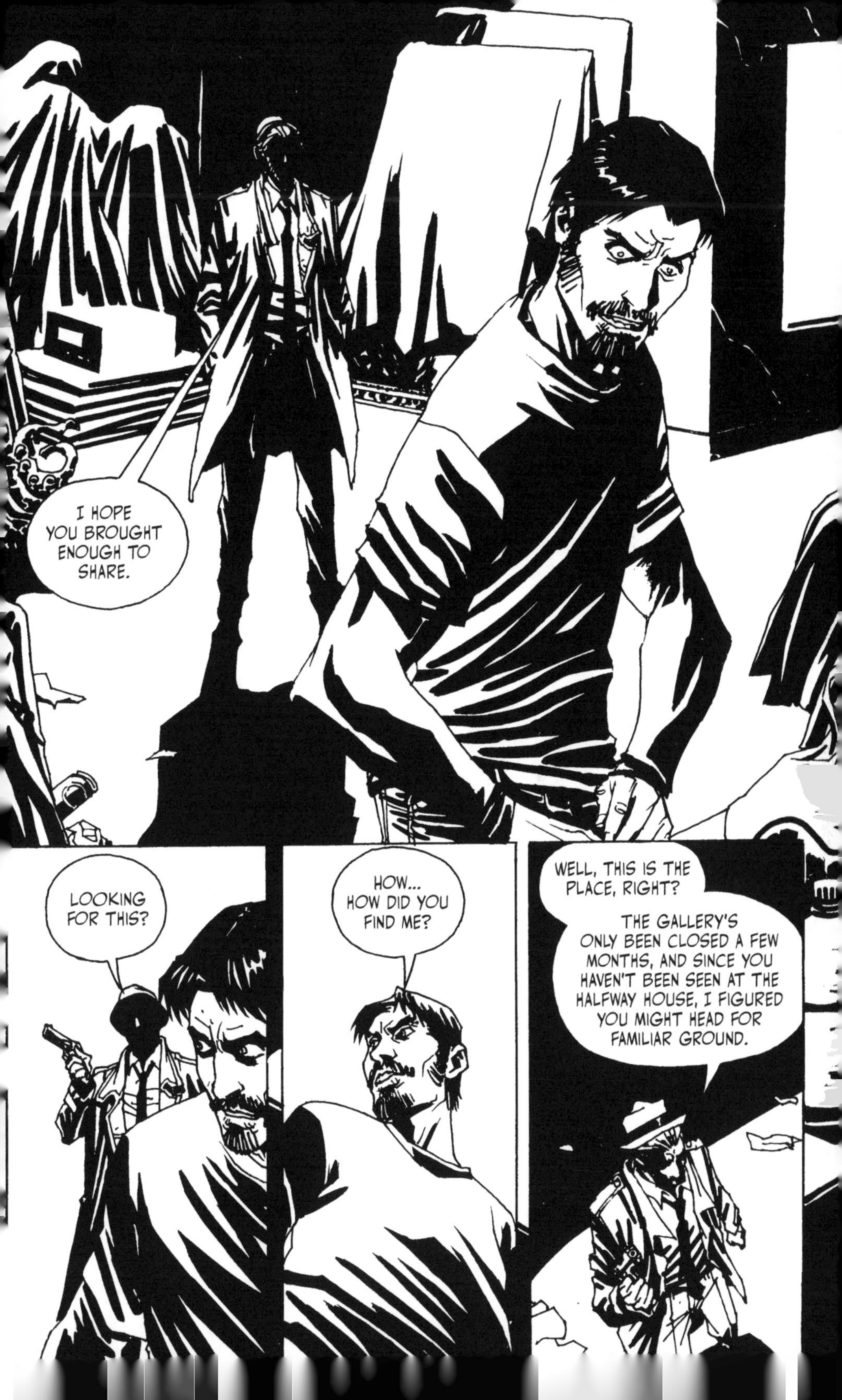
I HOPE YOU BROUGHT ENOUGH TO SHARE.
LOOKING FOR THIS?
HOW... HOW DID YOU FIND ME?
WELL, THIS IS THE PLACE, RIGHT?
THE GALLERY'S ONLY BEEN CLOSED A FEW MONTHS, AND SINCE YOU HAVEN'T BEEN SEEN AT THE HALFWAY HOUSE, I FIGURED YOU MIGHT HEAD FOR FAMILIAR GROUND.

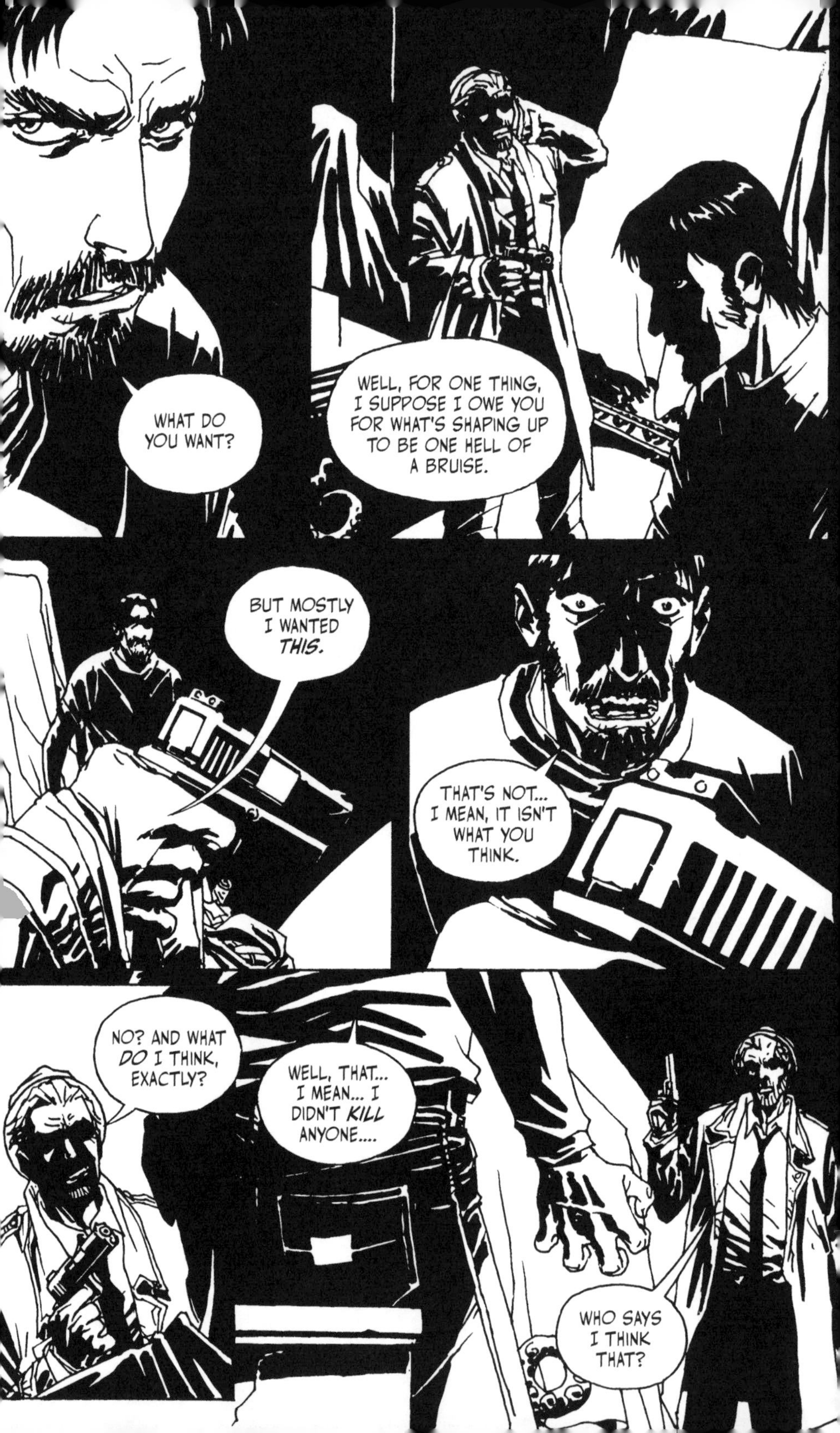
WHAT DO YOU WANT?
WELL, FOR ONE THING, I SUPPOSE I OWE YOU FOR WHAT'S SHAPING UP TO BE ONE HELL OF A BRUISE.
BUT MOSTLY I WANTED *THIS.*
THAT'S NOT... I MEAN, IT ISN'T WHAT YOU THINK.
NO? AND WHAT *DO* I THINK, EXACTLY?
WELL, THAT... I MEAN... I DIDN'T *KILL* ANYONE....
WHO SAYS I THINK THAT?

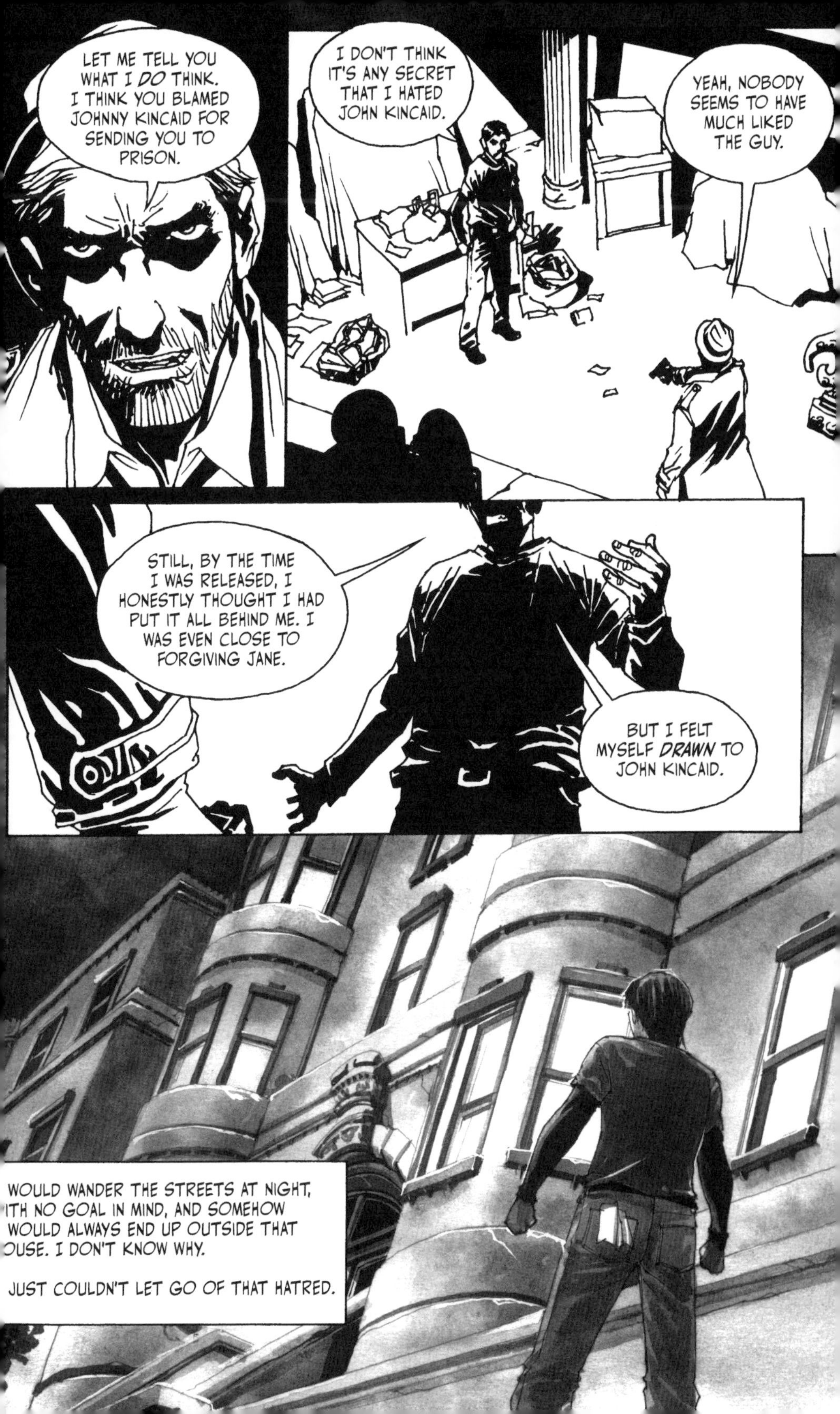
LET ME TELL YOU WHAT I *DO* THINK. I THINK YOU BLAMED JOHNNY KINCAID FOR SENDING YOU TO PRISON.
I DON'T THINK IT'S ANY SECRET THAT I HATED JOHN KINCAID.
YEAH, NOBODY SEEMS TO HAVE MUCH LIKED THE GUY.
STILL, BY THE TIME I WAS RELEASED, I HONESTLY THOUGHT I HAD PUT IT ALL BEHIND ME. I WAS EVEN CLOSE TO FORGIVING JANE.
BUT I FELT MYSELF ***DRAWN*** TO JOHN KINCAID.
WOULD WANDER THE STREETS AT NIGHT, ITH NO GOAL IN MIND, AND SOMEHOW WOULD ALWAYS END UP OUTSIDE THAT OUSE. I DON'T KNOW WHY.
JUST COULDN'T LET GO OF THAT HATRED.

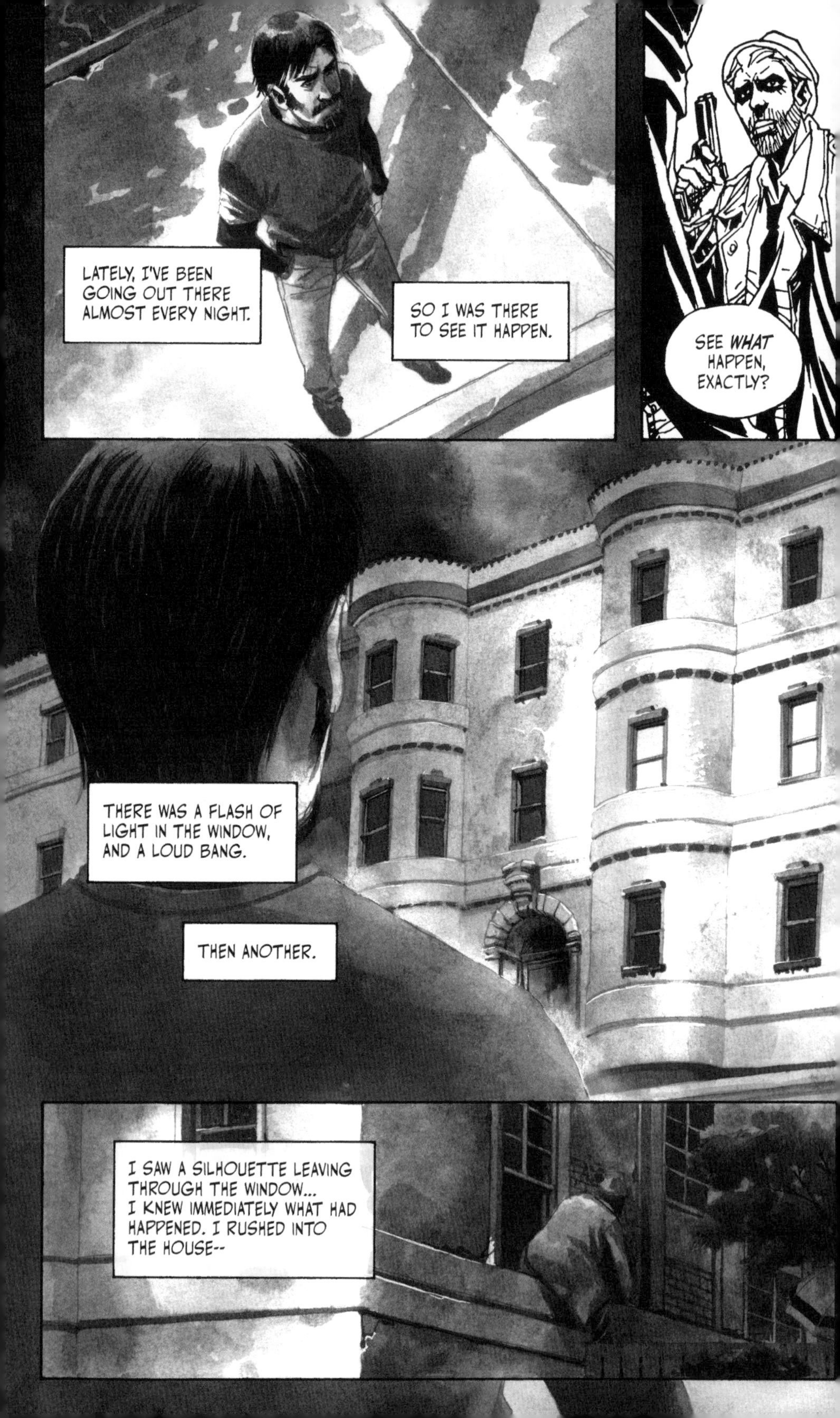
LATELY, I'VE BEEN GOING OUT THERE ALMOST EVERY NIGHT.
SO I WAS THERE TO SEE IT HAPPEN.
SEE *WHAT* HAPPEN, EXACTLY?
THERE WAS A FLASH OF LIGHT IN THE WINDOW, AND A LOUD BANG.
THEN ANOTHER.
I SAW A SILHOUETTE LEAVING THROUGH THE WINDOW... I KNEW IMMEDIATELY WHAT HAD HAPPENED. I RUSHED INTO THE HOUSE--

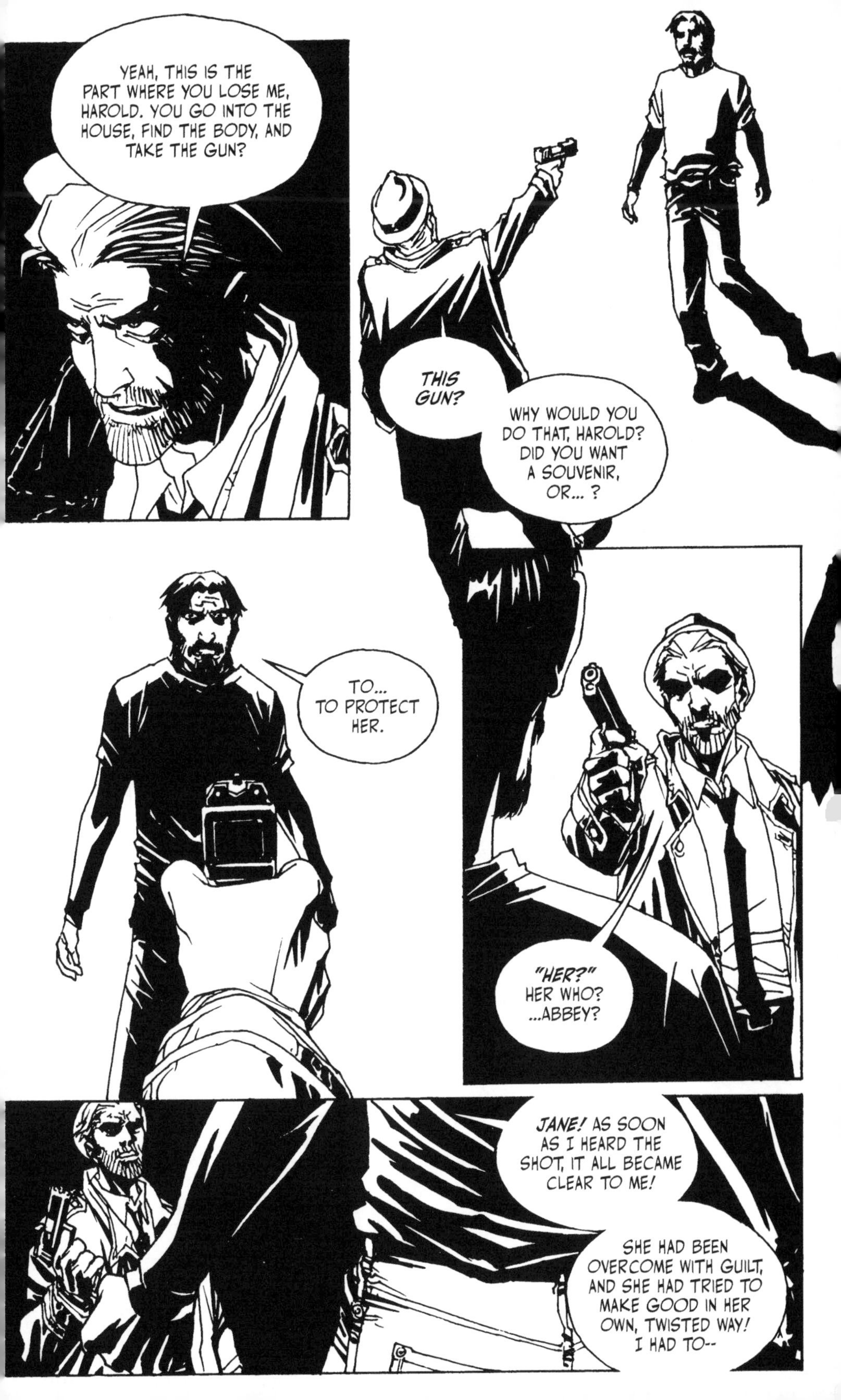
YEAH, THIS IS THE PART WHERE YOU LOSE ME, HAROLD. YOU GO INTO THE HOUSE, FIND THE BODY, AND TAKE THE GUN?
THIS GUN?
WHY WOULD YOU DO THAT, HAROLD? DID YOU WANT A SOUVENIR, OR... ?
TO... TO PROTECT HER.
"HER?" HER WHO? ...ABBEY?
JANE! AS SOON AS I HEARD THE SHOT, IT ALL BECAME CLEAR TO ME!
SHE HAD BEEN OVERCOME WITH GUILT, AND SHE HAD TRIED TO MAKE GOOD IN HER OWN, TWISTED WAY! I HAD TO--

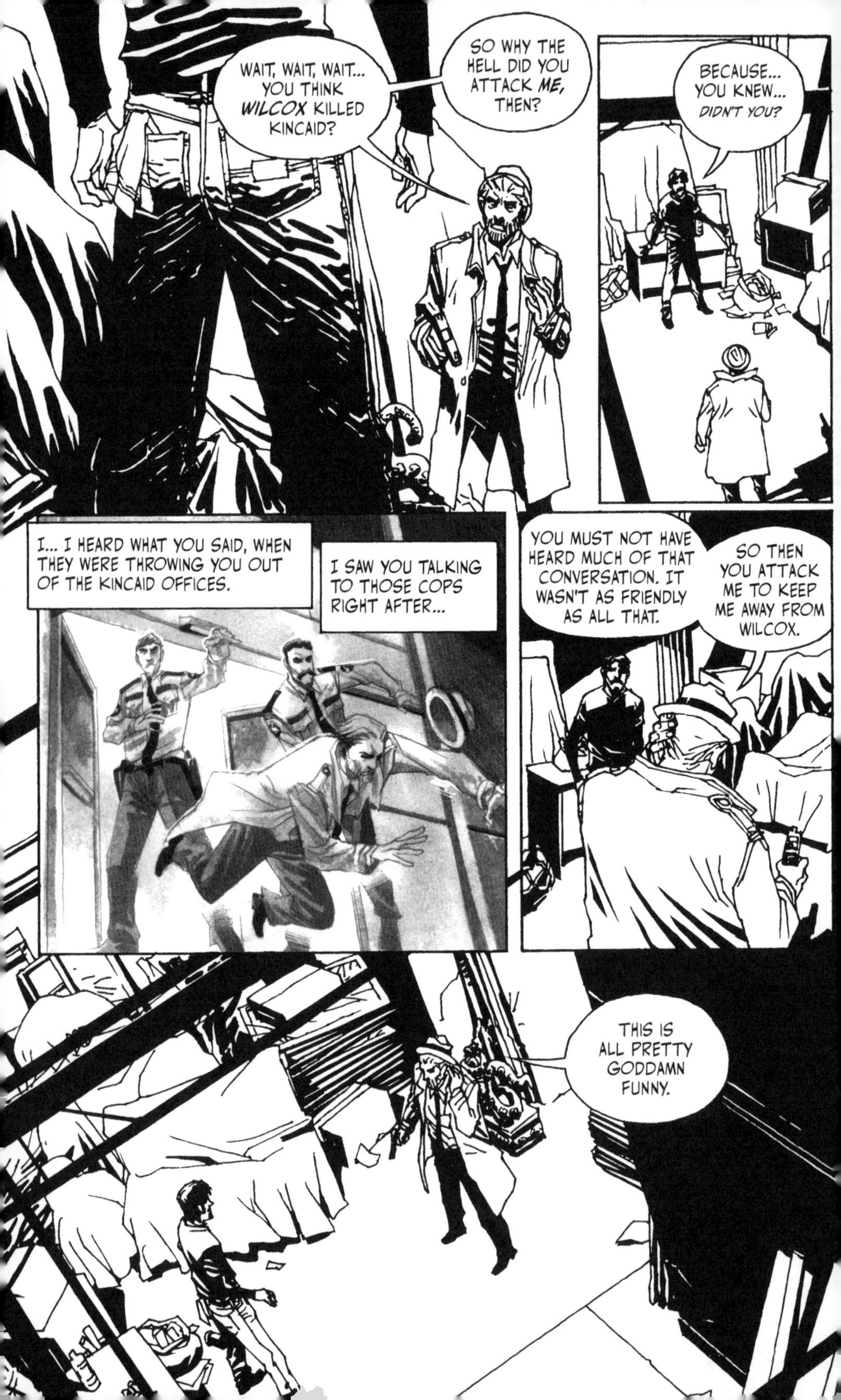

WAIT, WAIT, WAIT... YOU THINK *WILCOX* KILLED KINCAID?
SO WHY THE HELL DID YOU ATTACK *ME,* THEN?
BECAUSE... YOU KNEW... *DIDN'T YOU?*
I... I HEARD WHAT YOU SAID, WHEN THEY WERE THROWING YOU OUT OF THE KINCAID OFFICES.
I SAW YOU TALKING TO THOSE COPS RIGHT AFTER...
YOU MUST NOT HAVE HEARD MUCH OF THAT CONVERSATION. IT WASN'T AS FRIENDLY AS ALL THAT.
SO THEN YOU ATTACK ME TO KEEP ME AWAY FROM WILCOX.
THIS IS ALL PRETTY GODDAMN FUNNY.

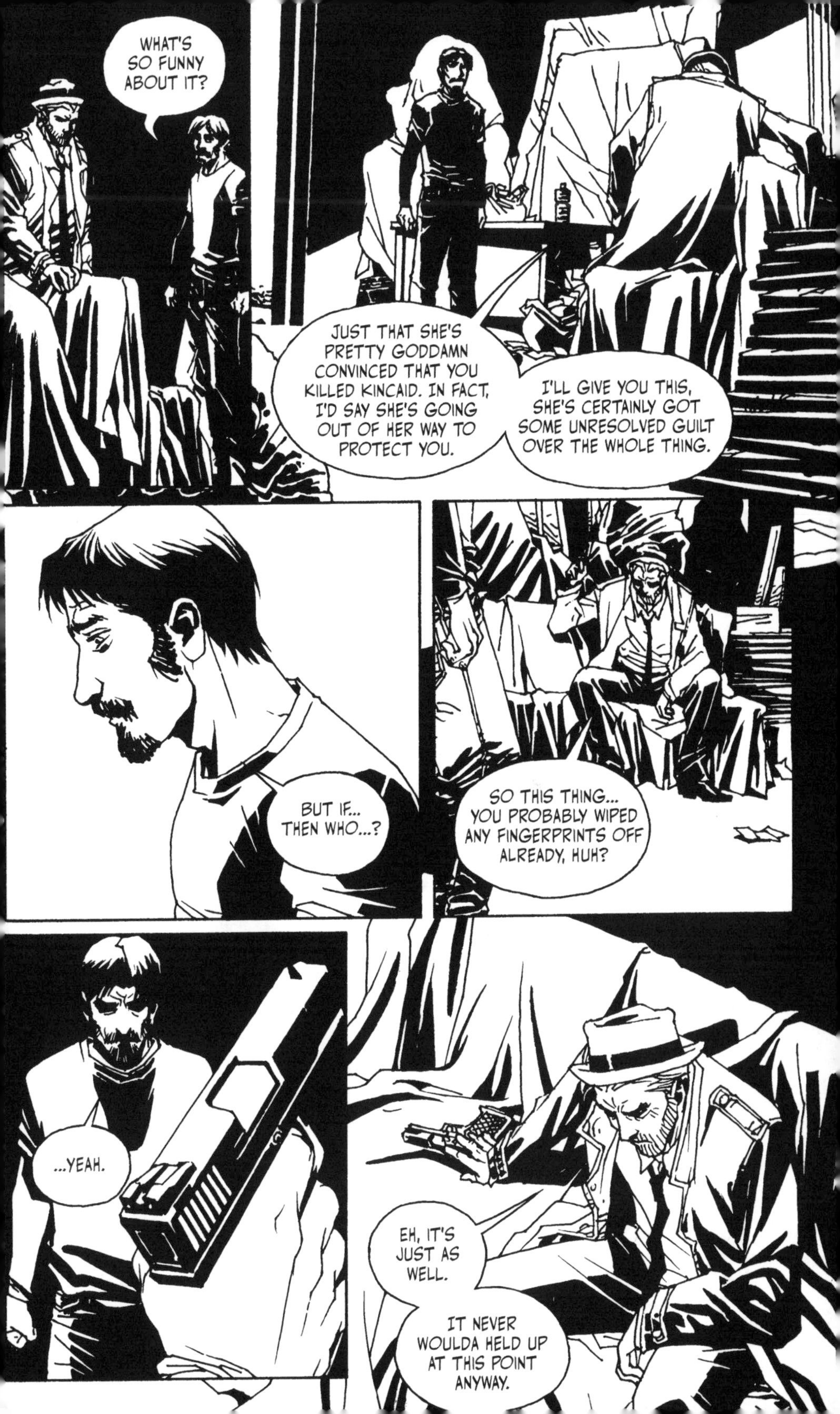
WHAT'S SO FUNNY ABOUT IT?
JUST THAT SHE'S PRETTY GODDAMN CONVINCED THAT YOU KILLED KINCAID. IN FACT, I'D SAY SHE'S GOING OUT OF HER WAY TO PROTECT YOU.
I'LL GIVE YOU THIS, SHE'S CERTAINLY GOT SOME UNRESOLVED GUILT OVER THE WHOLE THING.
BUT IF... THEN WHO...?
SO THIS THING... YOU PROBABLY WIPED ANY FINGERPRINTS OFF ALREADY, HUH?
...YEAH.
EH, IT'S JUST AS WELL.
IT NEVER WOULDA HELD UP AT THIS POINT ANYWAY.

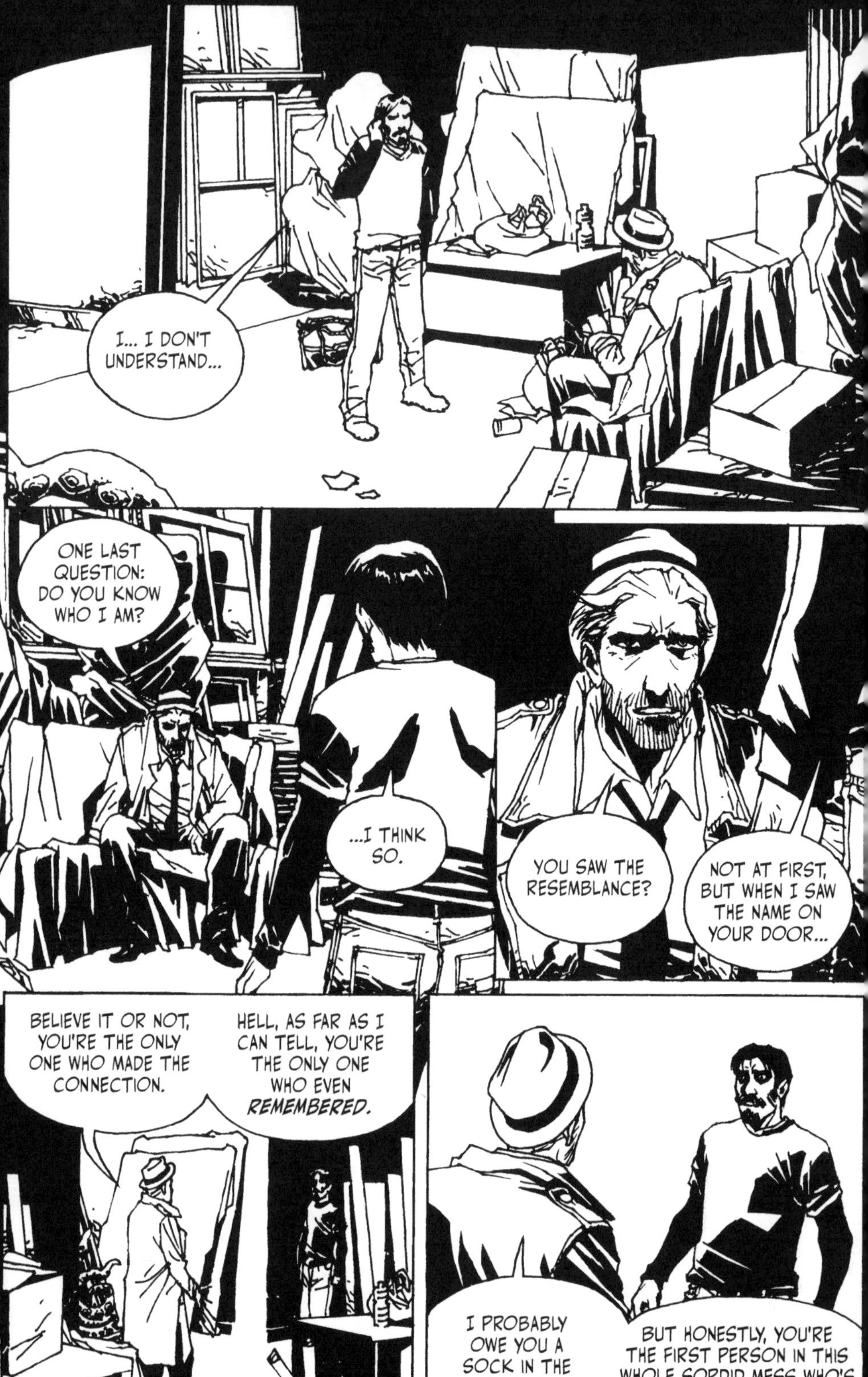
I... I DON'T UNDERSTAND...
ONE LAST QUESTION: DO YOU KNOW WHO I AM?
...I THINK SO.
YOU SAW THE RESEMBLANCE?
NOT AT FIRST, BUT WHEN I SAW THE NAME ON YOUR DOOR...
BELIEVE IT OR NOT, YOU'RE THE ONLY ONE WHO MADE THE CONNECTION.
HELL, AS FAR AS I CAN TELL, YOU'RE THE ONLY ONE WHO EVEN *REMEMBERED*.
I PROBABLY OWE YOU A SOCK IN THE GUT AND A BIT MORE BESIDES.
BUT HONESTLY, YOU'RE THE FIRST PERSON IN THIS WHOLE SORDID MESS WHO'S HAD THE DECENCY TO EVEN REMEMBER HIS NAME.

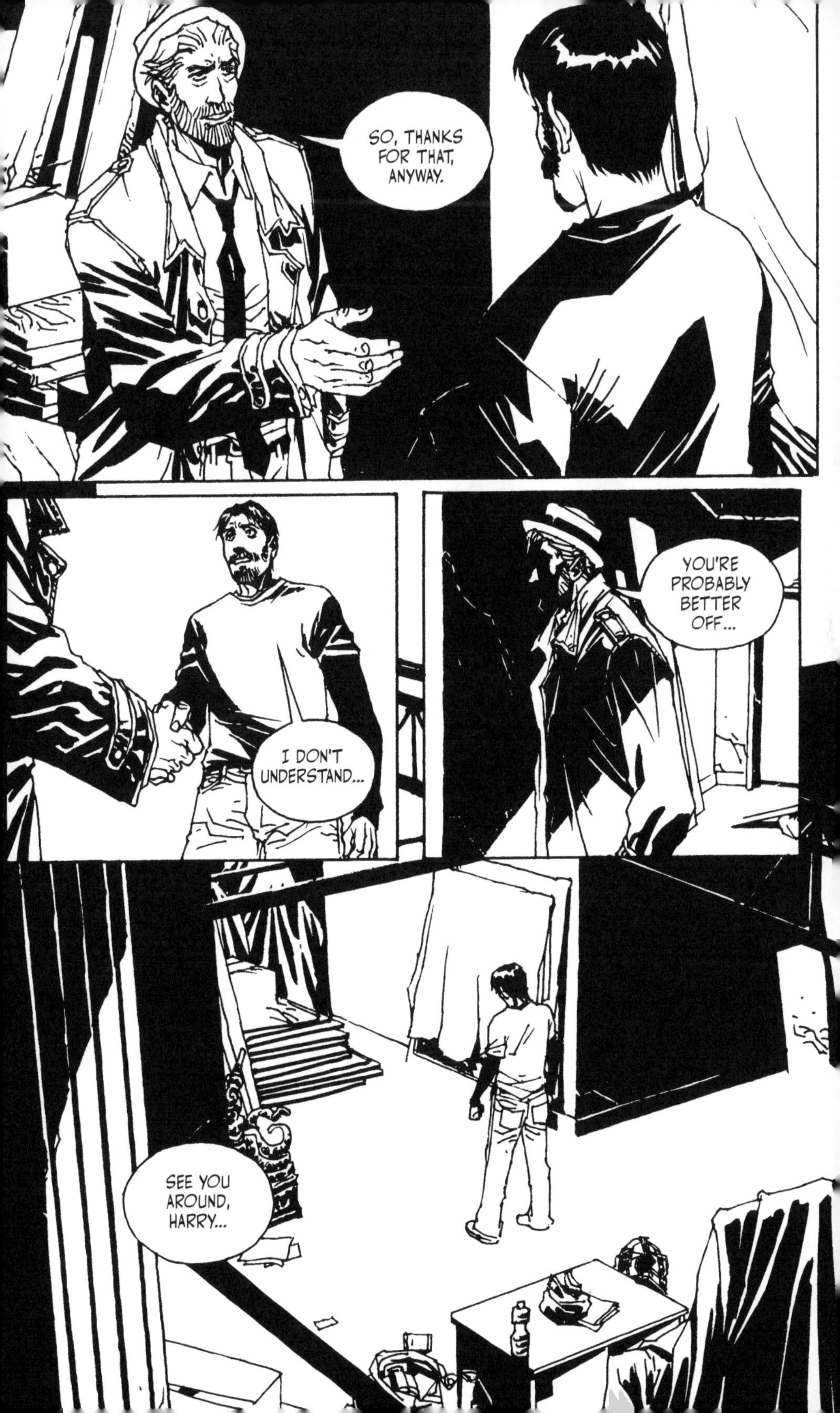
SO, THANKS FOR THAT, ANYWAY.
I DON'T UNDERSTAND...
YOU'RE PROBABLY BETTER OFF...
SEE YOU AROUND, HARRY...

NINE "AND HERE'S WHERE IT ALL GOES WRONG."

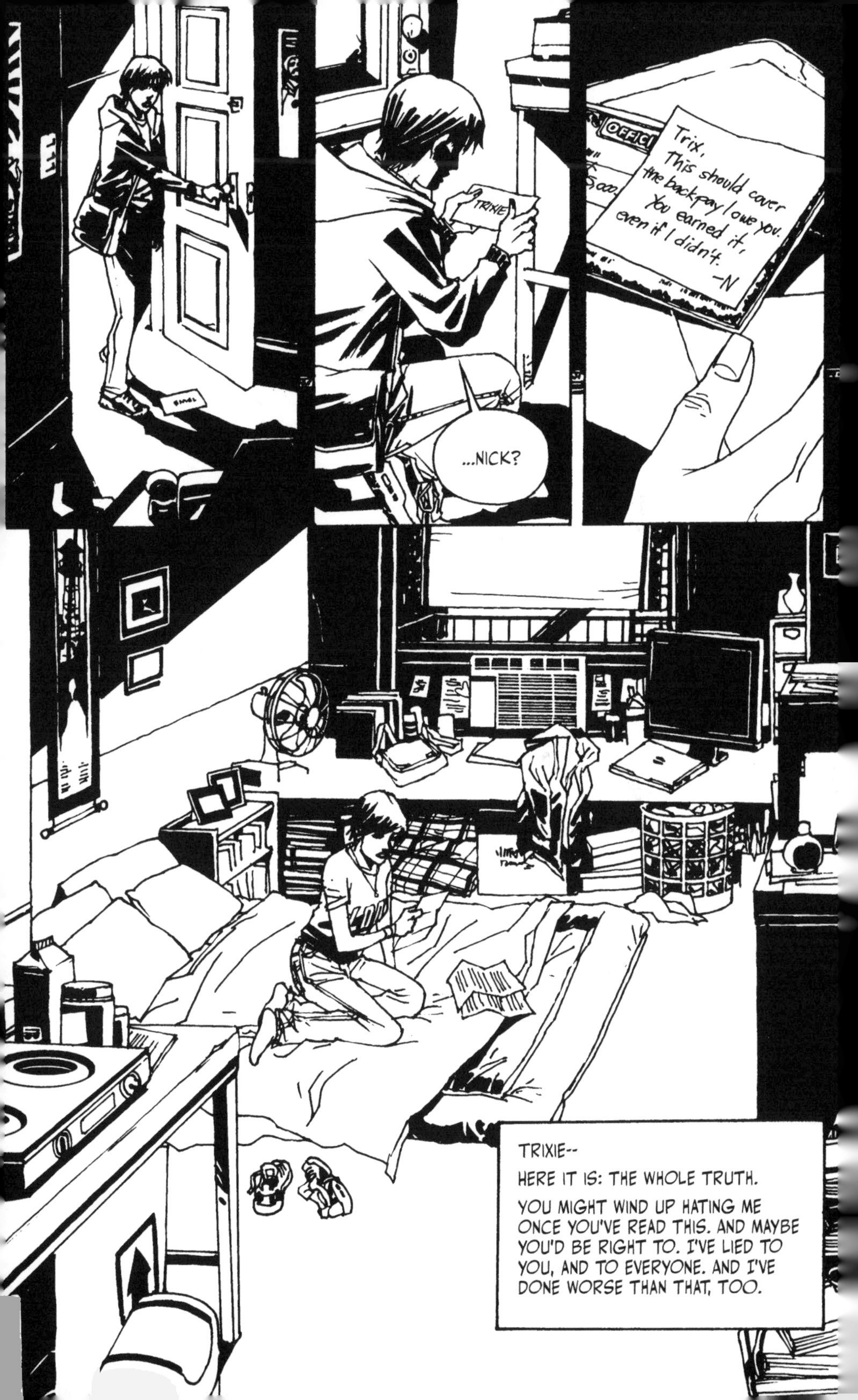

TRIXIE
Trix,
This should cover the backpay I owe you.
You earned it, even if I didn't.
-N
...NICK?
TRIXIE--
HERE IT IS: THE WHOLE TRUTH.
YOU MIGHT WIND UP HATING ME ONCE YOU'VE READ THIS. AND MAYBE YOU'D BE RIGHT TO. I'VE LIED TO YOU, AND TO EVERYONE. AND I'VE DONE WORSE THAN THAT, TOO.

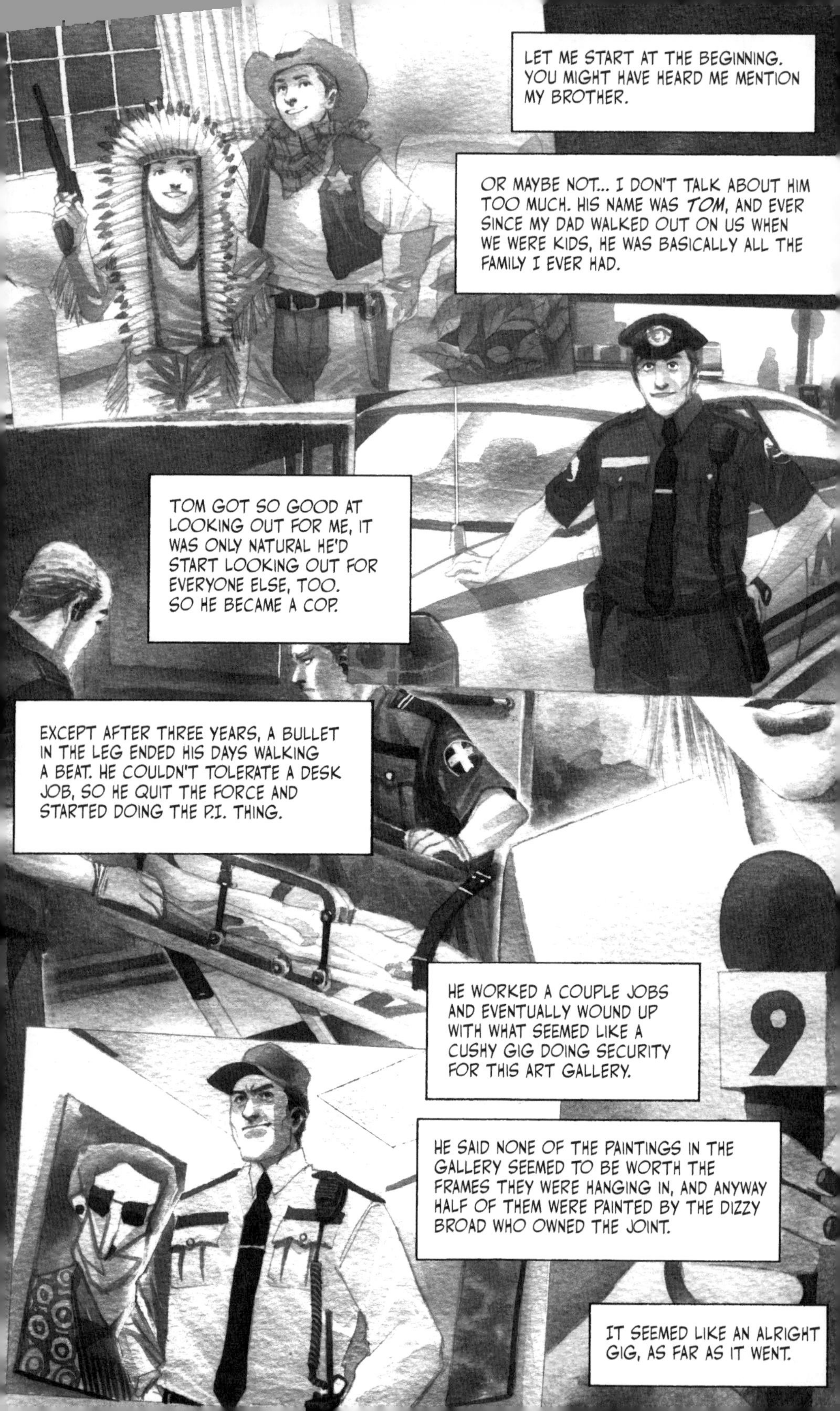

LET ME START AT THE BEGINNING. YOU MIGHT HAVE HEARD ME MENTION MY BROTHER.
OR MAYBE NOT... I DON'T TALK ABOUT HIM TOO MUCH. HIS NAME WAS *TOM*, AND EVER SINCE MY DAD WALKED OUT ON US WHEN WE WERE KIDS, HE WAS BASICALLY ALL THE FAMILY I EVER HAD.
TOM GOT SO GOOD AT LOOKING OUT FOR ME, IT WAS ONLY NATURAL HE'D START LOOKING OUT FOR EVERYONE ELSE, TOO. SO HE BECAME A COP.
EXCEPT AFTER THREE YEARS, A BULLET IN THE LEG ENDED HIS DAYS WALKING A BEAT. HE COULDN'T TOLERATE A DESK JOB, SO HE QUIT THE FORCE AND STARTED DOING THE P.I. THING.
HE WORKED A COUPLE JOBS AND EVENTUALLY WOUND UP WITH WHAT SEEMED LIKE A CUSHY GIG DOING SECURITY FOR THIS ART GALLERY.
9
HE SAID NONE OF THE PAINTINGS IN THE GALLERY SEEMED TO BE WORTH THE FRAMES THEY WERE HANGING IN, AND ANYWAY HALF OF THEM WERE PAINTED BY THE DIZZY BROAD WHO OWNED THE JOINT.
IT SEEMED LIKE AN ALRIGHT GIG, AS FAR AS IT WENT.

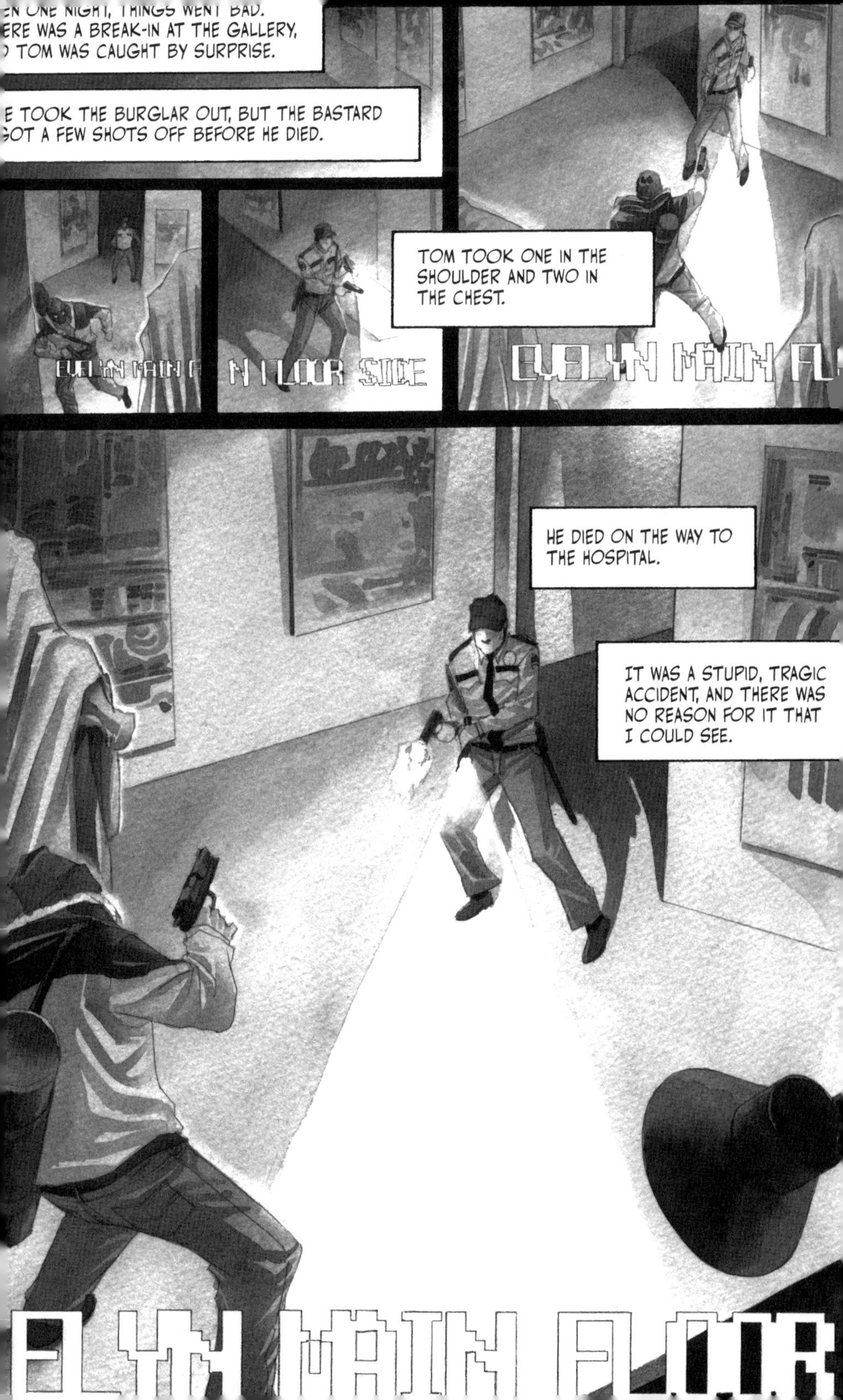
EN ONE NIGHT, THINGS WENT BAD.
ERE WAS A BREAK-IN AT THE GALLERY,
TOM WAS CAUGHT BY SURPRISE.
E TOOK THE BURGLAR OUT, BUT THE BASTARD
GOT A FEW SHOTS OFF BEFORE HE DIED.
TOM TOOK ONE IN THE SHOULDER AND TWO IN THE CHEST.
EVELYN MAIN F
N FLOOR SIDE
EVELYN MAIN FL
HE DIED ON THE WAY TO THE HOSPITAL.
IT WAS A STUPID, TRAGIC ACCIDENT, AND THERE WAS NO REASON FOR IT THAT I COULD SEE.
ELYN MAIN FLOOR

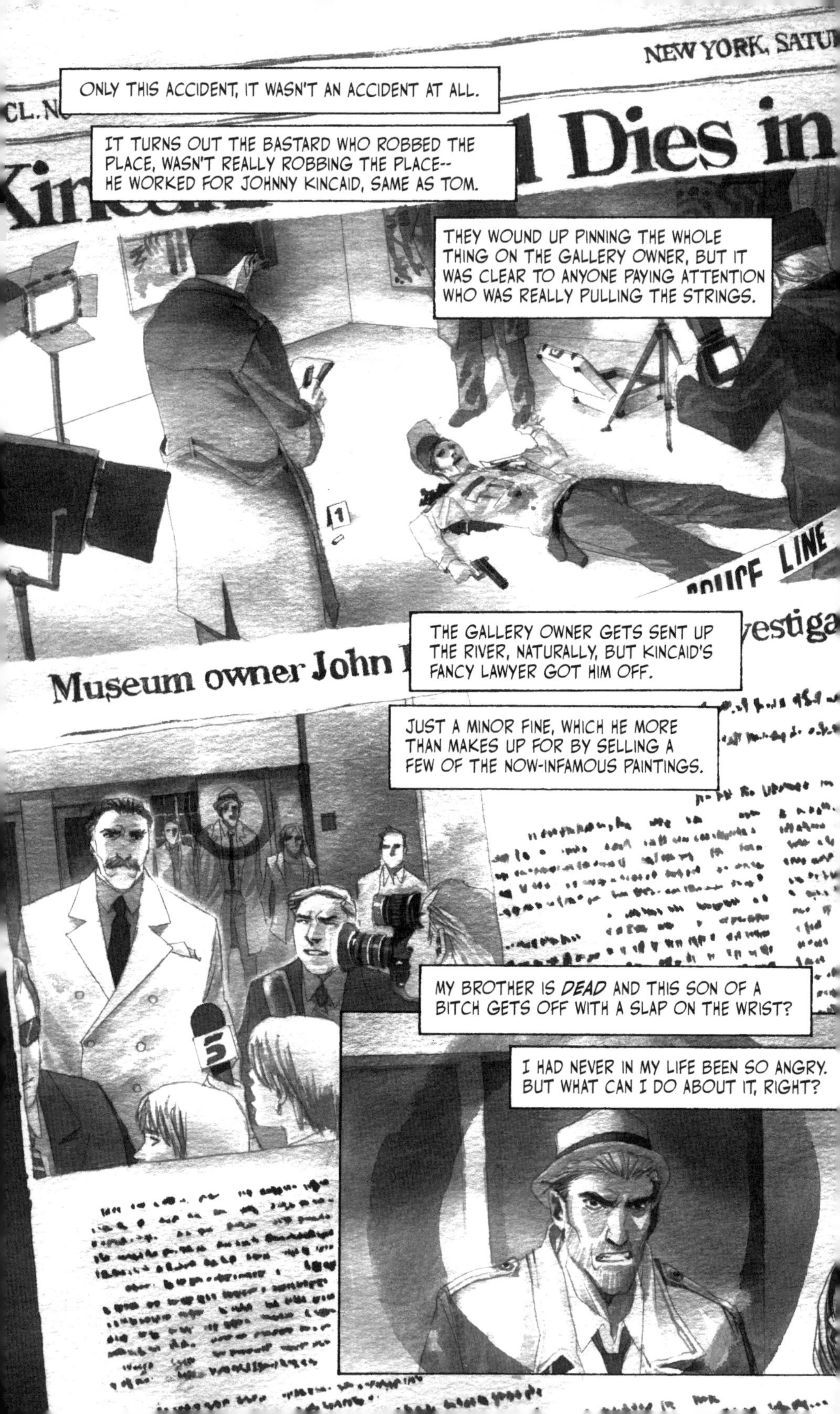
NEW YORK, SATU
CL. N
Kin 1 Dies in
ONLY THIS ACCIDENT, IT WASN'T AN ACCIDENT AT ALL.
IT TURNS OUT THE BASTARD WHO ROBBED THE PLACE, WASN'T REALLY ROBBING THE PLACE-- HE WORKED FOR JOHNNY KINCAID, SAME AS TOM.
THEY WOUND UP PINNING THE WHOLE THING ON THE GALLERY OWNER, BUT IT WAS CLEAR TO ANYONE PAYING ATTENTION WHO WAS REALLY PULLING THE STRINGS.
1
POLICE LINE
Museum owner John
vestiga
THE GALLERY OWNER GETS SENT UP THE RIVER, NATURALLY, BUT KINCAID'S FANCY LAWYER GOT HIM OFF.
JUST A MINOR FINE, WHICH HE MORE THAN MAKES UP FOR BY SELLING A FEW OF THE NOW-INFAMOUS PAINTINGS.
5
MY BROTHER IS *DEAD* AND THIS SON OF A BITCH GETS OFF WITH A SLAP ON THE WRIST?
I HAD NEVER IN MY LIFE BEEN SO ANGRY. BUT WHAT CAN I DO ABOUT IT, RIGHT?

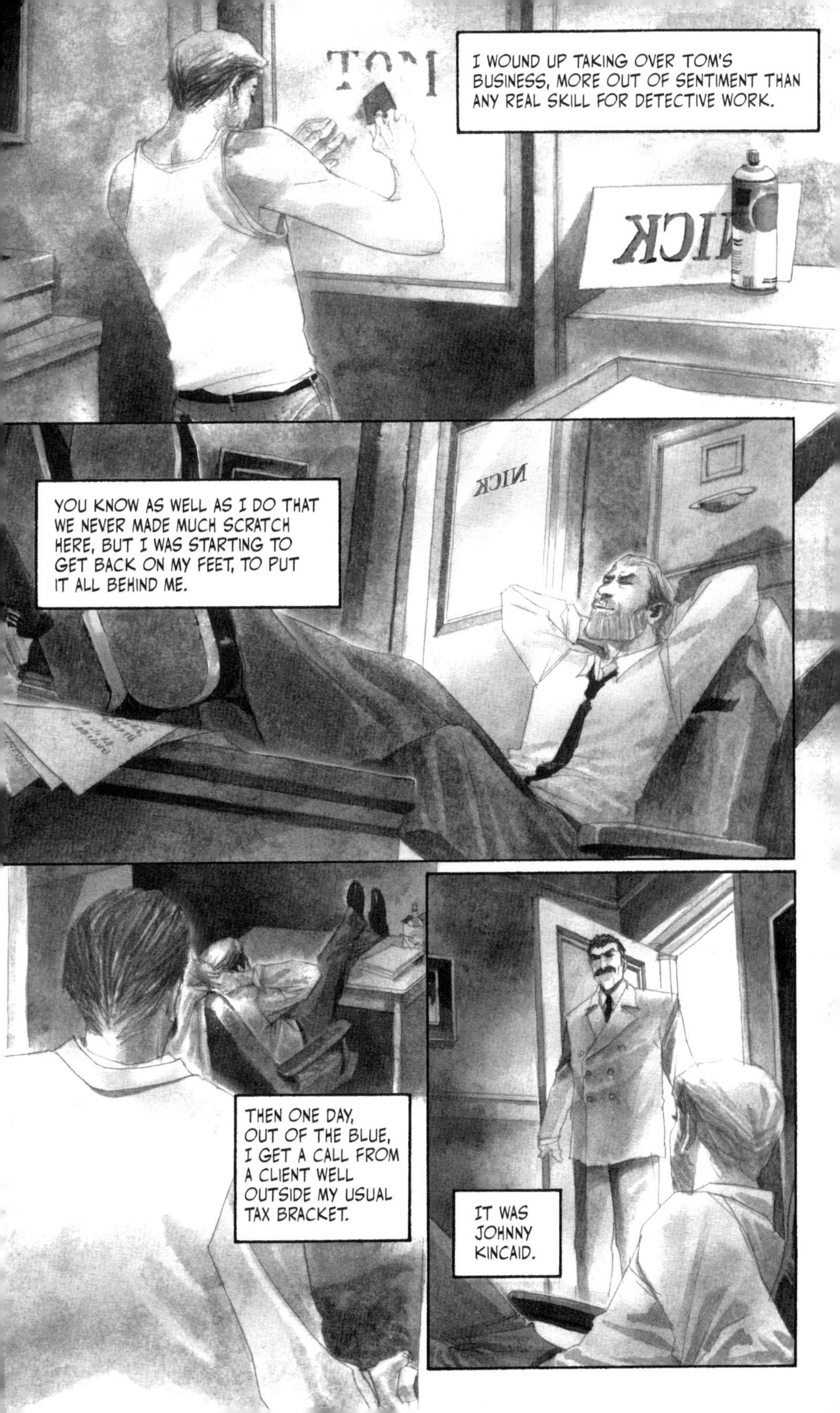
I WOUND UP TAKING OVER TOM'S BUSINESS, MORE OUT OF SENTIMENT THAN ANY REAL SKILL FOR DETECTIVE WORK.
YOU KNOW AS WELL AS I DO THAT WE NEVER MADE MUCH SCRATCH HERE, BUT I WAS STARTING TO GET BACK ON MY FEET, TO PUT IT ALL BEHIND ME.
THEN ONE DAY, OUT OF THE BLUE, I GET A CALL FROM A CLIENT WELL OUTSIDE MY USUAL TAX BRACKET.
IT WAS JOHNNY KINCAID.

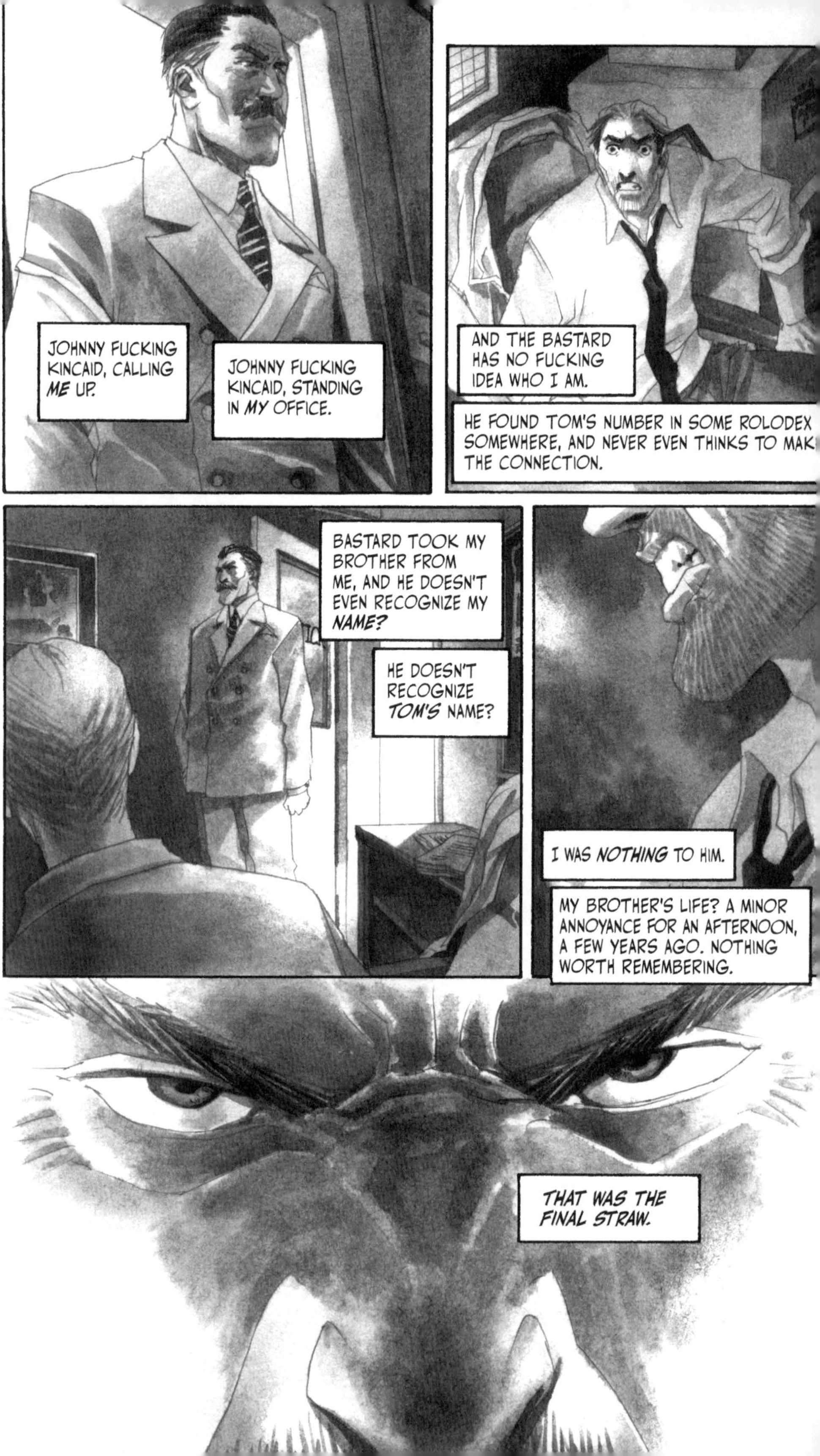
JOHNNY FUCKING KINCAID, CALLING *ME* UP.
JOHNNY FUCKING KINCAID, STANDING IN *MY* OFFICE.
AND THE BASTARD HAS NO FUCKING IDEA WHO I AM.
HE FOUND TOM'S NUMBER IN SOME ROLODEX SOMEWHERE, AND NEVER EVEN THINKS TO MAK
THE CONNECTION.
BASTARD TOOK MY BROTHER FROM ME, AND HE DOESN'T EVEN RECOGNIZE MY *NAME?*
HE DOESN'T RECOGNIZE *TOM'S* NAME?
I WAS *NOTHING* TO HIM.
MY BROTHER'S LIFE? A MINOR ANNOYANCE FOR AN AFTERNOON, A FEW YEARS AGO. NOTHING WORTH REMEMBERING.
THAT WAS THE FINAL STRAW.

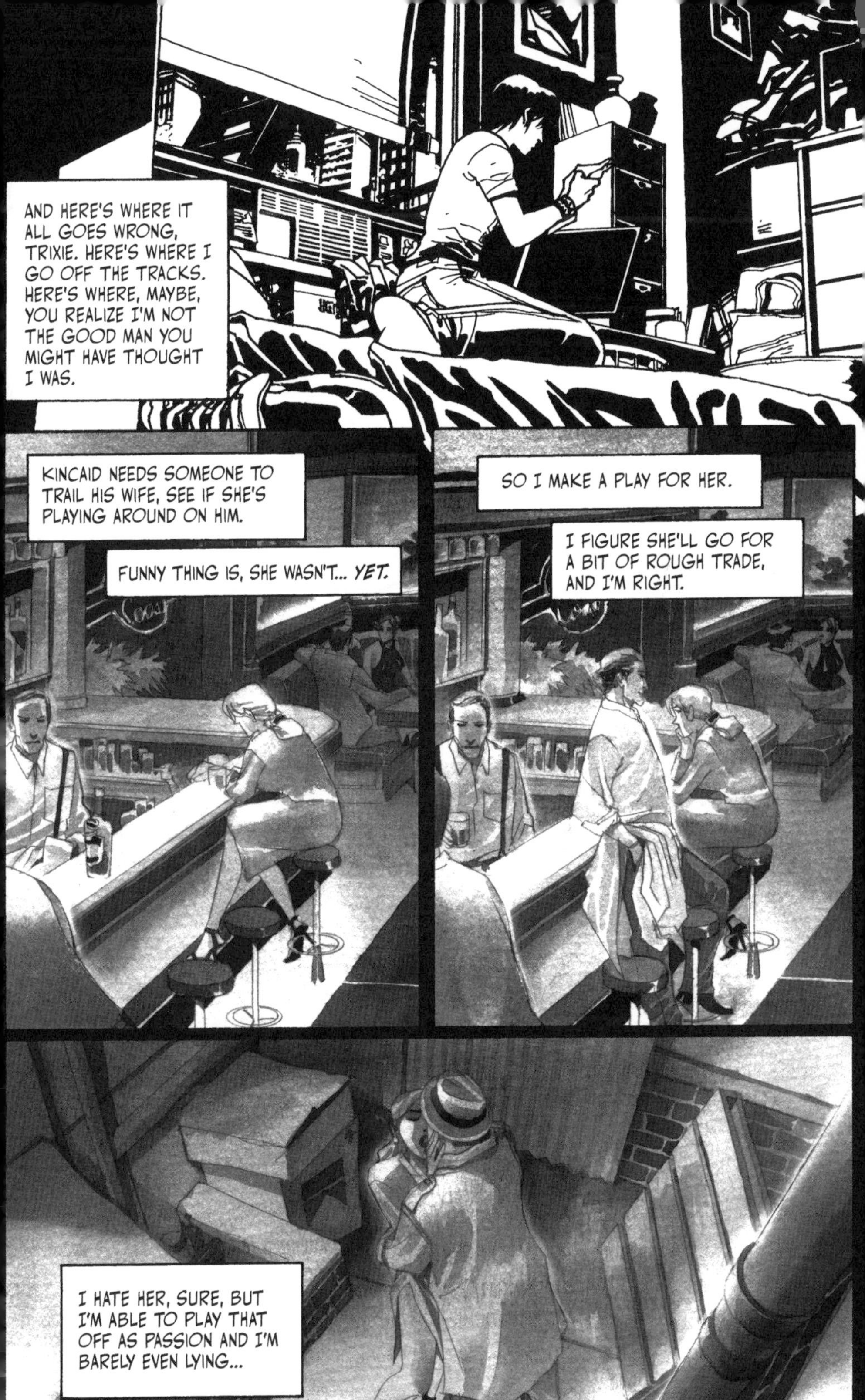
AND HERE'S WHERE IT ALL GOES WRONG, TRIXIE. HERE'S WHERE I GO OFF THE TRACKS. HERE'S WHERE, MAYBE, YOU REALIZE I'M NOT THE GOOD MAN YOU MIGHT HAVE THOUGHT I WAS.
KINCAID NEEDS SOMEONE TO TRAIL HIS WIFE, SEE IF SHE'S PLAYING AROUND ON HIM.
FUNNY THING IS, SHE WASN'T... *YET.*
SO I MAKE A PLAY FOR HER.
I FIGURE SHE'LL GO FOR A BIT OF ROUGH TRADE, AND I'M RIGHT.
I HATE HER, SURE, BUT I'M ABLE TO PLAY THAT OFF AS PASSION AND I'M BARELY EVEN LYING...

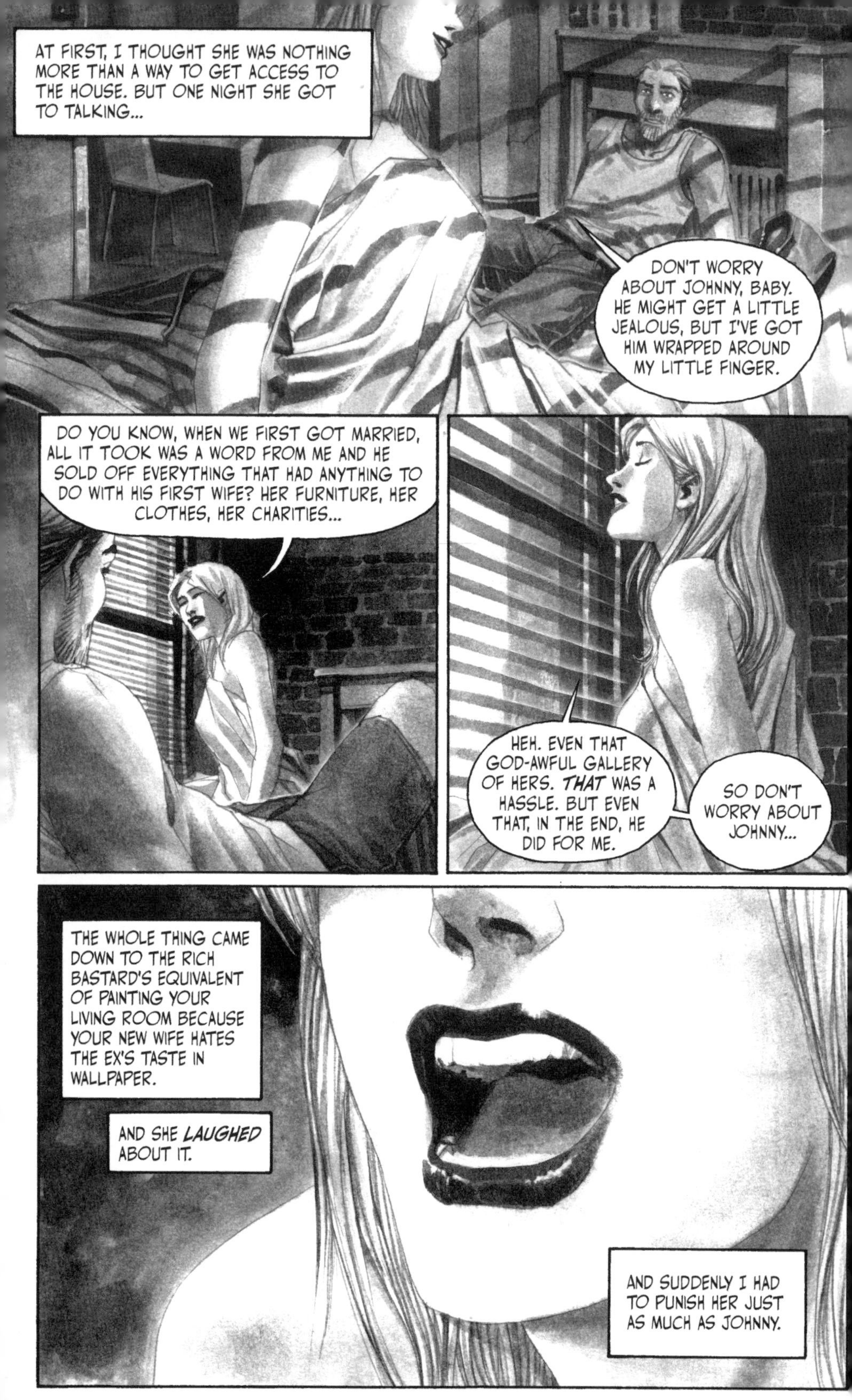
AT FIRST, I THOUGHT SHE WAS NOTHING MORE THAN A WAY TO GET ACCESS TO THE HOUSE. BUT ONE NIGHT SHE GOT TO TALKING...
DON'T WORRY ABOUT JOHNNY, BABY. HE MIGHT GET A LITTLE JEALOUS, BUT I'VE GOT HIM WRAPPED AROUND MY LITTLE FINGER.
DO YOU KNOW, WHEN WE FIRST GOT MARRIED, ALL IT TOOK WAS A WORD FROM ME AND HE SOLD OFF EVERYTHING THAT HAD ANYTHING TO DO WITH HIS FIRST WIFE? HER FURNITURE, HER CLOTHES, HER CHARITIES...
HEH. EVEN THAT GOD-AWFUL GALLERY OF HERS. *THAT* WAS A HASSLE. BUT EVEN THAT, IN THE END, HE DID FOR ME.
SO DON'T WORRY ABOUT JOHNNY...
THE WHOLE THING CAME DOWN TO THE RICH BASTARD'S EQUIVALENT OF PAINTING YOUR LIVING ROOM BECAUSE YOUR NEW WIFE HATES THE EX'S TASTE IN WALLPAPER.
AND SHE *LAUGHED* ABOUT IT.
AND SUDDENLY I HAD TO PUNISH HER JUST AS MUCH AS JOHNNY.

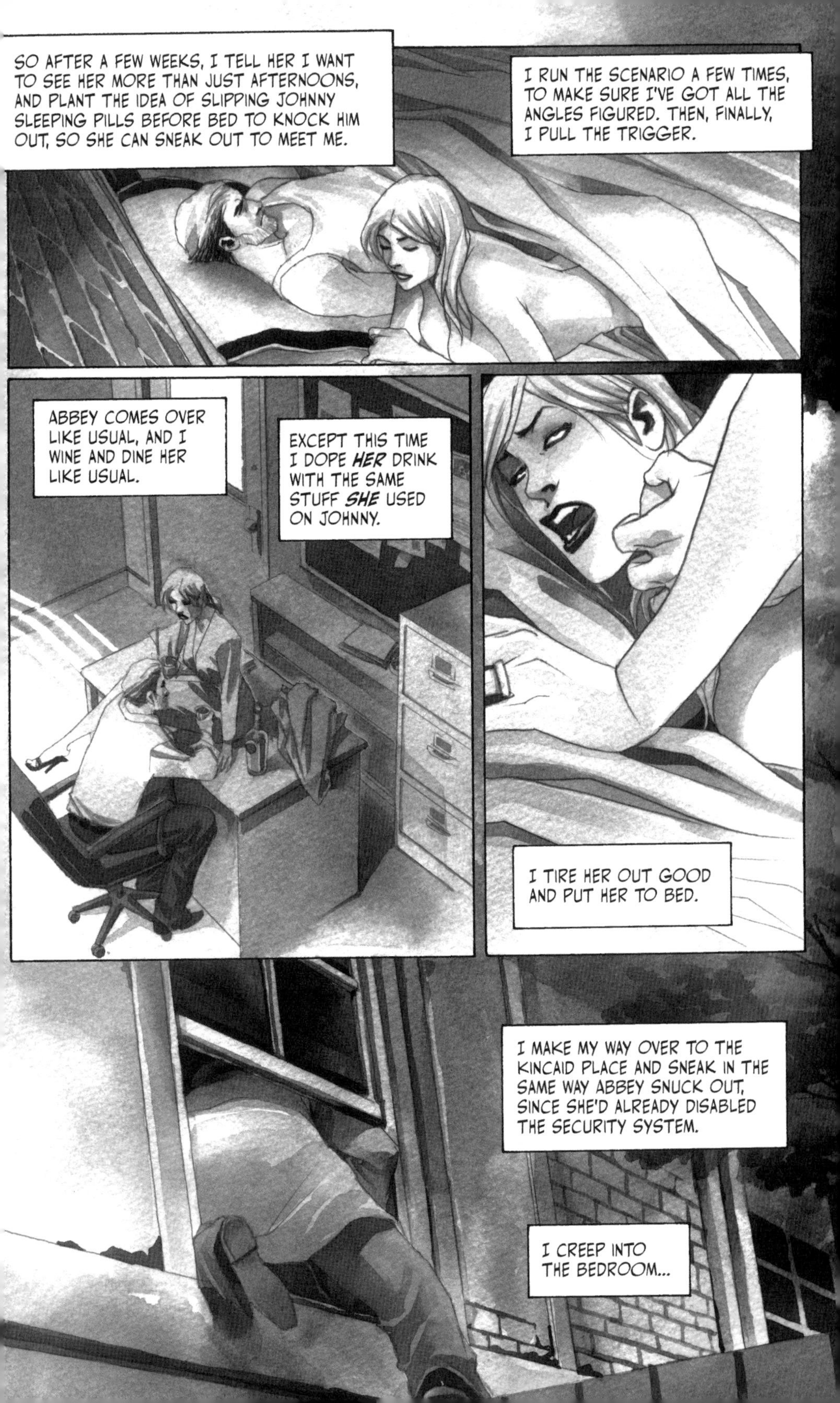
SO AFTER A FEW WEEKS, I TELL HER I WANT TO SEE HER MORE THAN JUST AFTERNOONS, AND PLANT THE IDEA OF SLIPPING JOHNNY SLEEPING PILLS BEFORE BED TO KNOCK HIM OUT, SO SHE CAN SNEAK OUT TO MEET ME.
I RUN THE SCENARIO A FEW TIMES, TO MAKE SURE I'VE GOT ALL THE ANGLES FIGURED. THEN, FINALLY, I PULL THE TRIGGER.
ABBEY COMES OVER LIKE USUAL, AND I WINE AND DINE HER LIKE USUAL.
EXCEPT THIS TIME I DOPE *HER* DRINK WITH THE SAME STUFF *SHE* USED ON JOHNNY.
I TIRE HER OUT GOOD AND PUT HER TO BED.
I MAKE MY WAY OVER TO THE KINCAID PLACE AND SNEAK IN THE SAME WAY ABBEY SNUCK OUT, SINCE SHE'D ALREADY DISABLED THE SECURITY SYSTEM.
I CREEP INTO THE BEDROOM...

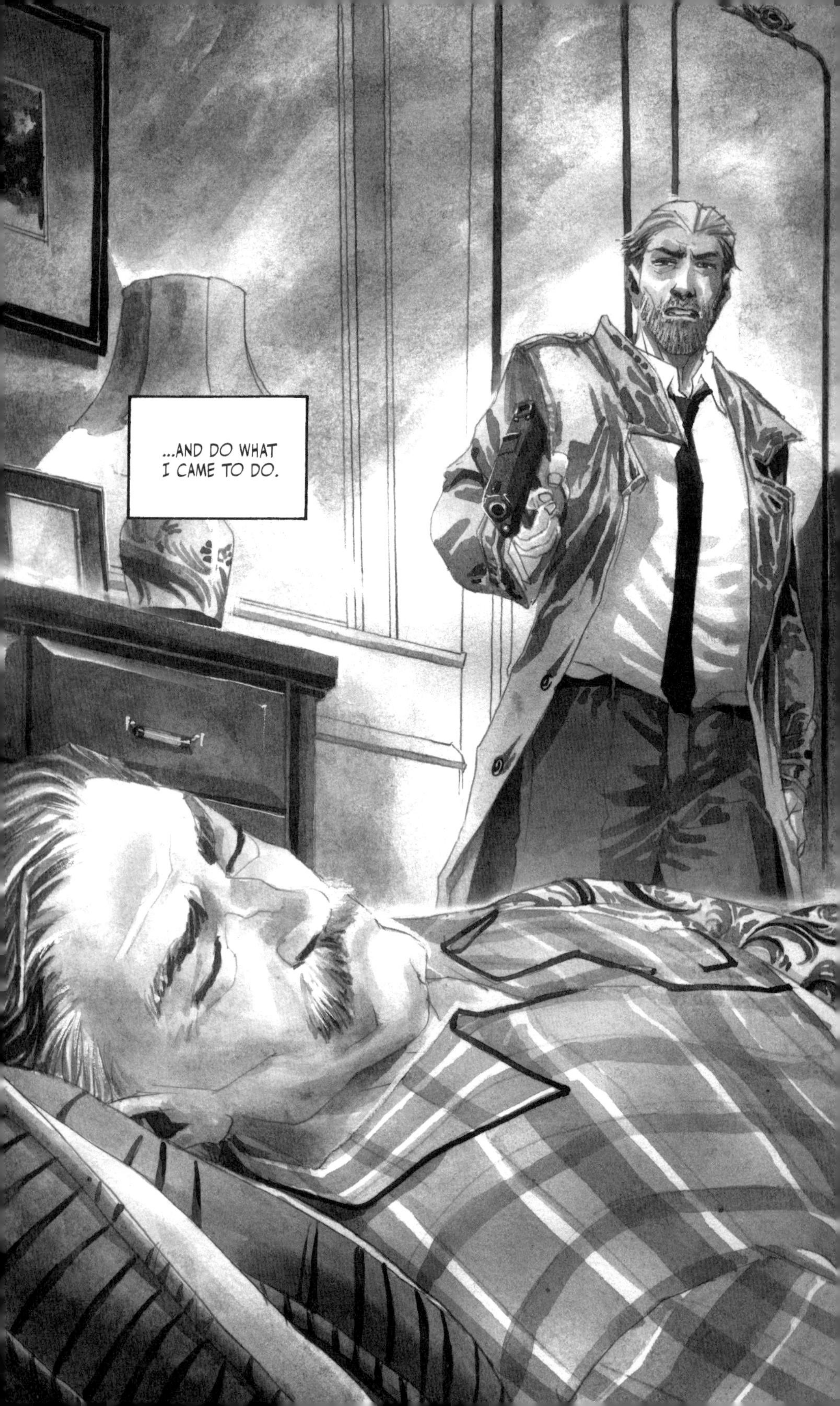
...AND DO WHAT I CAME TO DO.

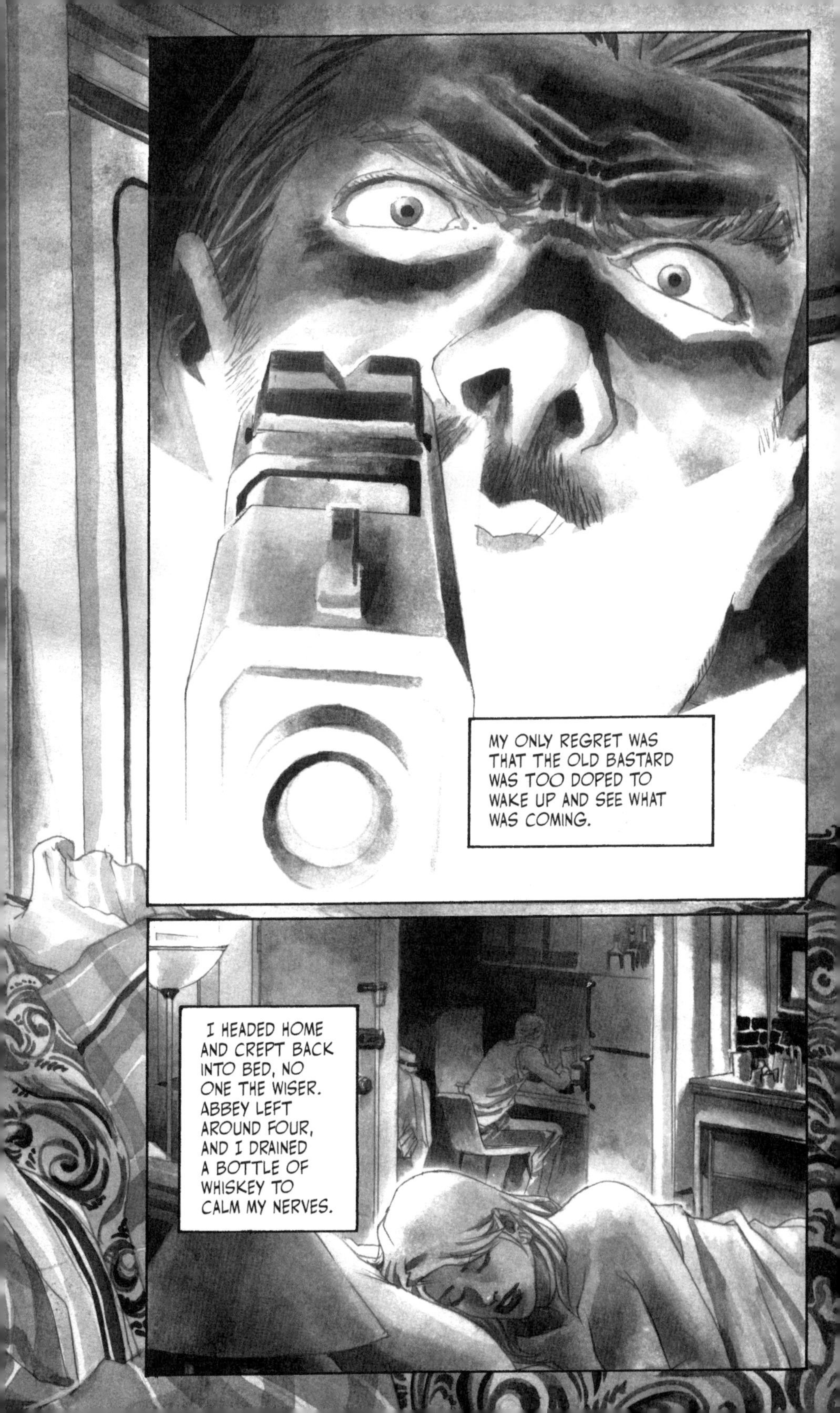
MY ONLY REGRET WAS THAT THE OLD BASTARD WAS TOO DOPED TO WAKE UP AND SEE WHAT WAS COMING.
I HEADED HOME AND CREPT BACK INTO BED, NO ONE THE WISER. ABBEY LEFT AROUND FOUR, AND I DRAINED A BOTTLE OF WHISKEY TO CALM MY NERVES.

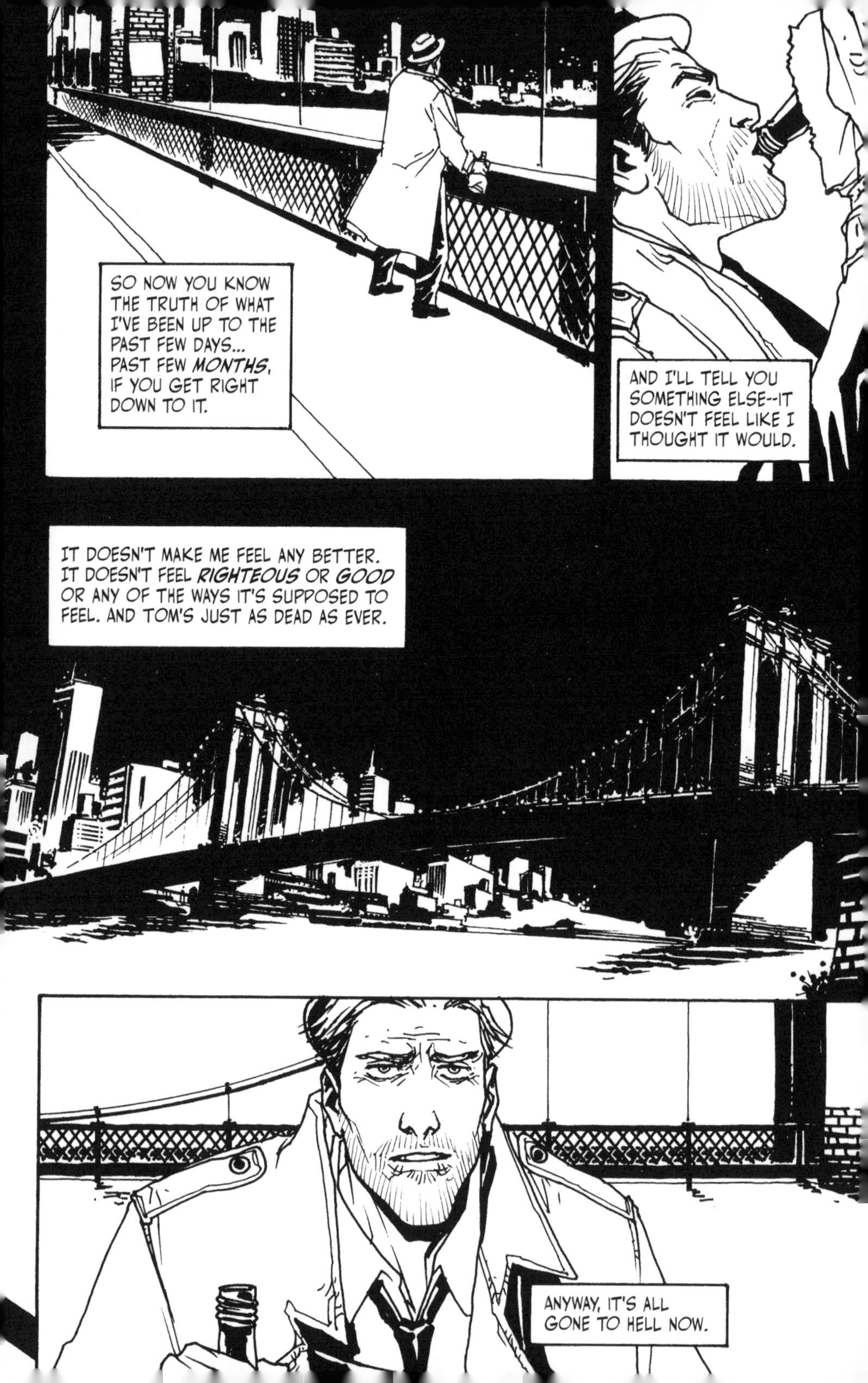
SO NOW YOU KNOW THE TRUTH OF WHAT I'VE BEEN UP TO THE PAST FEW DAYS... PAST FEW *MONTHS*, IF YOU GET RIGHT DOWN TO IT.
AND I'LL TELL YOU SOMETHING ELSE--IT DOESN'T FEEL LIKE I THOUGHT IT WOULD.
IT DOESN'T MAKE ME FEEL ANY BETTER. IT DOESN'T FEEL *RIGHTEOUS* OR *GOOD* OR ANY OF THE WAYS IT'S SUPPOSED TO FEEL. AND TOM'S JUST AS DEAD AS EVER.
ANYWAY, IT'S ALL GONE TO HELL NOW.

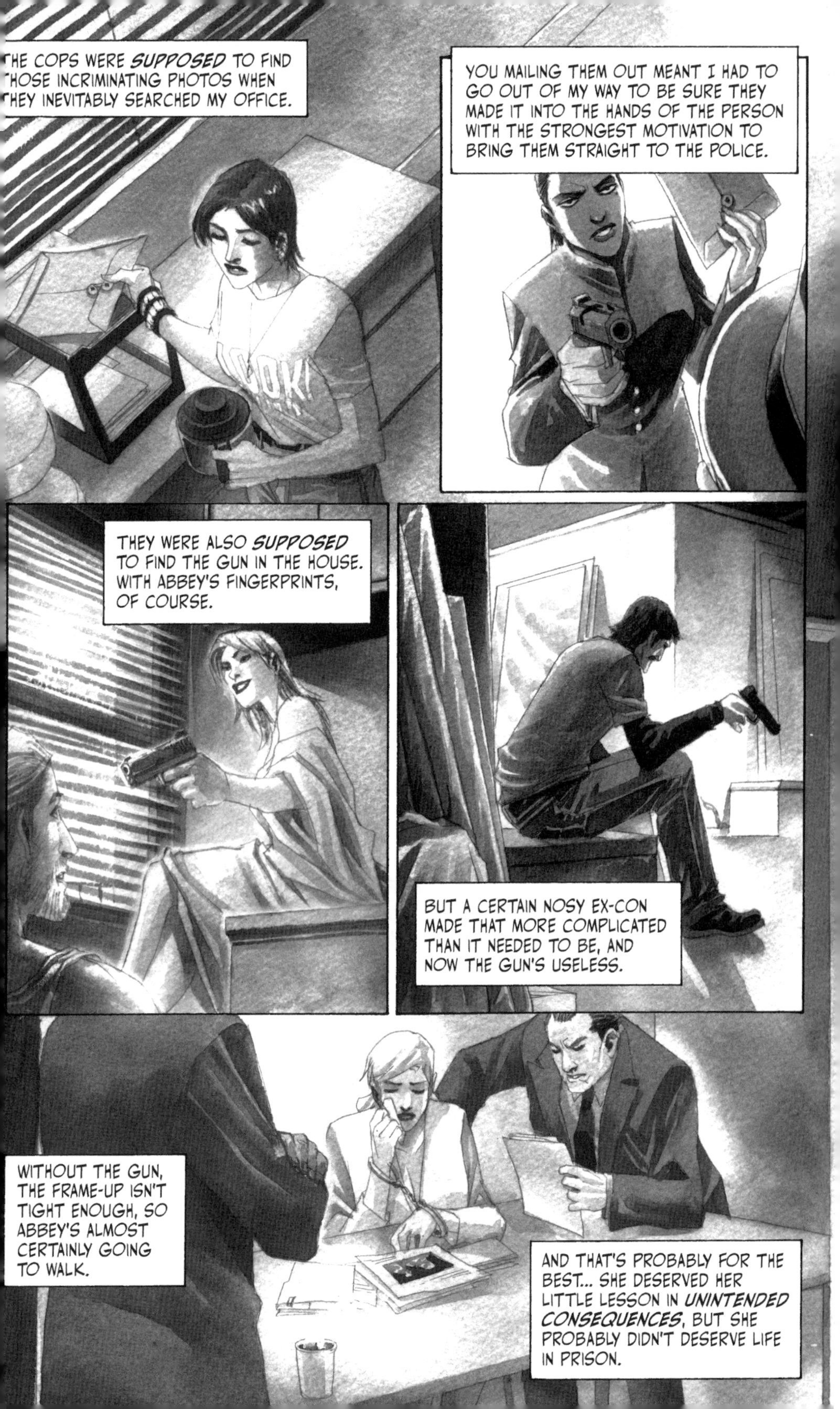
THE COPS WERE SUPPOSED TO FIND THOSE INCRIMINATING PHOTOS WHEN THEY INEVITABLY SEARCHED MY OFFICE.
YOU MAILING THEM OUT MEANT I HAD TO GO OUT OF MY WAY TO BE SURE THEY MADE IT INTO THE HANDS OF THE PERSON WITH THE STRONGEST MOTIVATION TO BRING THEM STRAIGHT TO THE POLICE.
THEY WERE ALSO SUPPOSED TO FIND THE GUN IN THE HOUSE. WITH ABBEY'S FINGERPRINTS, OF COURSE.
BUT A CERTAIN NOSY EX-CON MADE THAT MORE COMPLICATED THAN IT NEEDED TO BE, AND NOW THE GUN'S USELESS.
WITHOUT THE GUN, THE FRAME-UP ISN'T TIGHT ENOUGH, SO ABBEY'S ALMOST CERTAINLY GOING TO WALK.
AND THAT'S PROBABLY FOR THE BEST... SHE DESERVED HER LITTLE LESSON IN UNINTENDED CONSEQUENCES, BUT SHE PROBABLY DIDN'T DESERVE LIFE IN PRISON.

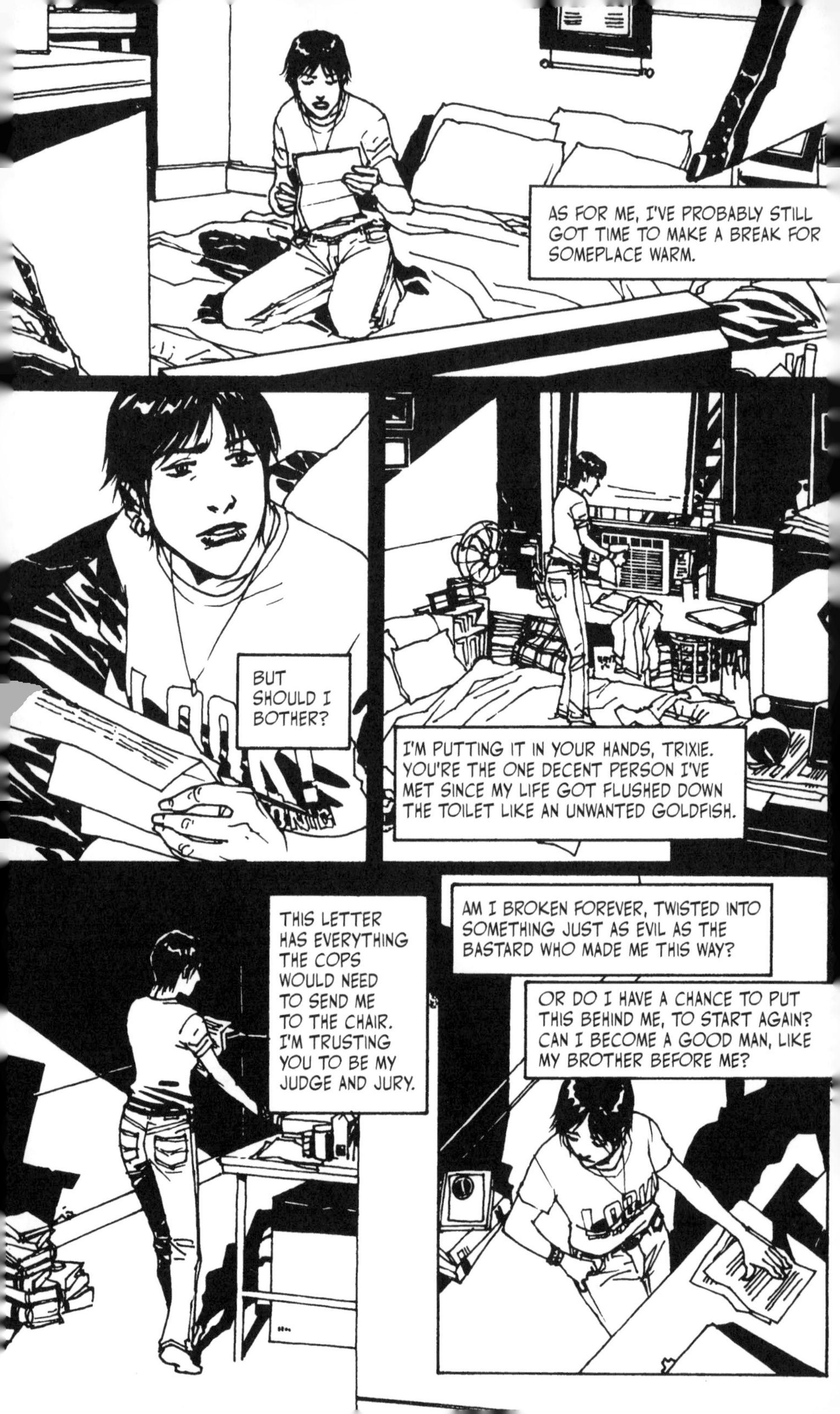
AS FOR ME, I'VE PROBABLY STILL GOT TIME TO MAKE A BREAK FOR SOMEPLACE WARM.
BUT SHOULD I BOTHER?
I'M PUTTING IT IN YOUR HANDS, TRIXIE. YOU'RE THE ONE DECENT PERSON I'VE MET SINCE MY LIFE GOT FLUSHED DOWN THE TOILET LIKE AN UNWANTED GOLDFISH.
THIS LETTER HAS EVERYTHING THE COPS WOULD NEED TO SEND ME TO THE CHAIR. I'M TRUSTING YOU TO BE MY JUDGE AND JURY.
AM I BROKEN FOREVER, TWISTED INTO SOMETHING JUST AS EVIL AS THE BASTARD WHO MADE ME THIS WAY?
OR DO I HAVE A CHANCE TO PUT THIS BEHIND ME, TO START AGAIN? CAN I BECOME A GOOD MAN, LIKE MY BROTHER BEFORE ME?

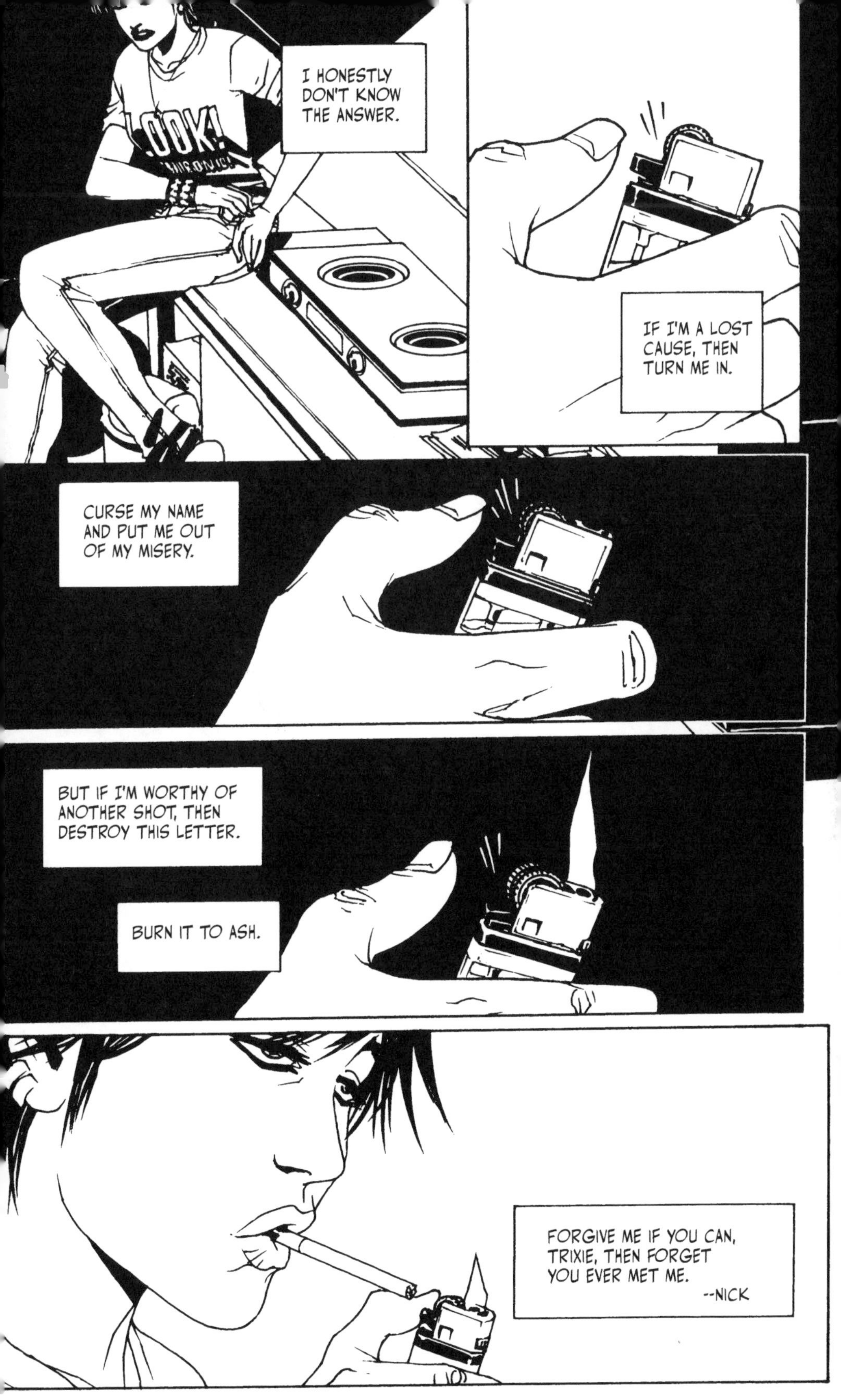
I HONESTLY DON'T KNOW THE ANSWER.
IF I'M A LOST CAUSE, THEN TURN ME IN.
CURSE MY NAME AND PUT ME OUT OF MY MISERY.
BUT IF I'M WORTHY OF ANOTHER SHOT, THEN DESTROY THIS LETTER.
BURN IT TO ASH.
FORGIVE ME IF YOU CAN, TRIXIE, THEN FORGET YOU EVER MET ME.
--NICK

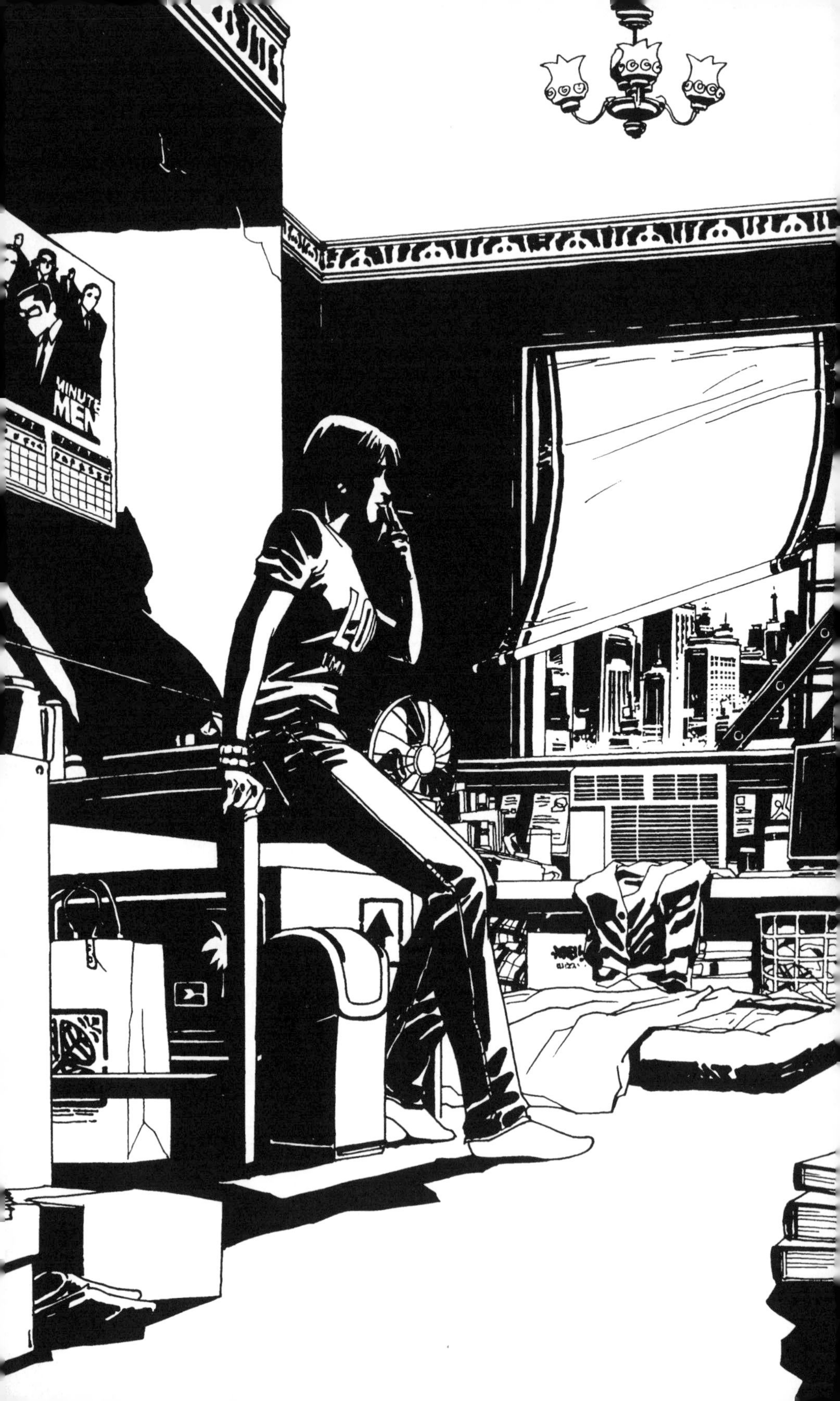
MINUTE MEN

THE END

ERIC SKILLMAN

STORY

is a Brooklyn-based writer, graphic designer, and art director best known for his design work on DVDs from the Criterion Collection and his design process blog *Cozy Lummox* (ericskillman.blogspot.com). Previous comics work includes the self-published comic series *EGG: Hard Boiled Stories*.

Liar's Kiss is his first book.

JHOMAR SORIANO

ART

is a Phillippines-based illustrator, mangaka, and father of three whose previous published works include *Mr. Grieves* for Seven Seas Books, for which he was a finalist (Top 19) for the First International Manga Award presented by the Japanese Foreign Affairs Ministry; *Arkham Woods,* also from Seven Seas; *Rumble to Kaga,* a backup feature for the monthly *Blade of the Immortal* series published by Dark Horse, and many more.

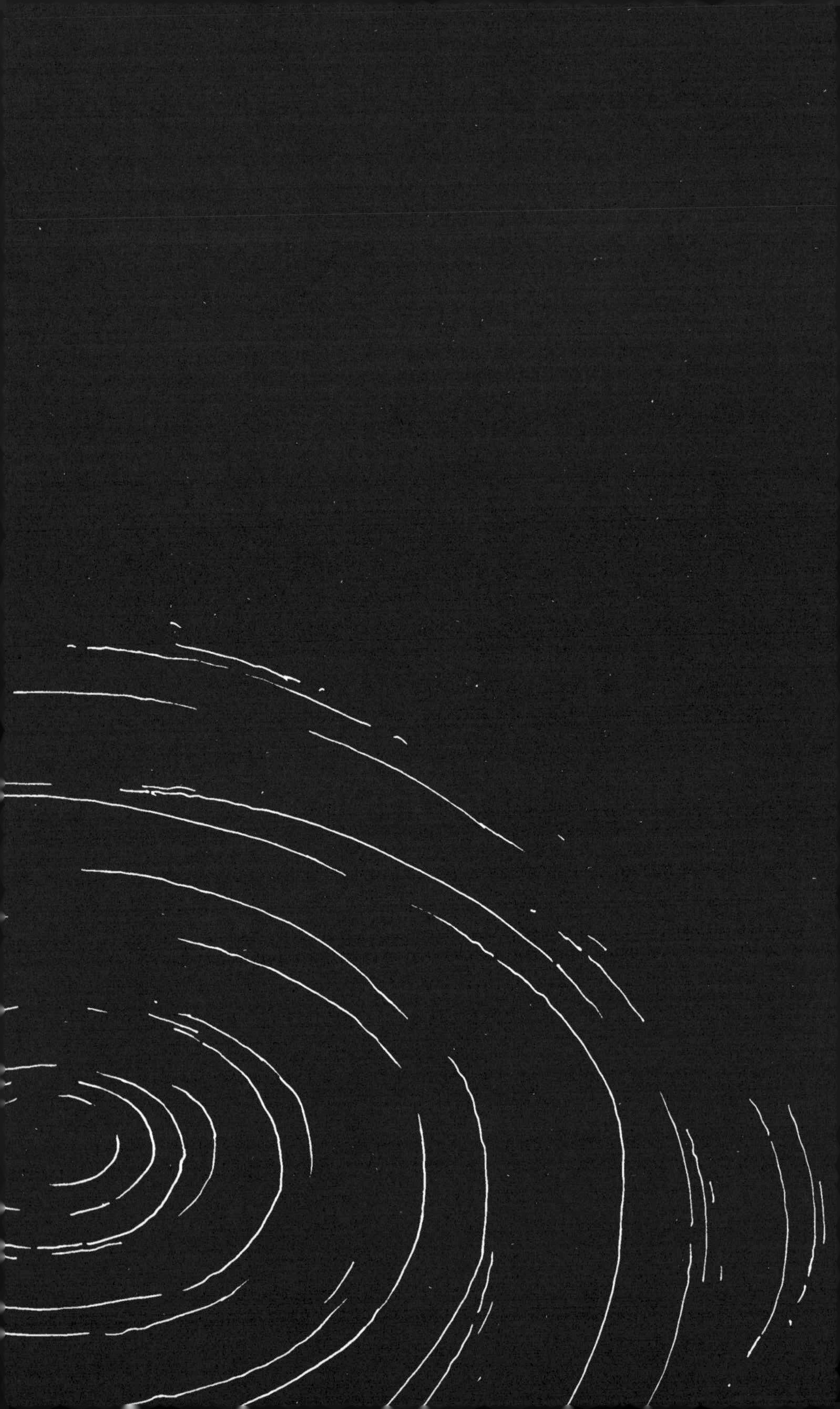